MISSION IN TODAY'S WORLD

Donal Dorr

Mission in Today's World

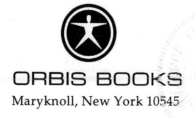

ORBIS BOOKS
Maryknoll, New York 10545

The Catholic Foreign Mission Society of America (Maryknoll) recruits and trains people for overseas missionary service. Through Orbis Books, Maryknoll aims to foster the international dialogue that is essential to mission. The books published, however, reflect the opinions of their authors and are not meant to represent the official position of the society. To obtain more information about Maryknoll and Orbis Books, please visit our website at www.maryknoll.org.

First published in 2000
in the United States by
ORBIS BOOKS
PO Box 308
Maryknoll, New York 10545-0308
www.orbisbooks.com

Cover by Bill Bolger
Origination by The Columba Press
Printed in Ireland by Colour Books Ltd, Dublin

Cataloging-in-Publication Data
available from the Library of Congress

ISBN 1-57075-339-3

Copyright © 2000, Donal Dorr

Contents

Introduction

At the heart of this book lies an ambiguity about the word 'mission'. At times the word has a rather restricted meaning where it refers mainly to work 'on the foreign missions'. At other times – or for other people – its meaning is much more general: it refers not so much to a particular kind of work as to a sense of being called to undertake some important enterprise, with a corresponding attitude of willingness to break new ground and to work on a new frontier, outside the established structures.

Up to about forty years ago there was a considerable overlap between these two shades of meaning, because the new frontiers were to be found mainly in 'the foreign missions'. In the past, foreign missionaries seemed almost to have a monopoly on frontier work. This gave them an aura of adventure and excitement when compared to the apparently more hum-drum everyday life of church workers 'at home'.

All this has changed radically. One reason for the change is that we have become aware of new and different frontiers – a point I shall return to in a moment. Another reason is that serious questions have been raised about the whole foreign missionary enterprise as carried out in the past. A third reason is that we have been very influenced by a distinction made about thirty years ago between 'mission' and 'maintenance'. We have come to believe that the difference between the two has to do not so much with the area in which we are working as with our own attitude and approach to the task we have taken on. So some people working in their home situations could have a radically 'missionary' approach, while some professional 'foreign missionaries' might well be lacking in the innovative spirit which would justify their claim to the word 'missionary'.

My aim in this book is to help to bridge the gap between the broad meaning of the word mission (where it refers mainly to attitude, approach and spirit) and the more restricted meaning (where it applies mainly to 'foreign missionaries'). I am writing here both about a pioneering approach and about 'frontier situations' including – but not confined to – foreign missionary work.

The book is written mainly out of my own experience. Trained as a missionary priest, I have devoted most of my life to work in what used to be called 'missionary areas' and to working as a 'resource-person' for foreign missionaries. But I have actually spent more time working in my own country than overseas and I have remained actively – though somewhat peripherally – involved in church work 'at home'. I have tried to distil this mixed experience into the chapters of this book.

There are two basic aspects to mission. The first is 'the mission of God' and the second is 'the mission of the church'. Four years ago I dealt with 'the mission of God' in a book called *Divine Energy*;[1] in it I gave an account of the sending and role of the Holy Spirit and the sending and work of Jesus, in our world. Presupposing the mission of the Spirit and of Jesus, I now go on in the present book to examine the mission of the church. This book is much less scriptural in style than the earlier book. The reason is that the mission of the church, though rooted in the New Testament, developed over the centuries. So when we come to evaluate it we cannot find quick easy answers in the Bible. But all through the book my aim has been to help Christians today to understand and continue the fundamental mission of Jesus, while recognising and relying on the multiform action of the Spirit who was at work in the world from the very beginning and who continues to inspire and empower us from moment to moment.

Over the past generation I have been in on-going dialogue about different aspects of mission with hundreds of foreign missionaries and 'home church' people. These are committed Christians who have worked their way through very radical changes in their understanding of the nature and purpose of mission, as well as though a major shift in missionary style and techniques. So the material of the book has been worked out over several years. Earlier drafts of many of the chapters have been circulated to members of the Irish Missionary Union. In the light of their responses I have corrected, expanded and re-edited the material many times.

I have tried to distil into words the lived wisdom of these partners in dialogue, and to put in a systematic form their emergent convictions which have not, perhaps, been fully articulated before. This encourages me to believe that at least some of it will be of interest to a wider readership, and will ring true to their experience. My hope is that the resulting book will go some way towards helping people to become more clear about what it means to live out the 'missionary spirit' in this period when the traditional missionary enterprise is under serious challenge and rich new opportunities for mission are opening up.

A Twilight Time
The most obvious of these challenges and opportunities has to do with foreign missionary personnel. For about a hundred years (roughly from 1870 to 1970), a very large number of missionaries came from the traditional mission-sending countries of Europe and North America to work in the 'young churches' of the other continents. Their ages ranged from the early twenties to the late eighties. Their age-profile remained fairly constant, since there was a steady influx of fresh missionaries to replace those who died or returned home.

Over the past generation, however, there has been a dramatic drop in the number of such foreign missionaries – a drop that is by no means compensated for by the growing number of missionaries going abroad from the more developed of the young churches. Perhaps even more striking than the drop in numbers is the change in the age-profile of Western missionaries. The great majority of them are already quite old and there is only a small trickle of younger people coming to replace those who die or return home. The result is that the average age of Western foreign missionaries is increasing very rapidly. It is quite evident that in fifteen years time, if present trends continue (as they almost certainly will), the number of active missionaries from the West will be very small indeed.

Clearly, we are coming to the end of a missionary era – one that began about the middle of the nineteenth century and lasted for 150 years. All of us who are concerned about mission need to advert to this historical background. Otherwise we are liable to assume that something has gone wrong – and that we are partly to blame for it, perhaps through a lack of missionary zeal on our part. Adopting this long perspective helps us to realise that what is taking place is not the ending of mission but only the end of a particular phase in the life of the church. It enables us to respond to new challenges and to find a richer meaning for the word 'mission' today. It also provides a background against which the members of the different institutes devoted to missionary work can look more closely at their own charism and tradition and then clarify or re-define the specific purpose of their institute.

New Attitudes, New Frontiers
One of the main reasons why this era of 'foreign mission' is drawing to a close is that the broad concept of mission has changed very radically in the past forty years. Ideas that were unknown or were given little emphasis in the past have now become major elements in our understanding of the mission of the church. In the first part of this book I focus on what is perhaps the most crucial of all these ideas, namely, the realisation that dialogue with other religions and spiritual outlooks is not opposed to mission but is a central aspect of it and a pre-condition to any other dimension of mission.[2]

There are four chapters in this first part of the book. In the first, I explore the whole notion of dialogue, with particular emphasis on an 'inner dialogue' to which every Christian is called. In the second chapter, I go on to illustrate this by noting some of the central beliefs and key values of several of the so-called 'world religions', namely, Judaism, Islam, the Hindu and Buddhist traditions, and Confucianism and Taoism; and I make some suggestions about what we have to gain from inner and outer dialogue with them.

Chapter 3 explores the interesting and difficult issue of dialogue with the primal religions, which in the past used to be called 'pagan' or 'animist' religions. I illustrate this treatment with examples from African religion and from ancient Greek and Celtic religion. In the fourth chapter I go on to examine the challenging and exciting question of the possibility of dialogue with the Western world of today. I suggest that there is room for a very fruitful dialogue, in which we can draw on, and share, the rich treasury of wisdom which the church has accumulated; but people will be open to such dialogue with us only if they find in us a sensitivity to their own deep values and respect for their spiritual experiences.

Then I move on to the second part of the book. In the six chapters which make up this section I take account of the fact that, alongside the notion of dialogue, there are other key entry-points into the whole notion of mission. Chapter 5 looks at mission as a process of evangelization – the attempt of the followers of Jesus to share in his task of bringing good news to the world. This leads on to Chapter 6 where I examine the notion of incult-uration – the whole issue of how the message of Jesus relates to and becomes at least partly embodied in the rich variety of cult-ures in the world. Next I move on in Chapter 7 to look at mission as a struggle for human liberation. In Chapter 8 I go on to con-sider mission as a project of reconciliation. The ninth chapter is devoted to an exploration of mission as an option for the poor.

The last chapter in this second part of the book (Chapter 10) is entitled 'Mission as Power from the Spirit'. In it I suggest that our mission involves sharing in different modes of power given us by the Spirit of God; and I outline ways in which some people move from a more active exercise of mission to a more contem-plative mode. This chapter provides a link between the present book and my earlier book, *Divine Energy,* in which I devoted a lot of space to the mission and work of the Holy Spirit.

There have been radical changes not only in our overall no-tion of mission but also in our understanding of mission in its more limited and specific sense as 'mission to the nations' *(ad gentes)*. These latter changes are my concern in the third part of this book, which has the title 'Re-Visioning Mission to the Nations'. I deal first, in Chapter 11, with the changes in attitude and approach which spring directly from the changes in the more generic concept of mission (examined in earlier chapters). I show how these attitudinal changes relate to the new images and models of mission which have arisen in recent years. In the twelfth chapter I go on to clarify the purpose of mission 'to the nations', making what I consider to be an important distinction between missionaries whose focus is on building up the church and missionaries whose main interest is in promoting what I call 'reign of God values'.

Chapter 13 is entitled 'New Frontiers'. In it I take up the question of how we should understand the concept of 'mission to the nations' today. Within the past generation we have be-come aware of many new 'frontiers' coming on to our horizons. These provide new and pressing challenges to Christians who are imbued with a missionary spirit, whether or not they are seen as 'missionaries' in the traditional sense. Some of the new 'frontiers' and challenges are political in origin – for instance, the enormous increase in the number of refugees in the world, the pressing problem of human rights abuses on a vast scale, and the urgent need for reconciliation which arises in areas where racism is rampant or where 'ethnic cleansing' or genocide has been practised or attempted.

Other 'frontiers' can be defined in social and economic terms – for instance, the vast urban slums surrounding so many cities today and the huge disparity in health care between the rich and the poor. Furthermore, the cultural and religious frontiers of the world are no longer thousands of miles away from us. Practically every country in the world has become far more variegated in recent times, with a great increase of cultural and religious pluralism within it. We have also become aware of the burning issue of injustice and poverty at the global level and of the challenges posed by ecological degradation and by patriarchy in society and the churches. All of these pressing problems call for a 'missionary' response from the church. The increasing secularisation of our world also raises 'missionary' questions, among which is the issue of dialogue with those who, in the midst of this 'secular' world, are engaged in a serious search for spiritual meaning. In this thirteenth chapter I give a variety of practical examples of people who have moved into these new spheres of mission 'to the nations'. This leads me on to give an overview of what I see as an understanding of mission 'to the nations' *(ad gentes)* which is appropriate in our present-day world.

Towards the end of the chapter I go on to look at some important issues which arise for institutes, societies, and congregations which have devoted themselves in whole or in part to 'missionary' work. How should they respond to the challenge of these new frontiers? And how can they integrate a response to these new frontiers with their traditional emphasis on foreign mission? I tentatively suggest some practical conclusions in regard to the policies of such institutes.

The final section of the book – Part Four – consists of four chapters in which I take up specific issues which arise for those who work as foreign missionaries, mainly in the so-called 'developing world'. Chapter 14 is entitled 'Missionary Strategy: Vehicles of Evangelization'. In it I spell out how different kinds of development work have embodied the good news for people in different situations; and I make some suggestions about an appropriate model and techniques which can 'carry' gospel values today. This leads on to Chapter 15, which examines the issue of the relationship between missionaries and development workers – how they differ from each other and how their work overlaps. Chapter 16 examines the question of when a particular task of mission *ad gentes* is 'completed' to a point where those who have undertaken it can and should move elsewhere. In the last chapter (Chapter 17), under the title 'Bringing it Back Home', I give some instances of fruitful ministries pioneered by missionaries who returned from overseas to their home churches. This leads on to a short exploration of some major issues which are likely to strike missionaries who have worked abroad and then come home and see their home church through 'missionary' eyes. I suggest a series of options which may give direction to returned missionaries who are eager to retain a missionary spirit and outlook while working fruitfully in their home church.

I take this opportunity to express my gratitude and appreciation to the leadership and members of the Irish Missionary Union under whose auspices this work has been done. I am particularly grateful to its Executive Secretary, Fr Tom Kiggins, for his unfailing support and encouragement. I am very much indebted to three friends for their painstaking critique of an earlier draft of this book. They are Pádraig Ó Máille, Paddy Duffy, and Victor Dunne. Each of them contributed very valuable advice and suggestions.

PART ONE

Mission as Dialogue

CHAPTER 1

Dialogue

As I said in the introduction, the notion of mission is so broad and rich that to understand it we need to approach the subject from a variety of different points of view. If I had been writing this book twenty years ago I would have begun with an account of mission as *evangelization*. But at the present time it seems more appropriate to devote the early chapters to an account of mission as *dialogue*.

The main argument for starting a study of mission with dialogue rather than evangelization is that it provides a corrective for the very one-sided notion of mission which people took for granted in the past. The emphasis then was almost entirely on the great work done by the missionaries and the great gift brought by them, with little attention paid to the *recipients* of this gift. One reason why the whole notion of mission has lost much of its glamour in more recent times is that people have become aware of how unbalanced this approach was. By starting with the notion that dialogue is integral to mission we take account of the fact that the Spirit is at work in the people being evangelized as well as in the evangelizers; and we acknowledge that there is a two-way exchange of gifts, between missionaries and the people among whom they work. Furthermore, the notion of dialogue conveys the impression that mission is not just a matter of *doing things for* people. It is first of all a matter of *being with* people, of *listening* and *sharing* with them.

The very notion of mission as dialogue is a direct challenge to an assumption that was sometimes made in the past that the successful missionary is one who to gets many converts and builds up the institutional church. Of course we can still find some crusading missionaries who are so convinced of the importance of the good news of Jesus Christ that they become preoccupied with the numbers of their converts. Their attitude is that dialogue between Christianity and other religions would be a distraction from their missionary work – though they would hardly dare to express it so crudely. Perhaps they are secretly afraid that their missionary enthusiasm would be weakened by engaging in religious dialogue. The irony is that the missionary enterprise is undermined much more by this kind of insensitivity than by devoting time and energy to understanding non-Christian religions. It is now generally accepted that, far from being opposed to mission, dialogue is in fact an integral aspect of mission.[1]

In my book *Divine Energy* I outlined a variety of ways in which the Spirit of God is at work in the world. In the very first chapter of the Bible we are told that at the beginning of creation the Spirit moved over the waters, bringing order out of chaos (Gen 1:2). Since then the Spirit has touched our lives through the influence of countless prophets, as well as through our own personal signs and dreams and all kinds of spiritual experiences. The various religions may be seen as attempts to give some institutional shape to such movements of God's Spirit and God's grace. In all of the religions we can find rituals, symbols and traditions which express or foster or embody people's religious experience. These symbols and rituals evoke in people a sense of the loving, healing presence of God in their own lives and in the wider world. But, like all human institutions, religions can become distorted and even corrupt. When that happens they may foster religious legalism, or arrogant fanaticism; or they may promote superstitious or quasi-magical practices.

This means that the non-Christian religions are channels of grace in some respects while in other ways they can lead people astray. However, when we look at Christianity, not in its ideal form but as it has actually developed through history, we have to make a similarly nuanced judgement about it. Undoubtedly, it has been and remains a powerful instrument of divine grace. Yet there have been situations where it has, at the same time, been a hindrance to authentic religious experience. That is why we hold as part of our Christian faith that the church is always called to allow itself to be reformed by God's grace. Both as individual Christians and as a church we must accept the pain of being called to conversion by prophetic people inspired by God's Spirit.

Dialogue between the religions is one of the most powerfully effective ways in which Christians and other religious believers can open themselves to the influence of the Spirit of God. Those who take part in inter-religious dialogue are submitting themselves and their own religious traditions to the judgement of God. The Spirit works partly by *enriching* those who engage in this dialogue; they grow in wonder and insight when they are allowed to share something of the religious experience of people from a different tradition. God's Spirit also inspires the partners in the dialogue to allow themselves to be *challenged* at a deep religious level. They are called to acknowledge that not only may they have much to learn in a positive sense from others but also that their own articulation of spirituality may be inadequate and even quite distorted in some respects. They are invited to admit that God's Spirit may use the other partner in the interreligious dialogue as a key instrument in showing up this distortion or inadequacy.

The Depth Dimension
There is a danger that we would think of inter-religious dialogue mainly in terms of an exchange of information. If we do so, then we may well feel we should leave it to the experts, the people who have a lot of knowledge about the different religions. But this would mean that we are treating religion in much the same way as geography or history or motor mechanics—that is, as a distinct area of knowledge with items of information, some of which we already know and others which we have not yet learned. That is a very mistaken approach. Religious faith cannot be fenced off into a separate domain. For it is concerned with all aspects of human living. Instead of thinking of it as a separate area of knowledge we could think of it as an exploration of the deep questions which underlie our everyday concerns.

For instance, when a child is sick, its parents normally go first to the doctor. But suppose the child dies, despite every effort the medical people can make. This death raises deep religious questions for the family. Why did God allow this innocent child to die? Why did this tragedy happen to us rather than to another family? Are we being punished by God for something we have done wrong? Often, the questions lead on to still deeper issues. Does God really care? And if God does care, is God really all-powerful? The death of a child may even lead parents to ask what is the meaning of life and to doubt whether their own lives are worth living. So there are spiritual or religious questions lurking behind people's everyday concern about sickness and health.

The same applies on a larger scale when a whole community comes up against major problems. For instance, one legacy of colonialism is that many of the poorer countries of the world are afflicted with widespread corruption in government. The problem is so pervasive that the ordinary citizens feel powerless to overcome it. This is a political and cultural problem. But it also has an important religious aspect. For there are some spiritualities and religious traditions which encourage fatalism in the face of evil and some which call for unquestioning submission to authority in the face of oppression and injustice. In sharp contrast to this, there are other spiritualities or religions which call people to struggle for liberation. They help people believe in their own goodness, their own power, and their responsibility both for their own destiny and for the well-being of their nation. They evoke in people the energy to resist oppression. The point I am stressing is that the *political* issue of challenging corruption also has a *religious* dimension. So religion cannot be fenced off from the political sphere any more than it can be partitioned off from the sphere of everyday personal and family concerns.

This point is expressed in more technical terms in a document issued by the (Vatican) International Theological Commission: '... religion is an *integral constituent* of culture, in which it takes root and blossoms. Moreover, all the great cultures include the religious dimension, as the keystone of the edifice they constitute ...'[2]

All this brings home to us the fact that inter-religious dialogue is not a marginal activity unrelated to everyday life. It affects – and is affected by – the political, social, economic and family issues that shape our daily lives. So it would be a serious mistake to assume that it can be left to specialists. It is a concern for all of us.

Different kinds of Dialogue
If inter-religious dialogue is to play an important part in the life of mission-minded people then it must not be confined to theoretical knowledge about the beliefs or practices of other religions. It has to be the kind of exchange which both nourishes people's faith and challenges them at the very deepest level.

This is not to play down the importance of the kind of formal intellectual dialogue which takes place in inter-religious conferences. There is no doubt that such meetings can foster better understanding between the different religions. But dialogue must not be left to the experts and church leaders who take part in such high-level gatherings. The meetings at official level play an important symbolic role and they can provide a stimulus and a focus for dialogue. However, they can easily be reduced to empty rhetoric unless they are underpinned by a more everyday type of dialogue.

The difficulty is that most people have no clear sense of how to go about this 'lower-level' dialogue. So, without minimising the significance of official inter-religious dialogue, I propose here to focus attention on the everyday informal dialogue in which we can all play a part.

In 1991 the Vatican issued a document entitled *Dialogue and Proclamation*.[3] In paragraph 42 of this document a distinction is made between four forms of dialogue:
– the dialogue of *life*, i.e. sharing of joys, sorrows and concerns;
– the dialogue of *action*, i.e. collaboration in furthering human development and liberation;
– the dialogue of *theological exchange;*
– the dialogue of *religious experience*, i.e. the sharing of spiritual riches such as ways of praying.

It is important for us to remember that, in varying degrees, all of us can be involved in the first, second and fourth of these. If we engage ourselves as far as possible in these less theological forms of dialogue, then we can in good conscience leave the theological exchange to the specialists who take part in scholarly conferences where they share the fruits of the intense study of the religions to which they have devoted their lives.

Where people of different religious faiths live in the same area, it should be normal to have 'a dialogue of life' and 'a dialogue of joint action'. In fact, these forms of dialogue should be far more common now than in the past, because in recent times the world has become much more pluriform as a result of emigration and immigration. Many areas which used to be religiously homogeneous now have significant numbers of people who belong to religious traditions very different from that of the majority. Sometimes these minority groups are left isolated, almost as though they were in a ghetto. In other situations, however, serious attempts are made to integrate them, while respecting their distinctive traditions.

If these attempts are to succeed, action at the social and political level is not enough; there is need for people to make a serious attempt to understand and respect each other's religious beliefs, values, rituals and organisation. So the dialogue of life and joint action leads on naturally to what the Vatican document calls 'the dialogue of religious experience'. The ideal is that there should not only be a sharing about each other's faith but an actual sharing of faith to whatever degree is possible, culminating, hopefully, in joint prayer-services where that is feasible.

Inner Dialogue

In addition to the four kinds of religious dialogue already mentioned, there is a less obvious but even more fundamental form of dialogue. It takes place not so much *between* one person and another as *within* each person. It is a question of seeking to 'get inside' the religious outlook of people of different religious traditions. What takes place is an inner dialogue of the heart, rather than a dialogue at the verbal or intellectual level. As the great theologian Paul Tillich says, '... every dialogue between religions is accompanied by a silent dialogue *within* the representatives of each of the participating religions.'[4]

It has become a commonplace to say that the difference between the religions is not that they provide different *answers* to the same fundamental question but that they set out to respond to different *questions*. I would like to express this insight in a somewhat different way. I suggest that each of the major religious traditions has a distinctive central core. Each of them focuses on a particular religious value or set of values. Consequently, each religion offers us a distinctive perspective on the deeper dimensions of life.

These different perspectives are by no means mutually exclusive. On the contrary, they tend to supplement and reinforce each other. We might even say that a fully comprehensive and integral spirituality will take all these different values into account. To live a rich and fully human spiritual life involves an appreciation of the various perspectives of different religions – and even an ability to shift at times from one perspective to another.

I have an image of a circle entitled 'The Deeper Issues'. The circle is divided into ten segments. Each of these represents a major religious value or need which lies at the heart of one or more of the religions of the world. (See the diagram below.)

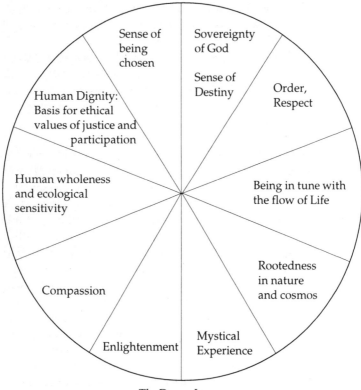

The Deeper Issues

The important point here is that all the 'deeper' (religious) issues cannot be reduced to just one basic issue, as some people mistakenly assume. Rather there is a whole constellation of concerns, all of which are spiritual or religious. As I noted earlier, none of these issues exists in a separate so-called 'religious' sphere. All of them are deeper aspects of our everyday interests and concerns. The various religions differ from each other mainly in the emphasis which they give to these major religious issues.

The key to engaging in a truly fruitful and challenging 'inner dialogue' with the different religions is to have a sympathetic understanding of their core values and interests. I am being profoundly disrespectful to another religion if I am interested only in discovering its attitude to the religious questions or values which are the main concern of *my own* religion. I need to broaden my horizon to take in all the various values or needs outlined in the diagram – and other values not mentioned explicitly there.

Provisos

I do not want to make a strict one-to-one correlation between each religion and one of the values listed on a segment of the circle in the diagram. This is because every religion focuses attention on more than one of these values; and also because there is a considerable overlap between the different values. The differences in 'tone' between the different religions comes largely (but not entirely) from the particular *constellation of values* which characterises each religion. Furthermore, different religions vary very much from one area to another and from one time-span to another. For instance, there can be no doubt that Western Christianity has undergone a major change of 'tone' since about 1960; it now puts far more emphasis on 'worldly' values such as justice, human rights, and ecological sensitivity than it did in the past.

Another point to remember is that the differences between religions does not arise only from differences in the values they accentuate. There are also major differences in the rituals and symbols they use, in the way they are organised and governed, and in the fundamental beliefs they stand for. What I am at present suggesting is not a comprehensive comparison of the different religions under all these aspects. I want rather to look at the values which are given prominence in various non-Christian traditions, with a view to promoting greater understanding in ourselves of these different outlooks. This better understanding can help us to learn from them. It can also enable us to become more aware of where non-Christians might be interested in some of what the Christian faith has to offer them.

I think it is quite likely that most readers who look at the diagram may say that the Christianity which they believe in is one which fosters *all* of the values in all the different sectors of the circle. Certainly, that is my own outlook. This raises the interesting point that at the present time one of the values which is most respected by many Western Christians is *openness to the values of other religions* (whereas fifty years ago we tended to be quite hostile to other religions and would have been inclined to look

askance at some of the values they stood for). So at this point we
have to distinguish between what I may call our *ideal*
Christianity (including the values I believe Christianity *should*
take account of and treasure) and the actual reality of Christianity as it exists in a particular area in a given time-period.

Each has a Gift

Having noted these provisos, I still think it is a very useful exercise to compare the religions on the basis of the values which are
promoted by each of them. In the next three chapters, I propose
to look briefly at a variety of different religions and philosophies
of life, and to identify, very tentatively, some of the religious
values or concerns which lie at the core of each. Chapter 2 is devoted to the topic of dialogue with six of what may be called
'world religions', namely, Judaism, Islam, Hinduism, Buddhism,
Confucianism and Taoism. In the third chapter I propose to explore the question of dialogue with the primal (traditional) religions. Then in Chapter 4 I shall go on to consider the issue of a
religious or quasi-religious dialogue with the religious and moral
'searchers' of the Western world today.

I am making the assumption that each of the great religions
puts its adherents in touch with one or more profound religious
values – and may well do so in a manner or a degree that makes
it unique. Furthermore, I assume that the uniqueness of each of
these religions puts it in a position to offer a vital and perhaps irreplaceable contribution to the religious experience and understanding of people of other faiths.

In other words, my starting-point is that each of the great
religions of the world has a special gift to offer to the others. No
religious believer has the right to say: 'Our religion is complete
in itself, in the sense that we have nothing significant to learn
from the others.' And this applies to Christians as well as non-
Christians. As Christians, we are called by the Spirit to open
ourselves, with eagerness and with humility, to engage in a dialogue of the head and of the heart with the followers of other
religions. In this way we can work towards a far richer, deeper,
and more rounded understanding of our own Christian faith
than we have at present. Indeed, if we take this invitation seriously, it is not just our understanding of the faith which will
deepen. Even our faith itself will grow and blossom in ways that
we could never have guessed.

In taking on this task of identifying key values in various religions, I am very aware of my own ignorance and of the dangers of over-simplifying and even misunderstanding them. I take seriously the warning of the scholar Eric Sharpe that 'there is a somewhat romantic attitude abroad these days, decreeing that imaginative sympathy is to be preferred over actual knowledge, where the Christian encounter with other religious traditions is concerned.'[5] But I think it is worth while taking the risk of over-simplification, because otherwise the spiritual treasures of the various religions may be available only to a small number of specialist experts. My hope is that what I have to say here may help people to locate within themselves the deep needs or values that are being responded to by the different religious traditions – and that this may lead them to a profound interior encounter with the core of these religions or worldviews.

QUESTIONS FOR REFLECTION

1. If you were not a Christian, what religion would you like to belong to? Why?
2. What do you consider to be central aspects of Christian belief which are not found in other religions?
3. Is there any aspect of any non-Christian religion which you find very attractive and valuable but which you consider to be incompatible with Christianity?

CHAPTER 2

Dialogue with World Religions

Dialogue with Judaism: The Covenant
In naming our partners in inter-religious dialogue it is natural
that we should start with the Jews, since they are the ones who
are 'nearest' to us. From both a historical and religious point of
view Christianity and Judaism spring from the same roots. But it
is crucially important that we should not imagine that dialogue
with Judaism is simply a matter of studying what we Christians
call the *Old Testament*. We need to be aware that even the use of
that title is not neutral – it implies a judgement that the Sacred
Writings of the Jews are incomplete and in some sense trans-
cended by our Christian *New* Testament.

Furthermore, we have to keep two other points in mind.
Firstly, Judaism has a whole wealth of very ancient religious
teaching and tradition over and above the books which
Christians call 'the Old Testament'. And, secondly, the Jews
have had a further 2,000 years of history since the coming of
Jesus; so Judaism today is a very different – and far more complex – reality than it was when Christians and Jews began to go
their separate ways.

Having noted the need to tread cautiously in relation to these
issues, I now take the risk of trying to identify a religious value
which provides a key to a sympathetic openness to the Jewish
religion. It seems to me that the notion of the Covenant *(berith)*
plays this central integrating role. It helps us to have some sense
of how Jewish people see themselves as a special, 'chosen' people. The Covenant implies fidelity on both sides – that God
promises to be faithful to the Chosen People and that they are
invited and challenged to remain faithful to God and to their
commitments.

A rich spiritual reward awaits us if we succeed in developing
a sympathetic understanding of the Jewish outlook. It will convince us of how important it is that we too have a sense of being

chosen by God. This awareness of being chosen helps us have a deep sense of our own worth and of the unique contribution each of us is called to make with our lives.

When the Jews first came to their 'covenant awareness' it was linked to a strong *inter-personal* experience of God. We see this, for instance, in the very personal way God called Abraham (Gen 12: 1-3, 7). It is even more clear when Moses is called and is taught to call God 'Yahweh' (Ex 3: 14-5). It is true that in more recent times some Jews no longer relate to God in such a personal way. Nevertheless, for me as a Christian to explore the Jewish sense of being 'chosen' gives me an opportunity to deepen my inter-personal relationship with God. Borrowing a phrase from Raymond Carver, we can find the deepest meaning of life in being able 'to call myself beloved, to feel myself beloved on the Earth'.

But we can also learn from Judaism that the sense of being chosen is not a purely personal or private experience. It is rather an awareness of being part of a whole community – a member of the chosen 'People of God'. It is not just that *I* am called but that *we* are called. In this way we are helped to avoid the modern tendency to turn religion into a purely private relationship between the individual and God. Eric Voegelin goes so far as to claim that already in the covenant with Abram/Abraham (Gen 15), the new domain of Yahweh is contained in germ. This new political order in which the Jewish people become the people of God originates in Abram 'through the inrush of divine reality into his soul and from this point of origin expands into a social body in history.'[1]

A crucial aspect of the Covenant—an aspect which as Christians we can easily overlook or play down—is its immediate link with 'The Land'. We may not agree with the Zionist understanding of the Covenant; and we may be appalled by the insensitivity of successive Israeli governments towards the Palestinians. But we have to accept that the concept of the Covenant does not sit easily alongside the easy distinction most people make nowadays between religion and politics. In fact we find ourselves compelled to recognise that, though this distinction is valuable and even necessary, nevertheless there are some situations where it is almost impossible to draw a clear boundary-line between politics and religion.

Dialogue with Judaism does not demand that we accept the

views and policies of the majority of Israelis today. But it calls us to find within ourselves a sense of how closely Jewish identity is bound up with Jewish history – which in turn revolves around repeated possession and dispossession of their own land. We need also to have a sense of how this history has always been experienced as a *sacred* history, the story of a whole people's ongoing and intimate relationship with a God who nevertheless remains transcendent.

By sharing in some degree in this Jewish worldview we may learn how to 'ground' our own sense of being chosen and we may integrate that sense into our everyday world and our history. For the Jews there is a fundamental link between 'being chosen' and having their own Land. From them we can learn that our spirituality is likely to remain shallow and rootless until we 'bring it down to earth' quite literally. External or internal dialogue with Judaism will teach us to recognise and appreciate our need for a *home country* whose history and geography provide us with roots and meaning and spiritual nourishment.

Dialogue with Muslims: Sovereignty, Destiny and Revelation
Dialogue between Christians and Muslims is probably the most difficult sphere of inter-religious dialogue today. Some of the difficulties spring from the long racial memories of bitter wars and crusades. Furthermore, there is at present a high level of political tension between 'the Muslim world' and 'the West' (which is still seen as in some sense 'Christian'). In the world as a whole, perhaps the most significant source of political tension arises from the fact that, since the death of communism, Islam provides the only really effective challenge to the cultural and political dominance of 'the West'. Moreover, *within* many countries in Asia, Africa and Europe there is serious strain in Muslim-Christian relations. In many countries the Muslims see themselves as having to 'catch up' with the Christians who often had a privileged role in the past; while in a few places (Pakistan, for instance) the Christians constitute a very poor and oppressed minority.

But the obstacles to dialogue are not just historical, political and cultural; they also arise in the strictly religious sphere. A key point is that both Christianity and Islam tend to be absolutist in their claims to possession of revealed truth.[2] Even though scholars on either side have done much work in exploring the sacred writings and history of the other religion, the fact remains that, quite frequently, each side puts forward an interpretation of the other religion which believers on the other side find quite unacceptable.

Faced with such an intractable situation it is all the more important that Christians should engage in whatever kind of dialogue is still possible. Most vital of all is the *internal* dialogue which enables us to have a sympathetic understanding of the religious values which form the core of Islam.

The word 'Islam' means 'submission'. At the heart of the Muslim faith lies the profound religious impulse of total surrender to the will of God. Linked to this is a very strong sense of God's total sovereignty, the utter conviction that all things are under God's control and therefore that whatever happens is willed by God.[3] These ideas are also central to Christian belief; so it should not be difficult for us to resonate sympathetically with Islamic believers, at least in these aspects of their core beliefs.

At times we Christians may feel that Muslims tend to understand God's sovereignty in a one-sided way which leads to fatalism. Many missionaries have had the terrifying experience of travelling in a bus or taxi whose Muslim driver refused to take elementary precautions on the grounds that he would die only at the time God has decided. I suspect that our exasperation with this attitude springs not merely from a fear of being killed but also from our awareness that a similar misguided understanding of destiny is not unheard of among some Christian drivers as well!

It would be grossly unfair to judge Islam as a whole on the basis of such an unbalanced application of the principle of God's sovereignty. It is clear that fatalism is an aberration and is not typical of mainstream Islam, either in its official teaching or in everyday living. Nevertheless, on this issue there remains quite a wide gap between the religious consciousness of ordinary Muslims and that of modern Western Christians. We are not, however, entitled to assume that *they* are wrong and *we* are right. In fact, Islamic belief in the sovereignty of God provides a very healthy challenge to the quasi-secularist attitude which, within the past generation, has become fairly common among Christians in the Western world.

Some years ago, when I was teaching in an inter-religious

institute of education in Africa, I asked a class of mature students what for them was the meaning of the word 'destiny'. It was very striking that all of the older, more traditional ones defined it as 'fate, or what happens to you'. In sharp contrast to this, all of the younger, more Westernised students defined destiny as 'what you make of yourself'. These responses brought home to me the radical shift of consciousness which was taking place within a few years – as a result of increased contact with 'the West', and perhaps especially with Western Christianity.

Here, then, is one point where religious dialogue with Muslims may prove fruitful – precisely because it points to an aspect of Christian belief where we may have compromised and weakened our faith. We may have failed to challenge – and perhaps even to notice – the assumptions of the prevailing secular Western culture. We may have come to take for granted that our destiny lies entirely in our own hands. Dialogue with Islam invites us to examine our consciences, to see whether we really believe in the power and sovereignty of God and are truly willing to entrust ourselves unreservedly into God's hands, while at the same time believing in the reality of our personal responsibility for our lives.[4]

The notion of prophetic revelation also lies at the heart of Muslim belief. Once again this is an area where there is a great deal of common ground between Christians and Muslims. Yet, paradoxically, this agreement tends to make the remaining differences even more intractable. When we engage in dialogue with Muslims on the nature of revelation we come up against the same problem as when we try to find a basis for communicating with Christian fundamentalists. We can understand this better when we know a little of the history of Islam. Within a couple of centuries of the time of Mohammed, orthodox belief came to be identified with a very literal reading of the Koran; and any kind of more liberal interpretation of the Koran was condemned as heretical. Since that time, mainstream Islam has been totally committed to seeing the Koran as the Word of God in a fundamentalist sense.

However, these difficulties should not lead us to minimise or play down the vital importance of our common belief in a transcendent yet personal God who has graciously chosen to speak to us. Furthermore, both Muslims and Christians believe that God's revelation is itself truly a divine reality which has mysteriously entered into our world. In seeking to have some sense of the role the Koran plays in Islam, it is not sufficient for us to compare it with the role played by the Bible in Christianity. The Koran in Islam has a role comparable to the role of Jesus in Christianity, since the Koran is seen as, literally, the Word of God, not just a created reality. As Wilfred Cantwell Smith says: 'Muslims do not read the Qur'an and conclude that it is divine; rather they believe that it is divine, and then they read it.'[5]

We have much to learn from the utter conviction of Muslims that God has truly spoken to us through the prophets. Living in our highly secularised world, we are constantly tempted to play down the reality of the prophetic Word. Fear of being seen as old-fashioned, or odd, or fanatical can inhibit us from proclaiming or witnessing to our beliefs.

In this atmosphere it can be quite helpful to be in touch with, or even to be aware of, the millions of Islamic believers who are quite unabashed in practising and preaching their religion. They inspire us to be less inhibited and shame-faced in relation to our faith. Furthermore, we sometimes have the opportunity to make common cause with Muslims in asking that the state should live up to the pluralism it professes, rather than reducing pluralism to secularism.

Dialogue with the Hindu and Buddhist Religious Traditions: Mysticism and Compassion

There is such an extraordinary richness and diversity in the Hindu and Buddhist traditions that there can be no question of trying to encapsulate their teachings and values in a few paragraphs. In any case, it is difficult to pin down any universally accepted body of teachings in either of these great religions.[6] This is partly because they do not give the same prominence to 'doctrine' as Christianity and Islam do. It is also because, over the centuries, each of these religions has branched out into different streams and traditions; and what is central in one branch of Buddhism or Hinduism may be quite peripheral or may even be denied in another branch. It is not possible to give universally valid responses even to such obvious questions as whether Hindus or Buddhists believe in a personal God or what priority they give to contemplation, or moral action, or religious devotions.

Mysticism

However, it is safe to say that one of the features common to several strands of both the Hindu and Buddhist traditions is a strong emphasis on mysticism. Indeed it is ironic that many people in the West who feel a real hunger for religious experience have sought to meet this need not by turning to the mystical tradition of the West but by looking to these Asian religions.

We cannot be really open to the contemplative aspect of the Hindu and the Buddhist traditions if we make the mistake of evaluating these religions in purely *moral* terms. Many people in the West, including many Christians, fail to realise that contemplation and mysticism are to be valued in their own right and not simply in terms of how they affect us at the ethical level – e.g. whether they cause us to be more just, more generous, or more loving towards others. Of course meditation and mystical experience do tend to make a person more moral. But the point I am stressing is that this is not their sole purpose – and may not even be their primary purpose. We must not reduce religion to morality.

It is particularly important not to make this mistake in regard to the Hindu and Buddhist traditions, since the distinctiveness and strength of both of these religions does not lie solely (and perhaps not even primarily) in the ethical values they inculcate, but more in the deeply *religious* values they embody. If we are to engage in effective dialogue with the Hindu or Buddhist traditions we must recognise *from our own experience* the difference between ethical values and religious values. We must know how important it can be to leave aside even very pressing moral concerns in order to 'go inside' and focus on religious values such as inner peace, or wisdom – or God.

In this strictly religious sphere, it can be enormously challenging and enriching to engage in an inner dialogue with these two Eastern religious traditions. *Challenging*, because it encourages us to let go of our inclination to value ourselves in terms of our achievements, or the good works we engage in, or even our high moral ideals. *Enriching*, because it affirms and strengthens the inner call we all experience at times to become more contemplative, to give 'quality time' to nourishing the spirit. Dialogue with the Hindu and Buddhist traditions can help us to listen to the inner voice which calls us to move inside, to sit still, to value meditation and the deep religious peace which it brings.

The call to reverse our priorities – to adopt a contemplative rather than an activist mentality – need not necessarily be seen as an invitation to do less work. We come nearer to the heart of the Hindu and Buddhist attitude if we think in terms of 're-nouncing the fruit of works'. This phrase is taken from the *Bhagavad Gita*,[7] which is one of the most profound of the Hindu sacred writings, composed over two thousand years ago. The passage suggests that we are hindered religiously not so much by our activity as by a utilitarian attitude which makes us calcul-ate the worth of our actions (and our own worth also) in terms of short-term consequences. The Buddhist tradition lays great em-phasis on the same point. Buddhists believe that a true inner freedom comes when we are able to choose what is right, with a certain indifference to the outcome.

In the *Bhagavad Gita* this inner freedom is the fruit of a pro-foundly religious experience, a sense of being wholly dedicated to God: 'Who standing firm on unity communes-in-love with Me as abiding in all beings ... that athlete of the spirit abides in Me.'[8] This is an experience which seems to be very close to what Christians would call total devotion to the will of God. In other strands of the Hindu and Buddhist traditions the notion of a per-sonal God is less prominent or even absent. But the idea of an inner liberation remains very important. There are different ideas about how one can attain this freedom of spirit (e.g. through asceticism, through yoga, through chanting, or breath-ing, or meditation).

There are also varying understandings of what it is that one is set free from, or has to let go of. In general terms, the liberated or enlightened person is released from *Karma*. This *karma* can be seen as the 'weight' of bodily existence or as the legacy or conse-quences of one's actions.[9] We might picture it as though it were sticky mud which pulls us back into a swamp; it clings to us be-cause we tend to grasp and cling on to the passing things of this world. Of course this image would suggest that the material world is like a swamp out of which we are trying to escape; and, from a Buddhist or Hindu point of view, that might not be too inaccurate. Both of these great religions tend to think of spiritual progress in terms of shaking off our entanglement with material things, including the human body.

Enlightenment

There are, of course, significant differences between the Hindu and Buddhist traditions. There is no need to go into these differences here. It may, however, be worthwhile recalling that the Buddha spent some years learning the practice of Hindu meditation. It brought him great peace of spirit. But it did not meet his deepest need because when he returned to daily life he still felt encumbered by his desires. That is why he went on to seek – and eventually to find – an 'enlightenment' which set him free from the burden of human desires.

This story poses a very deep and serious challenge to us Christians. Do we allow ourselves to admit how restless we are, how burdened and scattered we feel as we are dragged hither and thither by the welter of desires which flow through us? And are we really willing to let in the possibility that the way to be humanly fulfilled may be the *relinquishment* of our desires rather than their *attainment*? (When modern Western Christians engage in dialogue with these Eastern religions I think it is helpful to think of being burdened and weighed down not so much by the fact that we are material beings but by the multitude and power of our wayward *desires* for material things.)

The reason the challenge of Buddhism is so radical is that it calls us to be counter-cultural. Modern Western culture muffles the inner voice which calls us to the kind of freedom which comes through a letting go of desire.[10] So the first step in an authentic inner or outer dialogue with Buddhism is perhaps the most difficult: it is simply to recognise and uncover within ourselves the half-buried longing to be free of restlessness.

If we pay attention to this longing, it leads on to further profound questions. Should we seek an experience of 'enlightenment' which would enable us to transcend our desires? And what would this involve? Could we envisage some kind of mystical identification with God which would set us free of the many pulls which seem to be part of the fabric of human living? And how would this compare with the Buddhist 'enlightenment', which is usually described in more negative terms, without reference to God?

These are not issues with which Western Christians – or theologians – usually concern themselves. So the importance of dialogue with Buddhism is that it shows up blind-spots in the Western approach to religion and spirituality. We may never be able to find clear-cut answers to the questions it raises. But more important than answers is a willingness to make space in our lives for the questions. And, of course, we are missing the whole point of the dialogue if we seek to answer the questions in an abstract manner. The real challenge is to engage in an experiential exploration.

Compassion

So far I have been focusing mainly on the more *mystical* aspect of dialogue with Buddhism. But there is a further crucial element in Buddhism which is perhaps equally important. It concerns the *moral* response of the Buddha himself when he achieved 'enlightenment' – and of others who have followed his path. The 'Enlightened One', having been set free of the burden of desire and the constant rebirth it brings, may be moved by *compassion* for the multitudes of suffering people in the world. This compassion leads him or her to choose to postpone the full experience of the peace of *nirvana* in order to help others to find the way to enlightenment.[11]

From a Christian point of view, compassion is the basis for social and political action: we 'share in' the suffering of another and this drives us to ease the other person's pain or to tackle the causes of the suffering. Dialogue with Buddhism offers a different perspective on suffering and a different way of living out one's compassion. The Buddhist sense of the finite and passing quality of all things leads to a feeling of ultimate detachment. So the Buddhist may not feel the Christian's sense of urgency to change the situation; compassion may be experienced simply as a willingness to *be with others* in their suffering.

There are, then, two concepts of compassion: a Western active one which focuses on relieving the suffering of others; and a Buddhist one which may seem passive because it does not seek to change the outer world but which actually calls for 'work' of a very different kind. It invites one to find a way of being fully present to oneself and to others – and especially to those who suffer – which does not allow the evil in the situation to have its way, to triumph over the human spirit.

It is hard to resist the urge to compare these two positions with a view to deciding which is more correct or more valuable. But the whole point of this kind of dialogue is to avoid jumping to conclusions too quickly. In this case dialogue does not mean we have to abandon our commitment to human liberation. It does not require that we replace our ideal of liberation of the world by a notion of inner spiritual liberation. But the dialogue offers us an opportunity to deepen and enrich the quality of our compassion. It challenges us, firstly, to admit that in many situations we may be quite powerless to ease the suffering of others. Secondly, it reminds us that the word 'compassion' means, literally, 'suffering-with'. So, even in situations where suffering can be relieved by our action, we must not seek to by-pass the first step of really 'letting in' the pain of the other before rushing to 'cure' it.

Above all, perhaps, dialogue with Buddhism on this issue invites us to acknowledge the importance of liberation of spirit if we wish to bring liberation to the world – or to engage in any other form of mission activity. For our desire to help others can be 'muddied' by our need for approval, or an urge to prove ourselves, or other self-interested motivations; then the resulting action becomes distorted or even corrupted. So this inner liberation has a certain priority – as Jesus reminded us when he insisted that good fruit comes only from a good tree (Mt 7: 17-8).

Buddhism teaches us that to identify with others in their suffering is profoundly redemptive for both parties – even apart from any external effort to transform the situation. This lesson may help us Christians to come to a deeper understanding of God's response to our suffering. If I find myself scandalised by God's apparent failure to 'do something' about the appalling suffering in the world, perhaps it is because I have failed to really 'let in' that suffering; perhaps I am looking for an easy escape from it. Is it not ironic that Buddhism, which professes to have little or nothing to say about God, should in this way throw new light for us on one of the most profound aspects of our Christian faith?

Buddhist compassion is not limited to other human beings. The Buddhist (and Hindu) conception of *karma* is one where all living beings are linked. Animals may be reincarnated in human form and humans may be re-born as animals. So the compassion of the enlightened person extends to all living creatures. Dialogue on these issues with Hindus and Buddhists may give a new depth to the ecological concern which in recent years has become much more prominent in Christian spirituality.

Closely related to the compassion motif is the Buddhist emphasis on non-violence. This springs from a sense of reverence for others and for life in general. One of the lessons we in the

West can learn from Buddhism is the deep inner connection between the *religious* value of contemplative freedom of spirit and
a *moral* attitude of gentleness and non-violence. To engage fully
in dialogue with Buddhism is to find oneself invited to adopt an
approach to life which is radically different from the activist and
'go-getting' outlook which brings 'success' in the Western world.
This dialogue can help to ensure that Western or Western-educ-
ated Christians do not succumb to this Western inclination
which results in so much exploitation and dis-ease.

Dialogue with the Chinese Religions: Stability and Flow
There is some doubt about whether Confucianism should be
called a religion. Some would say it ought to be seen rather as a
philosophy of life because it appears to make little reference to
God or any transcendent power. However, it can be seen as a
partner in the kind of inter-religious dialogue with which I am
now concerned. It represents a particular outlook on life where
the value of stability is given a much higher priority than other
values. The Confucian philosophy of life lays great emphasis on
the importance of order or pattern in life. In this way it helps us
to appreciate that order is one of the fundamental values without which we cannot live a truly human life.

Harmony, dignity, stability, and respect – all these have a
high place in the Confucian value-system.[12] No wonder then
that there is a lot of emphasis on authority, first of all within the
family and then in the wider society. In order to have a sympathetic understanding of Confucianism – and indeed of the ancient Chinese culture – we need to appreciate the importance of
these values.

Over the past generation, we in the West (and the whole of
the Western-dominated world) have discovered to our cost that
we cannot take these values for granted. We see all around us
the fragmentation of society and the damage to individuals
which occurs when there is widespread breakdown of family
life and of the cohesion of local communities. There can be no
doubt that we have much to learn from external and internal
dialogue with the Confucian world-view.

Taoism
Taoism is another Chinese religion or worldview. For centuries
it has existed alongside Confucianism, and uses some of the

same language. Nevertheless, it is in many respects at the very opposite end of the religious spectrum.[13]

Both religions stress the importance of the *tao* – a word which means 'way' or 'path'. As used in Confucianism this word refers to the ordered pattern or way of life which gives dignity and a true quality of humanity to life. Taoism, as its name implies, gives an even more central role to the *tao*. But its conception of the *tao* is more cosmic than purely human. For the Taoist, the *tao* might be seen as 'the pattern of nature' or even, possibly, as 'the natural law'. But perhaps the most helpful translation of the word *tao* in its Taoist sense is 'the *flow* of life'.

The central point is that, in Taoism, the 'pattern' or 'law' of nature is not understood as being fixed or providing stability. Those who are in touch with the *tao* are people who can allow themselves to be carried along in the river of life, people who have an intuitive sense of where life is leading them. This means that while the Confucian *tao* represents stability, the Taoist *tao* implies spontaneity. But this spontaneity is not a purely arbitrary activity. It is, rather, the ability to know when *not* to act, not to interfere, not to try to control things, not to try to put our shape or stamp on the world, but to allow ourselves be borne along by the flow of life.

Dialogue with this Taoist point of view is of crucial importance for us today. Many religious people from the West – and people educated in Western ways – sense that some of our most intractable difficulties spring from the fact that we have become disconnected from the flow of life. For four centuries Western science has been dedicated to the effort to understand the world, not in order to *flow* with life but in order to *control* it, to 'master' the world. And its tools have been rationality and disciplined, organised, investigation. This has left us out of touch with the more spontaneous, creative and intuitive dimension of human life. We have gained knowledge at the expense of wisdom. Inner dialogue with Taoism may help us to be aware of this loss and may help us to come more in touch with the flow of life.

It is not just overtly religious people who have come to realise the enormity of our loss when we are no longer adequately in touch with 'the flow of life'. There is a growing understanding among psychotherapists that healing and well-being requires that we regain our connection with the *tao*, the flow of life.[14] Even in the business world of today there is a new appreciation of the importance of intuition. Management consultants, having more or less exhausted the possibilities of tools for rationalis-ation, have now begun to devise tools to develop the creativity and intuitive abilities of planners and workers.[15] This is a good example of how religious issues underlie our everyday secular concerns – even in the most unlikely places.

It is important, however, that we should not allow the inner dialogue with Taoism to be 'hijacked' by people who would like to 'use' what it has to offer but are unwilling to face its radical challenge to the dominant Western value-system. To become a follower of 'the Way' in the genuine Taoist sense is not just a matter of learning to use one's intuition in order to sense what is likely to happen. It is, rather, to let go of the need for power and prestige. It is to relinquish the frenzied activism and con-sumerism which drives the economy of the Western world. It is to return to a more placid and simple lifestyle, to know when to flow with life rather than trying to shape it to our design and for our comfort.

The dialogue with Taoism can also have important implic-ations in the sphere of ethics. Those who are in touch with the *tao* are not guided primarily by rules or laws. They have an inner sense of what is right and wrong. They know when to break the rules. This is not to say that they are lawless or immoral but rather that they recognise that life is constantly changing so that no fixed set of rules can provide an adequate guide for authentic human living.

QUESTIONS FOR REFLECTION

1. Is it really possible to be open to Judaism while disagreeing with Israeli policy?
2. Is it justified to use the word 'holocaust' to refer to other geno-cidal events besides the Nazi treatment of the Jewish people?
3. How would you define 'destiny'? How does it fit with human responsibility? Is there a difference on this issue between Christians and Muslims?
4. Does the Buddhist conception of compassion throw some light on the attitude of Mother Teresa of Calcutta and of Charles de Foucauld? Is the Christian always called to change the world?
5. What does the notion of 'the flow of life' mean to you? Do you experience it? What helps?

CHAPTER 3

Dialogue with Primal Religions

It is only in fairly recent times that we have come to speak about *primal* religions. A generation ago people in the West, including missionaries, spoke without embarrassment about 'paganism'. In doing so they were referring mainly to what is now called 'primal religion'. The word 'pagan' comes from a Latin word which means 'a rural person'. The word has been used for centuries in a derogatory way. It suggested that the religious beliefs of people living in 'country' areas or far from the so-called centre of civilisation are backward and misguided.

In recent times we have largely dropped the word 'paganism' from our vocabulary. It was replaced at first by the word 'animism', and then by the phrase 'traditional religions'. Nowadays, it is more acceptable to refer to 'primal religion(s)'. In line with this change of language comes a major alteration in the value we place on the traditional religious beliefs of, say, the Aboriginal Peoples of Australia, the indigenous peoples of North, Central, and South America, the peoples of Africa and of the Pacific, the ancient Celts, the so-called 'Tribals' of Asian countries, etc. One of the most significant changes in the whole area of the approach to religion and culture is the high regard in which these traditional or 'primal' religions are now held. In fact, we have reached a point where the uncritical rejection of these religions is often replaced with an equally uncritical adoption of their beliefs, values and practices.

Rootedness – In Nature and in the Community
To have some understanding of the spiritual experience of 'primal' peoples one needs to appreciate that for them *family* has a truly religious significance. There is a much stronger family solidarity than is customary in the West. And the 'family' extends far more widely than the nuclear family. Furthermore, those who have died recently are seen as part of the family and treated almost as

though they were still alive.[1] The more remote ancestors also play a vital role in the community; for the sense of being linked to them gives people a feeling of 'connectedness', of being situated within a continuum of family life which goes on from one generation to the next. So the connection with the ancestors is a key component in giving meaning to people's lives – it provides them with a sense of being rooted in the past and hope for the future.

'Primal' religion gives people not only a sense of being linked to the ancestors but also a feeling of 'connectedness' with the animal and plant world. One aspect of this is that certain categories of animal are given a sacred significance, and certain trees or rocks or caves or rivers are seen as 'holy'. But beyond that there is a sense of being part of nature as a whole and belonging to a living vibrant cosmos which has mysterious 'laws' of its own which we can perhaps glimpse and sometimes use to our advantage but never fully understand. These people have a very strong sense of the spirit world and of the active presence of divine or quasi-divine beings at work in our world. For them there is no sharp boundary between the spirit world and everyday life. Their world is alive with the presence of spirit.

There is a very significant difference between the Western and the primal ways of explaining what we see happening in the world. We in the West are content with a 'scientific' understanding of causality. Most primal peoples, by contrast, look for a *personal* explanation. Suppose, for instance, that a person is contracting malaria much more frequently than in the past. Western people are content with the explanation that people have failed to eliminate the usual breeding places where mosquitoes can hatch out. Primal people find such an impersonal explanation quite unsatisfactory. For them, it does not answer the key question why one person becomes ill while another is spared. For primal believers there must be a more personal cause. So their key question is: '*who* sent the mosquitoes?' In other words, they are not satisfied with an explanation which focuses on *how* the sickness occurred; they want to know *why* it happened.

Dialogue?
How can we engage in dialogue with primal religion? There are few, if any, spokespersons who have been appointed as its *official* representatives. There are, however, some gifted writers and

critics who have taken on the task of reflecting on their primal roots and articulating a partial interpretation of that 'world' to modern Western (or Westernised) society. Perhaps the most outstanding of these is the Nobel prize-winning Nigerian author Wole Soyinka, who has gone some way towards developing a very profound and sophisticated theology of certain parts of Yoruba traditional religion.[2] For the most part, however, it has been left to Western anthropologists and ethnologists to give us some account of primal religions. Most of them focus very narrowly on the details of the rituals and beliefs of a particular ethnic group. Occasionally, however, one or other of these scholars ventures to make some rather sweeping generalisations about primal religion, backed up by somewhat fragmentary evidence.

It is clear that in the case of primal religion we have to depend a great deal on the kind of 'inner dialogue' which I described in Chapter 1 above. We may now and then be privileged to meet somebody who holds on to the primal religious mentality and can articulate it in language that we can understand. But, for the most part, the dialogue has to go on *inside* us, as we struggle to be open to the values and beliefs which are embodied in people's behaviour rather than formally articulated. It is likely that it is in the effort to inculturate the Christian faith in indigenous cultures that we will begin to get some sense of the values of primal religion. (It is, of course, fairly easy to meet Western people who have decided to 'go back' to what they consider to be Celtic religion or ancient Earth religion; but there is a danger that the religious beliefs and practices of such people may owe as much to their own imagination and desires as to the historical reality.)

Primal religion puts little emphasis on formal articulated doctrine. It operates more in the sphere of myth, ritual, and celebration. It is hardly an exaggeration to say that traditional ritual ceremonies (incorporating dances, singing, sagas, and poetic myths) are the primal equivalent to the *creeds* by which we Christians define our religion. So, if we want to have inner or outer dialogue with primal religion we may have to pay less attention to our *ideas* and more to what we are *experiencing* and what is going on in our bodies and in our relationships with others.

An important first step in dialogue with primal religion is to recognise the price we in the West have paid for building our world around science and technology. We need to admit that we have largely lost the very 'grounded' sense of wonder of those who live close to the earth. We have undervalued the earthy wisdom of the traditional farmer. And we have failed to appreciate the intuitive abilities which are so necessary in everyday life and so valued by the peoples whom Westerners used to call 'primitive'. Dialogue with 'primal believers' may help us to recover these gifts. Conversely, a re-valuing of these gifts may make us more open to, and capable of, realistic and effective dialogue with primal religion.

Dialogue with primal religion is quite different from dialogue with a historical religion such as Islam or Judaism. For, as I suggested in my book *Divine Energy*, primal religion is not just one among many other religions but is the source from which all the historical religions spring and the place from which they draw sustenance:

> … primal religion … supports and is embodied in all the traditions … It is rooted in the religious capacity and longing which is common to all humankind. This deep underlying religious dimension of the human spirit is the point where we are most fully human. But it is also a matrix where the Spirit of God moves very powerfully. Here is where the Spirit intercedes for us and speaks to our spirits 'with sighs too deep for words' (Rom 8:26; 8:16) … [Here] we share in God's own life by drawing joy, hope, peace, life-energy and inspiration from the Spirit of God.[3]

Yoruba Deities

In primal religions it is quite common for people to believe in a variety of different gods or goddesses or deities. Western people find this really difficult to understand. We in the West tend to think that the major issue is, 'does God exist, or not?'; we find it hard to think that anybody would experience a need for a whole variety of gods! But if we are to come to a sympathetic understanding of primal religion we need to look at this issue.

I worked for some years in the Western part of Nigeria where the Yoruba religion still has a very strong influence, despite the fact that most of the local people would identify themselves as Muslims or Christians. In fact this traditional system of belief and cult was so strong that when African people from all over the continent were carried off as slaves to Brazil the Yoruba religious beliefs and practices became a unifying factor for them all.

The spiritist cults of Brazil (Umbanda, Maconda and Candomblé) have taken over the Yoruba deities and there are probably now more people who believe in them in Brazil than in Africa. When I worked for a short time in Brazil I found it interesting to discover that I could find far more people who proclaimed and practised their belief in these deities in an open and public manner than I could back in Nigeria.

Yoruba religion has a great variety of deities. Two of the best known are Ogun, the god of iron, and Sango, the thunder-god (spelled Xango in Brazil). The water goddess Oshun is associated especially with the Oshun river. There is also a pre-eminent god called Olodumare. Christians – and many Western scholars – have tended to explain the role of the lesser deities by analogy with the role played by the Madonna and favourite patron saints in Italian or Latin American popular piety. They see them as 'intercessors' who play a kind of mediating role with God; and Boladji Idowu, the author of the best-known book on Yoruba religion, sees the god Olodumare as equivalent to the Christian God.[4]

No doubt there is some element of truth in this approach. But my suspicion is that it is far too simple. It does not give any real insight into the inner meaning of the deities. Furthermore, it does not account for the role of certain significant aspects of Yoruba religion. For instance, Ifa, the deity or spirit associated with oracles and divining, has more in common with the Greek Delphic oracle than with any Christian saint. (Ifa has also been used as a more generic term for the overall Yoruba religion.) Furthermore, there is a mischievous divinity called Eshu— which Christians incorrectly assumed to be equivalent to the devil.[5] And Shopona was a deity associated with smallpox; he seems to have faded out of existence since this disease was more or less eradicated in recent times; but it is difficult to see how such a divinity could be equivalent to a Christian saint. As for the question of one supreme God: it may well be that Idowu and other Christian scholars were interpreting Yoruba religion too much in the light of their own Christian belief.

A more fruitful approach might be to look at the Yoruba religion and similar primal belief-systems in terms of the actual religious practice of those who belong to the cult of the different divinities. For instance, a certain number of traditional believers belong to the cult of Ogun, the god of iron. This has the effect of making them feel that a certain quality of iron is infused into them; they experience themselves as tough, able to resist pressure from other people or from the environment in which they live. Others belong to the cult of Sango. This gives them a different kind of power – the kind of energy that is associated with thunder and lightning, rather than iron.[6] Similarly, each of the other deities is associated with a particular kind of energy which generates in its devotees a particular mood or mode of being.

Celtic Deities

There are many similarities between the Yoruba divinities and those of ancient Celtic peoples. Here I shall just mention some of the divine or semi-divine figures which were worshipped in pre-Christian Ireland. First, the female deities: There was a goddess associated with the river Boyne, called Bóinn in Irish. She is a mother-goddess.[7] She can be compared to the river-goddess Oshun in Yorubaland. Flidais appears to be a different manifestation of the mother-goddess, but seems to have a special concern for deer and other wild animals, so it has been suggested that she represents 'the wilder aspect of that divinity';[8] in this her role corresponds to some extent to that of Artemis among the Greek deities. There is a goddess of the soil called Danu or Ríogain or Mor Ríogain. Since her task includes protection of the land she is also a goddess of war, who empowers those whose side she is on, and who screeches terrifyingly over the battlefield.[9] Then there is Brighid who seems to be another manifestation of the land goddess Danu. As such she guarantees agricultural prosperity. She also has the special role of suckling (i.e. inspiring) poets. When Ireland became Christianised Saint Brigid (who has the same name) took her place and was given many of her functions.[10] Medb (which is the Gaelic spelling of the common Irish name Maeve) is a goddess who personifies sovereignty and who sleeps with the young hero who is destined to become king.[11]

Among the male Celtic gods we may mention Lugh who is associated with the harvest festival of Lughnasa, which is the Irish word for the month of August. The play and film *Dancing at Lughnasa* by the Irish playwright Brian Friel shows how the power of this pre-Christian festival, and of the god who animates it, endures down to the present day as a source of life and wild exuberance. Then there is Goibhniu who is a god of smithcraft,[12] corresponding to some extent to the Greek god Hephaestus. There is a divinity of healing and health called Dian Céicht. He was greatly honoured because the healing of sickness was a crucial aspect of Celtic religion, as of all primal religions.

Greek Gods and Goddesses

It is clear that each of the various Celtic gods and goddesses, just like the Yoruba deities, is associated with a special sphere of activity and a specific kind of energy. The same applies in the case of the ancient Greek divinities. Here I shall just give some brief examples from among the Greek Olympian 'sky-gods', while noting that ancient Greek religion also included the pre-Olympian Chothonian 'earth-gods', as well as the mysterious Moira, which represents Destiny or Fate and which seems to be independent of, and in some sense superior to, all the gods.

Aphrodite is the goddess of love, of beauty and of joy. She affects men and women by filling their hearts with love and desire. She is manifested particularly in beautiful, desirable, charming, loveable women. She is associated above all with sexual love, but also with friendship, and with the beauty of nature. She has nothing to do with marital fidelity; in fact when her energy comes into play men and women are likely to desert their marriage partners and run away with the object of their infatuation. So her kind of love can bring disaster. For instance, the great war described in Homer's *Iliad* came about because Helen, the wife of Menelaus, king of Sparta, deserted her husband to elope with Paris, prince of Troy.

In sharp contrast to all this is the nature of the goddess Athene. Though she is a goddess of battle she does not inspire people into mindless passionate fighting. She is rather the epitome of reason, of the thoughtfulness which curbs and inhibits passion. And she is always near at hand to inspire presence of mind in those she favours. Men and women who come under her influence manifest practical wisdom and prudence.

The god Hermes is very different from both Aphrodite and Athene. He is a god of the night. In the world of Hermes the night provides opportunities for making money, for being lucky, for taking advantage of others, perhaps for playing tricks on them, or even stealing. So Hermes is a kind of patron to merchants, travellers and tricksters.

Each of the Greek gods or goddesses can be seen as the unifying power of a whole constellation of objects, events and experiences; so each of them gives meaning to a whole 'world'. These deities are not themselves objects with the visible world, but they are 'real' – in fact far more real than the everyday objects around us. For we do not experience any object in isolation but only as part of a wider 'world' in which it has its meaning and reality. A chair only has meaning in a world where people sit down; the notion of a parent only makes sense in a world where there are children; a book can only be understood in the context of a world where people read; and so on. Perhaps a more practical illustration of the same idea is the variety of quite different ways in which a valley in the mountains can be experienced. A lover may experience the valley as a place of beauty to be shared with the beloved; a military strategist sees it in terms of defence; an engineer may see it as a possible site for a reservoir; and a mystic may experience it as an invitation to find closer union with God.

In terms of primal religion, each of these different experiences is attributable to a particular god or deity. It is the gods which give meaning to our world – and not just one meaning but a variety of different meanings which come to the fore at different times. The night has a radically different meaning in the 'world' of Aphrodite, the goddess of love, than it has in the 'world' of Hermes, the god of chance and wealth and opportunity.[13]

In so far as they affect us humans, it is helpful to think of Aphrodite, Athene, Hermes and the other Greek gods and goddesses as sources and manifestations of a variety of different moods or modes of being. 'The gods ... are the personification of those mysterious forces which through their often violent interaction produce the harsh patterns of human life – the rise and fall of nations, the destructiveness of the earthquake ... but also the sweetness of passionate love, ... the extra strength that surges through a warrior's limbs at the moment of danger.'[14] They are *personifications* but they are not *persons* in the strict sense. This means that they are not individuals who are subject to moral constraints, who take account of the welfare of others, who are capable of self-criticism or able to question their own nature. 'Each one is a separate force which, never questioning, moves blindly, ferociously, to the affirmation of its own will in action.'[15] So it is more accurate to see them as different types of energy rather than as different personalities.

Spiritual Energies or Powers

This notion of a deity as a type of spiritual power or energy applies also to the Yoruba deities which I referred to above. For instance, Ogun is the source and personification of 'iron energy', of toughness. His spirit, his energy, inspires and imbues black-smiths, those who go to war, and those who do difficult physical work, such as road construction. In the primal world 'spirit' and 'energy' and 'power' are all more or less the same reality. Furthermore, those who experience the world in this primal way do not make the kind of sharp distinction made in the West between *personal* and *impersonal* powers; so it is not possible to get a clear answer to the question, 'is Ogun a person?'

When I was engaged in pastoral work in Africa I was struck by how frequently people said to me 'I was taken by a spirit of anger' (or by a spirit of lust, or envy). A European is inclined to see such remarks as figures of speech. But I suspect that such remarks are remnants of an older religious mentality, one where people experienced themselves as influenced – perhaps even 'possessed' – by spirits or powers.[16] I say they are 'remnants' because it seems that Christianity subsumed all the more positive aspects of such experiences, leaving only the negative ones to linger on without being integrated with the Christian world-view.

What all this suggests is that, for adherents of primal religions in ancient Greece or in tribal societies in the non-Western world, there is no gap between the material world and the spiritual world; spiritual energy permeates every aspect of life. The 'natural order' is not opposed to 'the supernatural'. Instead, nature is experienced as an integral reality which includes, on the one hand, what we can see or hear or touch and, on the other hand, various kinds of spiritual power or energy which we can 'feel' or experience and which have a profound influence on our lives.

It is to be expected, then, that people would set out to under-stand and control spiritual energies, just as they learn to manage the growing of plants and the herding of animals. Some people are believed to be more effective than others in 'managing' these spiritual powers; such people are recognised as shamans or div-iners or healers – or sometimes as magicians or wizards or witches. The spiritual powers remain mysterious, however; even though they do not constitute a separate sphere which is seen as distinct from everyday life. They are rather the controlling forces of everyday life, what we might call the depth dimension. As I have said, diviners or shamans or healers learn ways of 'using' these powers. But the reality is that it is more true to say that people are controlled by the powers than that the powers are controlled by people – even by the most effective shamans or diviners.

It now becomes quite understandable why different people become involved in the cult of different gods or deities. Take the case of Greek or Nigerian warriors who sometimes experience themselves as 'taken over' by a kind of 'battle fury', to such an extent that they find themselves filled with courage and quite ready to risk their lives in the heat of battle. If the warriors interpret this experience to mean that they are inspired or empowered by the Greek war-god Ares or the Yoruba god Ogun, then it is not surprising that they would seek ways of invoking this power again when they come to face another battle. So soldiers are likely to be devotees of their warrior god and to become involved in whatever ritual or cult is associated with this god. The cult can be looked at in two ways. From one point of view it is a celebration and honouring of this mysterious spiritual energy or force which surpasses ordinary human power; but from another point of view it can be seen as an attempt to use or harness this power. Much the same can be said of those who engage in the cult of Aphrodite or any of the other gods.

I should mention in passing that this attitude does not seem very different from that of Catholics who have a great devotion to, say, Padre Pio. Their devotion includes both an honouring of this saintly person and an attempt to gain some benefit from him. But devotion can go much further than this. It can move in two very different directions. At times devotion can take a direction that borders on the magical; in such cases the devotee is trying to 'harness' the power of the saint. On the other hand, there is a deeply authentic kind of devotion which is not at all magical or superstitious but is almost mystical. It seeks – and sometimes finds – some sharing in the life, the energy, the spirit of the holy person to whom one is devoted. I know a deeply religious woman who has a great devotion to Padre Pio. In times of great difficulty she occasionally has a sense of being in living contact with his presence. She experiences this presence in the form of a beautiful aroma which envelops her and brings her unutterable consolation and peace. In some respects this is a typically 'primal' experience; yet it is fully integrated into her Christian faith.

I suspect that such experiences are far more common than we realise. Perhaps the reason we church ministers do not hear more about them is that they do not fit well with our rather cerebral theology. One of the benefits of dialogue with primal religion may be that we come to a better understanding and appreciation of such experiences. On the other hand, I believe that it is only by being open to listen to such religious experiences among our own Christian people that we can begin to have some sense of what is involved when the adherents of primal religion engage in the cult of various deities.

Possession

As Christians we tend to take it for granted that being 'possessed' by a spirit is unusual, bizarre and evil. But people who practice primal religion quite frequently want to be possessed. One obvious example is the war-dance ritual where warriors set out to be empowered and 'taken over' by a deity or spirit of battle which will give them courage and also, perhaps, give them immunity to the weapons of their enemies. Much more common are rituals in which a shaman or 'medicine man/woman' deliberately sets out to be filled with and inspired by a god or spirit in order to be able to act as a diviner – for instance, to discover the cause of some sickness or evil which is troubling an individual or a whole village.[17]

Spirit possession can also have a healing effect. For example, in parts of Zambia young women who are under a lot of stress occasionally become 'possessed'. This is accepted as a fairly normal part of life. It offers the young woman an opportunity to opt out of everyday life for a while and to go through a kind of catharsis which may have the effect of relieving the strain. I have often thought that it serves much the same function as the 'primal therapy' or 'holotropic breath-work' which has become fairly common in the West in recent years. In each case the normal barriers are broken down or suspended for a time in order to allow the person get access to, and work through, material that would normally be considered unacceptable, for instance, very painful memories from the past. I should add, however, that when this kind of work is done as therapy in the Western world the person is usually encouraged not to go so deeply into the altered state that he or she loses all sense of the everyday world; the aim is rather to achieve a kind of dual consciousness, so that the cathartic work may have an immediate effect in the person's 'normal' world. In primal religion, on the other hand, it appears that 'possessed' people usually lose all personal contact with their 'normal' world; it would seem that the link to that everyday world is held for them by the community and by those who specialise in working with them.

In many traditional primal religious celebrations there are extended bouts of intense dancing which do not have any purely 'practical' function such as healing or triumph over enemies. The aim of the rite is strictly religious – it is to shift the participants into a state of altered consciousness where they achieve a condition of spiritual exaltation. For the participants this indicates that they are touched or even possessed by a deity or spirit. Some of the Pentecostal churches in Africa, Asia and Latin America (as well as various 'prophetic' or 'healing' sects such as the 'Aladura') have adapted this practice and given it a Christian interpretation: the adherents of these sects set out to become possessed by the Holy Spirit.

Witchcraft

Fifty years ago there was a ready market for films and periodicals such as *The Wide World Magazine* which depicted the barbarous religious practices of tribal peoples in a lurid and bizarre manner. In sharp contrast to this, people nowadays tend to romanticise primal religion, seeing it in terms of an idyllic harmony with nature and the earth. Each of these presentations, of course, owes more to the imagination of Western people than to the reality. The truth is that we have much to learn – or re-learn – from primal religion, but people who live according to this pattern also suffer a lot of spiritual oppression and their lives are often marked by fear of spiritual evil.

There are various sources of fear and evil. One notable cause of distress for many people is the havoc which they believe is caused by the spirits of recently deceased relatives who are dissatisfied with the way their family treated them before or after their death. Another major source of trouble is disharmony in the community which brings all kinds of illness and evil into people's lives. But in my experience by far the greatest source of fear and evil is witchcraft. It would be difficult to over-estimate the impact which witchcraft, or even suspicion of witchcraft, has on the everyday life not only of primal believers but also of

Christians who come from a primal background, or a culture where witchcraft is taken seriously.

This is the sphere where I find the widest gap between my own religious consciousness and that of my African friends. Some years ago in West Africa a close friend of mine told me he had discovered that his daughter was a witch; he was afraid to let her out of his sight for fear she would do irreparable damage.

Some time previously, a fellow missionary who was an ethnologist was staying with me. An African teacher came to visit me and the three of us got talking. The conversation turned to witchcraft. The teacher assured us that he did not believe in witches. My ethnologist friend drew him out skilfully and before long this teacher was sharing what he really believed, rather than what he thought we Westerners would want him to think. He told us that he had discovered that his own wife was a witch and that she had left him to practise her craft elsewhere; and he ended by saying, 'I heard that the woman died.'

In such circumstances I find in myself a very strong inclination to make a judgement, to say this is right, that is wrong. It is as though I try to control the situation by trying to fit it into a moral grid of readymade judgements. But witchcraft is so foreign to my present Western culture that it will not fit easily into my pre-existing frameworks of understanding or evaluation. Of course I have no doubt that it is evil and does enormous harm in the cultures where people believe in it. I find it important to be reminded that not all spiritual energy is good – that there are people who cultivate a kind of spiritual power which is destructive and is used for evil purposes.[18]

I do not know how best to deal with witchcraft. I find it salutary to recognise that this is one of many areas where I am ignorant, inexperienced, and have no readymade answers to give people. My limited experience indicates that if I take too much account of it I only increase its power—just as the efforts of the Inquisition in Europe to extirpate witchcraft gave it more credibility and caused it to increase. My African friends have a sense that it is their very belief in the power of witchcraft which gives it a power over them – a power which does not seem to touch me.

But it would be very naïve to draw the conclusion that the power of witchcraft is purely psychological. There is here an evil spiritual power which, in my Christian view, can ultimately be overcome only through the power of Christ whose dominion is universal. But I am shocked by the insensitivity of some Western evangelists who come to preach to tribal peoples and draw in large crowds by presenting their message in terms of a confrontation between 'their' Christ and 'the forces of evil' (as defined by them). In dealing with witchcraft it seems better to rely not on mass crusades but first of all on careful listening and humble dialogue, and then, where appropriate, on personal witness to one's belief in the all-embracing care of God and the power of Jesus Christ.

Transcendent?

The conclusion which emerges from all that I have said is that primal religion is not 'other-worldly' in the same way as religions such as Christianity, Islam, or Judaism set out to be. And it is not as inward-looking as the Hindu and Buddhist traditions. Primal peoples are not at all dualistic; and this applies also to people who still retain a primal form of religious consciousness even though they are officially Christian or Muslim.

We are accustomed to think that religion is concerned with the *transcendent.* But it would appear, at first sight, that I am now saying that primal religion has no conception of the transcendent. In one sense this is true. But in a more important sense it is not true at all. We need to distinguish between two levels of transcendence.[19] There is first of all the sacred dimension of the world around us. For primal people this is at least as real and as obvious as the everyday objects around them; and they do not make any clear distinction between 'the sacred' and 'the secular'. But from the point of view of the rather secularised Western world, this 'sacred' aspect of the world *transcends* or goes deeper than the visible tangible objects around us.

The second level of transcendence applies above all to the God of the Christian, the Muslim or the Jewish believer. It does not imply that God is absent from our world. But it indicates that God is not limited to this world or identical with it but always remains 'beyond' it. It is not clear to what extent primal religions have such a conception of God. Almost all African religions have some notion of a Supreme Being who is 'beyond' our world and is normally accessible only through intermediaries. But these religions do not have a formal theology so it is difficult if not impossible even to discuss the question whether this Supreme Being is transcendent in the same sense as the Judeo-Christian God or the Muslim Allah.

Perhaps the major source of difficulty in understanding primal religion and engaging in dialogue with it is the fact that we in the West have partly lost our sense of the sacredness of the world. It seems that one reason for this is precisely because we have put so much emphasis on the transcendence of God. It seems as though this divine 'other-worldly' transcendence somehow monopolised the sphere of the sacred, leaving our everyday world largely bereft of its sacred or spiritual quality. However, I would prefer to qualify this statement: I think that this secularisation of our world occurred more in the realm of scientific and theological theory than in the actual everyday experience of people who were less scholarly.

Over the past three centuries, the emptying of the sense of the sacred and of the mysterious dimension of life gradually percolated 'downwards' from the scholars to the middle classes and to the world of industrial workers . It was a long time before it had a big effect on the peasants – and it is only as the peasants of Europe have gradually disappeared that secularisation has had its full impact on the West. And even still there are remnants of a deeply religious consciousness in many 'ordinary' Western people; these are half-submerged and are largely ignored by most scholars (including theologians). In recent years many Western theologians made the very mistake which is often attributed to primal peoples: they saw God as so transcendent and distant that they found little room for God in their everyday experience of life. Putting it in very crude terms, one might say that the transcendent God first 'hoovered up' all the sacredness of life; and then this God became more and more remote and eventually more or less disappeared from everyday life!

However, things are not as bad as might appear at first sight. First of all, the process of secularisation has taken place more at the level of articulation and theory than in the actual experience of 'ordinary' people. So one aspect of the way forward is to look more closely at the 'spiritual' experiences of people and to value them more highly. Secondly, many Western people are becoming aware of how empty and meaningless life becomes when it lacks a sacred dimension, or when the depth aspects of life are not properly acknowledged. This has led to a great (and sometimes naïve) interest in primal religions of all kinds – perhaps especially Celtic religion and Native American religion.[20] So, as the process of secularisation advances, it is being challenged by a more recent growth in interest in 'spiritual' realities. It is at this point that I see a convergence between primal religion and the deeper dimensions of modern Western life. That is the topic I wish to consider in the next chapter.

QUESTIONS FOR REFLECTION

1. Have you had the experience of being *inspired*? Who or what do you think is the source of inspiration?
2. Can you identify aspects of your own religious experience which you would consider to be 'primal'?
3. What is your attitude to witchcraft? Do you think somebody could bewitch you – and if so what do you think is the source of this power? Could you guard yourself against witchcraft?

CHAPTER 4

Dialogue with the Western World

How does one engage in religious dialogue with a secularised world? The first step is to recognise that to be 'secularised' does not necessarily mean that one has no sense of God or of the sacred. There would not be much point in seeking dialogue about spiritual issues with people who have no interest in things of the spirit. The secularisation of the West does not mean that most people have lost interest in spiritual matters. It is true that in Europe (much more than in North America) there has been a great decline in church practice, that very many people do not belong to any church, and that the churches have lost a lot of the credibility which they had in the past. But many people who have become disillusioned with church, and perhaps with all official religions, have a deep interest in spirituality – even though not all of them would use the word 'spirituality' to describe the deeper aspects of their experience, or the profound questions that concern them, or the fundamental values to which they are committed.

I want to argue here that Christians should see the Western world as a prime candidate for religious dialogue – but only under certain conditions. The first of these conditions is that the dialogue be conducted in a style and language that finds echoes in people's everyday experience, rather than in an old-style 'churchy' language which leaves them cold.[1] The second condition is that the dialogue should begin, not with the transcendent God or with other-worldly questions, but with the deep spiritual dimensions of everyday life. It is at this point that there is a convergence between two worlds that seem at first sight to be very different from each other – the world of the adherents of primal religion and the modern 'secularised' world.

'Searchers' and 'Deep Ecologists'
The dialogue must focus on the concerns of those who take part

in it; and these concerns vary a great deal from person to person. There are some people in the Western world today who are engaged in a very serious and conscious search for spiritual meaning and values. These 'searchers' are people who have become quite disillusioned with the competitive, exploitative and ruthless style of much of modern living; and have devoted themselves to finding an alternative way of life. Such people will be interested in sharing with us and listening to our experience of meditation or mysticism or divine energy and spiritual healing – provided we can talk from personal experience rather than giving them book knowledge or abstract theology.

There is an increasing number of people in the West who have committed themselves to respect for the earth and to living in harmony with nature. Some of them are interested in what has come to be called 'deep ecology': they seek to develop or rediscover the more spiritual or religious dimensions of care for the earth. They are intensely interested in the rituals and myths of various primal religions – for instance mid-winter or mid-summer celebrations, initiation rites, funeral celebrations, and the 'spirit quest' of Native American peoples or the Dream World of Aboriginal people.

They are quite likely to have a negative view of Christianity, seeing it as the monotheistic, patriarchal, legalistic religion which ruthlessly wiped out as much as possible of the earlier religious beliefs and practices, which were centred on Mother-Earth and which gave a far more prominent role to women. But they will be interested in a dialogue which indicates that Christians have something to offer in relation to respect for nature and living at peace with others and with all of creation. They may be particularly interested in the way in which in Ireland, down to the present day, Christianity has managed to accommodate itself to the continued celebration of the four great seasonal festivities of the primal Celtic religion: the Spring festival of Brigid on February 1st, the celebration of the beginning of Summer in May, the harvest festival in August, and the festival of the dead in November.[2] What was lost and what was gained when Christianity took over in the Celtic lands – and in so many other places where primal religion was partly replaced by, and partly subsumed into, Christianity? This is a topic of particular interest and urgency today.

Moral Values, Moral Virtues

It must be acknowledged, however, that only a minority of people in the West today are seriously engaged in a conscious search for religious meaning and values. On the other hand, there are many deeply committed people in our world whose primary interest is not in such overtly 'spiritual' values but rather in moral and political values. I think of one friend of mine who has devoted her life and all her energy over the past ten years to working with refugees in Liberia. Or there are those well-known people (and others who work behind the scenes) who have dedicated their lives to the victims of the Chernobyl nuclear disaster. In giving themselves totally to this cause they seem to find resources of energy which appear almost superhuman. Much the same applies to those who find the meaning of their lives in living with autistic people in the Camphill communities or to living with people who have learning difficulties in the l'Arche houses inspired by Jean Vanier. There are courageous journalists and lawyers who campaign tirelessly for human rights. There are theologians and church ministers who have sacrificed comfortable positions to make 'an option for the poor'. The list goes on and on.

Some of these dedicated people are Christians or belong to some other religion; others have no religious affiliation. What they have in common is that their lives are built around some noble moral value which has inspired them and almost 'taken them over'. It has lifted them 'out of themselves' in the sense that they are willing to give up comforts and careers to follow their cause. In a 'primal' world, people would have no hesitation in saying that a god or goddess or a spirit had touched their lives, inspiring and perhaps even possessing them. We in the West today do not use that language, but the reality is the same.

The kind of people I have in mind have devoted themselves to some virtue such as justice, love for the poor, the vindication of human rights, care for the earth, etc. It is interesting to note that the word 'virtue' means, literally, 'power'. So one might say that they have dedicated themselves to a spiritual power. Perhaps it would be more accurate to say that a spiritual power has taken them over, enthused or inspired them to a point where it has become the central purpose and meaning of their lives. From that point of view, there is not much difference between them and primal people who are 'taken over' by a deity which, as we have seen in the previous chapter, is a spiritual power or energy which is not personal in the strict sense.

A Source of Meaning and Purpose
In a primal culture various categories of people such as shamans, warriors, and lovers devote themselves to a god or goddess who then inspires, directs, enlivens and gives purpose and meaning to their lives. In much the same way many modern Western people devote themselves to rich spiritual values or virtues and find in them a meaning, a purpose, a driving force and a source of energy. They find themselves enthralled, almost 'possessed' – and are often quite willing to serve their values 'unto death'. In this way they are saved from the emptiness, meaninglessness, and selfish individualism which is fairly common in our world.

People can be 'taken over' and driven by other spiritual powers which are not so obviously 'good'. There are people who are sports fanatics and people whose ruling passion in life is to climb mountains. Some scholars devote their whole life and energy to the study of an arcane subject. And it would seem that some people find the meaning of their lives in doing battle with others; in a primal culture they would be seen as devotees of a god of war.

Another example: a friend of mine recently gave up a safe and comfortable career to marry, at a time and in a situation which many thought quite 'crazy'. If this had happened in ancient Greece, people would have had no doubt that it was the work of Aphrodite. Nowadays we simply say, he fell in love and decided to follow his heart rather than taking the safe option. The reality of what happened is the same, even though we label it differently. The significant point here is that what happened was not something that we would normally see as 'religious' – in fact many people would not even see it as 'good'!

Something similar happens in cases where people devote themselves single-mindedly and whole-heartedly to art. There are poets and dramatists, painters and sculptors who may well have made a mess of their 'ordinary' lives but who are inspired to create great works of art. Even in our secularised Western world it is considered normal to speak of such people as touched by the Muse – though most of us probably see that as a figure of speech. For the artists themselves, however, the experience of being inspired is very real.

All these are examples of the kind of experiences which feature in primal religion. Surely this indicates that our so-called 'secularised' world may have more in common with the primal world than one would have expected. And we may conclude that this kind of event provides an opening for religious dialogue with the modern Western world. For we are talking of situations where people give their lives to a spiritual power of some kind and where the power in return gives them life.

Religious Dialogue about Moral and Political Values
In order to engage in meaningful religious dialogue of this kind we need to find a language which will help both partners to recognise the 'depth dimension' or spiritual aspect of these experiences of devotion, dedication and inspiration. If the Christian partners fail to name this dedication as truly spiritual then they will be unable to see how it can be a basis for *religious* dialogue; they will want to hasten on to 'other-worldly' topics which may be of no immediate interest to those on the other side. If modern Western people do not have an appropriate language, they are unlikely to notice just how important it is to be rescued from aimlessness or self-absorption by commitment to some spiritual virtue, or value, or 'power'.

One advantage of the kind of dialogue proposed here is that it can help us to re-connect morality with religion. I am taking it for granted that morality has its own integrity as a personal response to ethical values such as justice, truth, or love. But when we recognise this 'autonomy of morality' there is a danger that we assume that moral and political values such as social justice and concern for human rights are not matters about which we can have *religious* dialogue. The effect would be to confine spirituality to a rather limited sphere of very 'private' religious values and practices such as meditation or the search for inner wisdom.[3] By naming moral values and virtues as spiritual energies or 'powers' to which one can be devoted, I hope to widen the sphere of religious dialogue very considerably. From this point of view the sharing of experiences and views about fundamental moral values can be seen as a genuine religious dialogue.

Issues of the Last Two Centuries
Looking back on the past two centuries, we can identify several major areas which could and should have been occasions for

fruitful religious dialogue between the Christian churches and modern society. But, sadly, in most cases what took place was 'a dialogue of the deaf'. The French Revolution brought the notion of democracy into the arena and for the next hundred years there was a very polarised debate about this issue. The leaders of the Catholic Church took a strong anti-democratic stance and failed – or refused – to see the deep spiritual values embodied in democracy. They remained blind to the enrichment brought to the lives of those who devoted themselves whole-heartedly to promoting democracy. It took a further fifty years before the Catholic Church came fully to terms with the values of the democratic state.

On the issue of human rights, the story was much the same. The quality of the 'dialogue' over a very long period is indicated by a statement made by a pope about ninety years ago: 'We have heard enough of the rights of man but what about the rights of God?' It is only within the past generation that leaders of the Catholic Church have spoken out strongly in favour of human rights and made it a central emphasis of Catholic social teaching.[4]

Even more striking is the absence for over a hundred years of a truly open dialogue on the issue of socialism. It is quite evident that church leaders on one side and Marxists on the other got locked into blind opposition to each other's positions. Some Protestant Church-people showed an openness to socialism early in the twentieth century. But in the Catholic Church the first serious attempt by a pope to engage in dialogue with Marxism came in Pope John Paul's 1981 encyclical 'On Human Work' (Laborem Exercens). Even after that, the Vatican has shown itself quite unsympathetic to liberation theology and in this way missed an opportunity for very fruitful dialogue within the church itself.

A more recent example of a 'dialogue of the deaf' is on the issue of the ordination of women. On one side stands the official Catholic Church, the Orthodox Churches, and significant segments of the Anglican and Protestant Churches. On the other side is the main body of 'the women's movement' (including very many committed members of all the churches), as well as many men and a large number of theologians. The argument has become very acrimonious. The Vatican imposes heavy sanctions on those who refuse to accept that this whole question is a closed issue. Those on the other side tend to see the theological arguments put forward against the ordination of women as an ideological defence of patriarchal and clerical power; and they fail to recognise how far the church has moved in recent years on 'women's issues'. Furthermore, they often fail to appreciate the major contribution which the church has made down through history towards the recognition of the gifts and dignity of women. (I think, for instance, of the way in which over the past century devoted missionary teachers – Sisters and lay people – have changed the lives of millions of young women in the so-called Third World and, in doing so, have raised the status of women to a level which it never had before.) The breakdown in communication between the women's movement and many of the churches has done enormous damage to the church itself. Just as the church lost the working classes in the nineteenth century, it is now losing the allegiance of a very large number of women who used to be 'the backbone of the church'.

Why have the churches failed so notably to open themselves to sensitive dialogue on such fundamental spiritual issues? Probably because behind the debate was a power-struggle. Protagonists on either side of each of these major issues sensed that they had a great deal to lose if they failed to win the argument. Church leaders –particularly those of the Catholic Church – allowed the church to become allied to authoritarian and unjust regimes. The result was that they became blinkered in their views. Much of what they said and wrote on these controversial issues was simply a defence of entrenched positions, even when they were convinced that they were engaged in an unbiased search for the truth. The conclusion is obvious: if church-people are to be open to genuine dialogue they must not allow themselves to get tied into power-structures which they feel they have to defend at all costs.

At the present time the church finds itself engaged in debate or dialogue about a number of major topics, such as questions relating to ecology and development, the women's issue, the nature of human sexuality, and bio-ethical issues including questions about when human life begins and ends, and about cloning and gene-manipulation. Unfortunately, on several of these issues the battle-lines have been drawn up; and even on less polarised issues such as ecology there is no great openness on either side to real dialogue.

If the church is to exercise its mission to engage in dialogue with the world, it must be more open to the notion that the Spirit speaks not only in the church but also in the world – even in our present Western secularised and sinful world. In fact all the evidence is that the Spirit has been speaking very powerfully in this world, quite outside the context of the institutional churches. The lead in the struggle for social justice was taken by people outside the church. On ecological issues, too, the lead did not come from church authorities. (The ecological theologians Thomas Berry and Matthew Fox were treated as rather maverick figures in the church.) Many – perhaps most – of the great moral and political ideals which inspire people today came from non-church sources – and sometimes in the teeth of fierce opposition from church-people. Examples are the concepts of human rights and of gender equality.

Spiritual Hunger

Nevertheless, the church has much to offer the Western world at this time. For there is a real spiritual hunger for ultimate meaning and values. We live at a time when the West is exercising an economic, political and cultural imperialism over practically the whole globe. The driving forces of this imposition and expansion are dis-values such as competitiveness, exploitation, and greed. Under the pressure of this apparently unstoppable system, people's traditional ways of life are collapsing and ancient belief-systems are being eroded and losing credibility.

In many respects we find ourselves in a situation similar to that which prevailed shortly after the time of Christ. At that time, too, the expansion of an imperial power (the Roman Empire in that case) had undermined people's traditional value systems and ways of life. Then, as now, the imperial power was not content to control people's lives but sought also to impose its own belief-and-value system on all. People were required to worship the empire – just as nowadays we are expected to give allegiance to 'the laws of (capitalist) economics'. Then, as now, many people were in this way turned into idol-worshippers. But in that period, just as today, a lot of people found that their lives were becoming drained of meaning and purpose. They were searching frantically for some alternative system of meaning and for worthy spiritual values by which to live. The mystery cults and gnostic teachings provided a partial answer. But

Christianity offered a more satisfying faith-system which met both the 'private' and 'public' religious needs: 'private' needs for life-giving religious experience and wisdom; and the 'public' need for a spiritual power which could effectively challenge even the Empire itself. This helps to explain the rapid expansion of the very early Church.[5]

This pattern could, in principle, be repeated today. The rapid growth of Islamic fundamentalism is an indication of the hunger of people in the Muslim world for an effective alternative to Western capitalist ideology. Many people in other parts of the world, not least in the West itself, feel a similar hunger; but few in the West feel drawn to meet it with any kind of fundamentalism. The Christian faith could provide answers to many – provided they are not distracted from its core by 'baggage' which has become attached to it, and provided it is embodied in a language and ritual which speaks to their hearts. Furthermore, their need will not be met if the Christian faith is presented in a mode of old-style one-way mission. It will be appreciated only if it comes to them in the context of genuine and humble dialogue, where Christians are willing not only to share their own faith but also to learn from the profound spiritual experiences and wisdom of those who profess little or no formal religious beliefs.

A Treasury of Old Things and New

I have been dealing with issues where there are tensions in the dialogue between the church and the Western world. But now it is time to look at some of the many topics which could provide opportunities for a very rich dialogue. These are aspects of life on which the church has valuable experience and insights to contribute to interested people in the West. I shall group them under three headings: (a) Rites of Passage, (b) Moral and Political Values and (c) Religious Symbols and Practices. In relation to all of them I shall focus particularly, though not exclusively, on the prospective contribution of the Catholic Church because it is the one I know best.

(a) Rites of Passage

By rites of passage I mean significant stages of life, such as birth, marriage, sickness, and death. Over the centuries the church has developed profound rituals and ceremonies which bring out the deep meaning of these experiences and help people to respond to them in a fully human way. For instance, the ritual of baptism includes the notion of sponsors, where family friends willingly commit themselves to care for the spiritual welfare of the child. The marriage ritual is one of enormous solemnity and power – expressed, for instance, in the words, '....for richer, for poorer, in sickness and in health, as long as we both shall live.' Also very valuable is the tradition of having a 'wake' when a person dies – an all-night vigil which combines communal support and sympathy with reminiscences, prayer and a certain amount of muted conviviality. Then there is the funeral liturgy which helps relatives and friends of the dead person to let in the reality of the death and begin the process of becoming resigned and resuming everyday living. (Unfortunately, there is a tendency nowadays to omit some of the more powerful aspects of the ritual – for instance, the singing of the *Dies Irae*, and the throwing of clay on the coffin in the grave with the words 'ashes to ashes, dust to dust'; and funerals nowadays are often more private than in the past.)

The whole issue of how we account for illness and how we respond to it is one of those 'depth' topics which are of as much concern to people in the Western world today as they are to those who live in a primal culture. It is an ideal subject for dialogue, and one where Christianity has much to offer. It may often be better to begin the dialogue not with theology about why God allows sickness and evil but with much more practical matters such the value of the Christian tradition of having a ritual anointing of people who are seriously sick. Even very secularised people often recognise that such an anointing can be a very moving occasion – and very effective in helping sick people, and their friends, cope with the illness. Dialogue about it could easily lead on to a sharing on more profound issues around the spiritual aspects of healing.

It frequently happens that a community of people feel the need to celebrate some important event in the life of the group, or to make a solemn beginning of some joint enterprise, or even to foster a deeper harmony and sense of solidarity in the community. If such people are Christians – and more particularly if they are Catholics – they almost automatically decide to organise and celebrate a special eucharist in such situations. Here they have ready to hand a very rich ceremonial and ritual which meets all these deep spiritual needs and which can be 'tailored' to the particular occasion by the choice of suitable readings, prayers, and symbols. Those who are 'unchurched' may have to start from scratch in constructing rituals for such occasions – and they probably will not have any rich tradition to draw on. So they may be open to dialogue on this whole topic of celebration and spiritual community-building.

People with little or no church affiliation often turn to the ancient Christian rituals to celebrate the turning-points of life; for these rituals give expression to the sacredness of such experiences. There is here an opening for a fruitful dialogue about the meaning of such sacredness. But Christians must not assume that they are the experts on experiences of the sacred who already have all the answers. They must be open to learning from others and to be willing, together with them, to adapt existing rituals and design new ones in accordance with the aspects of the situation which the partners in the dialogue find sacred.

(b) Moral and Political Values

Perhaps the most striking moral value which could be a topic for dialogue between Christians and 'secular' people is how to respond to the plight of the poor. Over the centuries the church has garnered a wealth of experience in this regard. Those who are concerned to respond to, or alleviate, or overcome poverty today have much to learn from the diverse spiritualities which have animated Christians on this issue. These range from the approach of those in the Middle Ages who set up the 'Lazar houses' for the care of people suffering from leprosy, to the radically new approach of Vincent de Paul (in his time), to the more recent (and very diverse) spiritualities of Mother Teresa of Calcutta, Jean Vanier, and Charles de Foucauld.

The concept of an option for the poor was developed by Christians who were in dialogue with Marxism. They brought into the dialogue a rich new notion which, as I shall say in Chapter 8 below, owes more to the Bible than to Marxism. The values underpinning such an option have already had an effect far beyond the Latin American Catholic ambience in which the notion first emerged; and the topic is one of great relevance for a dialogue with committed people in today's world.

This leads on to the issue of liberation. Of course the struggle for human liberation is a moral-political issue rather than a strictly religious matter. But behind the immediate ethical and political questions lie background issues which are truly spiritual and religious. When we look at the hope and the energy which animate those who engage in the struggle for liberation we have to ask: 'Where does this power and this hope come from?' A lively dialogue on such issues developed in Nicaragua and in South Africa where so-called 'secular' activists struggled together with Christians against oppression; and interest in the topic is by no means confined to places where tyranny prevails.

A further moral-political topic that should be of general interest is the recent practical experience of *team leadership* practised in so many religious orders in the church (especially in women's congregations). This new model of authority is of enormous relevance to all the institutions of our world, from multi-national companies to small businesses, and from government departments to medical bureaucracies and educational establishments. It is an area where religious orders and congregations have something very valuable to contribute to the wider society. There are two aspects which are significant: the very idea that authority is seen as *leadership* rather than as control; and the experience of exercising this leadership in teams rather than bureaucratically or hierarchically. Also relevant to secular institutions is the further experience of religious congregations and societies in re-defining their purpose and mission corporately through large assemblies or 'general Chapters'.

Still in the political sphere, there is another very sensitive topic about which we could have dialogue. It is the centuries-long attempt by church leaders to defend orthodoxy through the Inquisition. How does this compare with the attempt of Marxist-Leninists to preserve 'the party line'? And, if the church's experiment with 'thought police' has proved immoral and unviable, how can we hope to develop at least a minimum measure of practical consensus on major public issues of morality – for instance, on the morality of nuclear weapons, or of genetic modification of plants, animals and humans, or on the attitude of the state to abortion or euthanasia? Does the church's historical experience of having a 'Holy Office' to safeguard orthodoxy have anything to teach us and our partners in dialogue about how to cope with the rigid orthodoxies of today in, say, departments of economics or philosophy in the universities, or the so-called 'liberal agenda' of much of the media?

If people are looking for yet another topic for dialogue in the political sphere, then it might be very interesting to take up the question of the Crusades. What have we learned from this channelling of religious fervour into militant action? It is well to remember that we still have 'crusaders' in our midst today – for instance, animal rights activists, eco-warriors, militant nationalists, and the governments which continue to bomb Iraq even as I write these lines. Do these 'crusaders' of today's world have anything to learn from the history of past crusades?

Another moral topic which may be of interest to secular people is that of fidelity. In situations where society as a whole had a strong belief in a personal God it was customary to call God to witness our commitments – for instance, in the making of marriage vows. What basis can people nowadays find for the sacredness of such commitments? And how absolute should such commitments be? Where the situation changes (e.g. where one partner in a marriage develops schizophrenia) should people still feel bound by the 'vows'? This is a good example of a moral question which leads on to deep religious issues.

(c) Religious Symbols and Practices

Finally we come to the matter of specifically religious practices. My starting-point here is the fact that, even within our secularised world, very many people experience a need for some spiritual practice or some sacred space or time or some object which opens them up to a deeper dimension of life. This is an area where the treasury of the church (especially the Catholic Church) is so rich that it is almost overflowing.

We can begin with the very many styles of meditation and prayer which have been used by generations of believers in the past. These include the mantra-like prayers of the rosary or 'the Jesus prayer', the public or private recitation of the breviary (built around the psalms and scripture readings), and solemn liturgical celebrations of the eucharist. They also include discursive meditation, Ignatian 'contemplation' of the mysteries of Christ's life, the prayer of quiet and mystical prayer, as well as personal or communal *lectio divina*. What a rich menu this is, a menu from which each person or group can choose the style that suits their own temperament.

Alongside this, the church has a wealth of experience in relation to appropriate postures for prayer and meditation (kneeling, bowing, genuflecting, stretching out of hands, etc), as well as in relation to ascetical practices such as fasting (or celibacy?) which may dispose one to pray or meditate more effectively. Why is it that people in the West who become interested in the practice of meditation nearly always turn to the East and seldom ask or hear anything about the rich tradition that is available nearer home? Does it perhaps indicate that the churches are focusing their attention on issues where people do not want to hear them rather than on a topic where they might well find willing partners in dialogue?

Then there is the whole concept of 'a sacred place' – not just churches and prayer-rooms, but holy wells, holy mountains, way-side shrines, holy islands, and sacred journeys (pilgrimages). All of these were very common in the Ireland in which I grew up. Even though Ireland has now become quite secularised, there is still a great interest in sacred places, where people have an opportunity to step back from the routine and pressures of daily life. We can also note the sense of the sacred generated by stained glass windows and sacred vestments. Very striking, too, is the power of the tabernacle, the sanctuary lamp, and the monstrance as sacred objects which become focal points for meditation. Furthermore, even today many Irish homes have a 'St Brigid's cross' made of rushes pinned to the door as a sign of protection. There are other holy objects, ranging from medals and blessed candles to rosary beads, from statues and icons to the relics of saints, and from holy water to incense. As Christians became more secularised in recent years they tended discard or downplay such objects. So they are surprised to find that many unchurched people in the West are using these or similar objects to nourish their spirits. This provides an interesting topic for dialogue.

The Christmas crib still has an almost magical power to entrance people and give them a sense of the sacred. The crib – like the pictures of the Sacred Heart – remind us that from a Christian point of view the incarnation is the focal point for everything that is sacred in our world. In the person of Jesus there is a convergence of the full transcendence of God with the lower level of transcendence (the depth dimension of worldly realities) to which I referred in the previous chapter. Christians see the incarnation of Jesus as the definitive presence of God in our world – a presence which is foreshadowed and prepared for in the myriad of intimations of transcendence found in everything we find sacred. So in one sense the incarnation ensures that our respect for holy objects is not idol worship. But from another point of view the incarnation of Jesus is just the peak moment of a more generic incarnation – a presence of the divine which permeates all of creation. The whole topic of the sacred and sacramental dimension of our world is a rich area for joint exploration and dialogue.

Counter-Cultural Communities
Quite a lot of idealistic people in the West today – many of them with no church affiliation – are interested in forming countercultural communities. In dialogue with such people and groups the church has a rich experience to draw on. Over the centuries the church has built up a great deal of practical wisdom about the management of such communities. I am referring here to such issues as how best to organise the common ownership of goods, how to foster the practice of a simple lifestyle, what are the most appropriate models of formation for those who wish to join, and how to manage the governance of such communities in a respectful and participatory manner. Some of this wisdom has even become embodied in law – either in the official Canon Law of the church itself or in the Constitutions and Directives of various religious congregations. If church people develop a truly open and sensitive tradition of dialogue with interested 'searchers', they may come to see such laws as a rich resource – a record of approaches that work well and ones that run into trouble – instead of cringing with embarrassment at the very notion of Canon Law!

Furthermore, the whole concept of the 'charism' of a community could be a topic of great interest for such communities of 'searchers'. They may welcome the opportunity to hear and share about the many different spiritualities which have been built around such charisms – and to explore how a particular spirituality can become embodied in a tradition which is handed on to succeeding generations. It can be very helpful for those who would like to form a community to explore the structures that have been developed over the centuries to support those who feel called to live in contemplative communities as distinct from those whose call is to a more active life of service of the poor, or those who wish to live as hermits. Furthermore, there is the fascinating topic of how reformers within each of the great traditions have at times felt a call to restore the charism of their group to its pristine purity.

Religious Leadership and Authority

Another subject for dialogue which some people in the so-called 'secularised' West may find fascinating is the very notion of a 'minister of religion'. Is there need and room in the secularised world for spiritual leaders or people who can speak with some kind of sacred authority on issues concerning the meaning and purpose of human life? How could one become qualified to play such a role? What gives such a person authority? Is authority different from credibility? What are the similarities and differences between a shaman, a guru, an imam, a priest in the Jewish tradition, and a Christian ordained minister, etc? What about religious charlatans – how can they be dealt with in a pluralist world such as ours?

Spiritual Experiences

A further possible topic for dialogue is the whole area of intense spiritual experiences such as visions or special 'messages'. Nowadays it is not uncommon to find people who have such experiences, even though they may have little or no attachment to any church. Frequently they have no idea how to handle these experiences; they are afraid even to talk about them lest people think they are going crazy. Over many centuries, the church has developed a wise pastoral approach in relation to such happenings. The official church does not authenticate such visions or messages but neither does it deny that they may be valid. The distinction made in the church between a 'private' and a 'public' revelation is itself an important contribution, because it lessens the pressure on individuals to go public with their personal spiritual experiences.

Providence and Guidance

The final item I want to mention as a possible topic for dialogue is one of the most important of all. It is the question of a sense of providence and of guidance. Traditionally, Christianity has preached a very 'strong' doctrine of providence, namely, that God's care and love are active at every moment and in every event of our lives. One traditional way in which the intimate personal quality of this care has been communicated is through the belief that each one of us has been given a personal guardian angel, who watches over us. As children we learned to pray to this angel, 'ever this day be at my side, to light and guard, to rule and guide'. As the prayer indicates, we learned to believe that God, through the angel, was not only protecting us but also guiding our choices.

One of the obvious aspects of secularisation in the West today is a widespread lack of belief that God is at work in the detail of our lives. Even within the church the doctrine of the providence and guidance of God seems to have become somewhat attenuated. Yet ironically, at this very time when public belief in the doctrine is absent or weakened, the question of a very personal sense of providence and spiritual guidance has come quite strongly to the fore. Many people have the feeling or conviction that they are 'being looked after', either on special occasions or over a long period. And many people have a distinct sense at times that they are being guided in their choices by some benign spiritual power. Television programmes about Guardian Angels have become remarkably popular. In this situation there is an opportunity for fruitful dialogue between Christians and non-Christians as they explore together their experience of being cared for and guided and/or their hunger for such an experience. My own experience in dialogue of this kind indicates that a revival of our belief in angels as 'spirit guides' can be a very good starting point.

As I suggested at the beginning of this chapter, the place to start the dialogue with many Western people may not be with our transcendent God but with the depth dimension of everyday life – the spiritual experiences which people have or the profound questions which they are asking about the meaning of their lives and the values they feel called to live by. This is the holy ground on which we can walk together with reverence and humility as we share and search together for the mystery which illumines our lives. Here is perhaps the most striking place where the Christian mission has to be exercised in the mode of dialogue.

QUESTIONS FOR REFLECTION

1. Suppose a person who is not attached to any church asks your advice about developing a practice of meditation, what would you say?

2. Christian faith has been understood as a call to struggle for liberation, but also as a basis for putting up with injustices imposed by legitimate authority. How would you explain this to an interested agnostic?

PART TWO

Key Entry Points for
an Understanding of Mission

CHAPTER 5

Mission as Evangelization

The previous four chapters have been concerned with dialogue as a fundamental aspect of mission today. Now I am moving on to look at the notion of mission from a variety of other points of view. My hope is that each of the six chapters in this second part of the book will throw light on a different facet of the notion of mission. In the present chapter I begin with the very rich concept of mission as evangelization.

Literally, the word 'evangelization' means 'bringing good news'. The phrase is used 24 times in the synoptic gospels. The classical expression of this 'good news' is summed up in St Luke's gospel in the words put in the mouth of Jesus as he read the words of the prophet Isaiah:

> The Spirit of the Lord is upon me, because he has anointed me to bring good news to the poor. He has sent me to proclaim release to the captives and recovery of sight to the blind, to let the oppressed go free, to proclaim the year of the Lord's favour.' .... Then he began to say to them, 'Today this scripture has been fulfilled in your hearing.' (Lk 4:18-21)

There are three key aspects to this text. First, the good news is of liberation for people who are poor or oppressed or disadvantaged. Secondly, this liberation is something new which is being brought by Jesus. Thirdly, it takes place through the power of the Spirit of God.

St Paul gave a central place to this concept of good news, using it as a general label or description for the basic content of his preaching (e.g. Gal 1:11; 2:2, 7, 14). The phrase is used in this sense about 60 times in the Pauline epistles. Some key passages in the epistles spell out what Paul regards as the core of his preaching. It is that people are now for the first time hearing about something previously unknown – a mystery which was hidden in past ages but has now been revealed to all the nations (Rom 16:25-6; cf. 1 Cor 2:7-10). The mystery is essentially Christ

himself in whom the fullness of God dwells (Col 1:19) who contains and reveals all the treasures of God's wisdom and knowledge (cf. Col 2;2). The good news is that God has a plan, an
'eternal purpose', which is brought into effect through Jesus
(Eph 3:11). The divine plan involves allowing us human beings
to have access to God through Jesus (Eph 3:12). Perhaps the
most crucial point of the good news, for Paul, is that this free access to God through Jesus is not confined to Jews but is now
open to all peoples (Eph 3:4-6). So the plan is to unite all peoples
and all things in Christ (Eph 1:9-10), to bring reconciliation and
peace through Jesus Christ (Col 1:20).

Given this very solid foundation in scripture, it is not surprising that Christians should frequently talk about 'bringing the
good news' or 'preaching the good news', as a fundamental description of the church's task in carrying on the mission of Jesus.
The Greek words for 'good news' have also been taken over into
modern languages; and in fact there are two English versions:
the words 'evangelism' and the word 'evangelization'. Of the
two, the word 'evangelism' has a much longer history in
English. It is a word much favoured by the evangelical wing of
Protestantism – people who put a great deal of emphasis on getting people to listen to, and read, the Bible. For a long time it was
associated with the great preaching crusades of evangelists such
as Billy Graham – and also with the work of street preachers.[1]

The word 'evangelization', on the other hand, is a word with
more Catholic associations. It is really a transliteration of the
equivalent word in the Latin languages. About thirty years ago
the word 'evangelization' came into widespread use among
Catholic theologians and church leaders in continental Europe. I
think the reason why it became so popular is that it was used instead of the word 'mission', at a time when the word 'mission'
was running into some trouble. Vatican II had broadened the
meaning of 'mission' to cover the whole work of the church.
Catholic writers were beginning to say, 'the church is mission'.
But theologians realised that for many Catholics the word 'mission' still conjured up an image of working in foreign non-
Christian areas. In this situation the fine scriptural word 'evangelization' seemed more fresh. It did not carry any of the old
'baggage' of the word 'mission',[2] so it could be used to describe
the fundamental work of the church in *any* situation, at home as
well as abroad. Furthermore, the text from Luke's gospel (quoted

above) which links 'good news' with the liberation of captives, meant that the word 'evangelization' could be used to convey a sense of the comprehensiveness and integral quality of Christianity – that it is not just a message about 'spiritual' affairs or about the next life but involves also a commitment to transform this present world.

But in translating these ideas into English, why did Catholics not settle for the well-known word 'evangelism' instead of carrying over the word 'evangelization' from continental languages? I think it was because the meaning and overtones of the word 'evangelism' seemed too narrow to convey what Catholic theologians meant by the Latin word *evangelizare* and its equivalents in other languages. There was a sense that the word 'evangelism' was associated too much with very evangelical Protestants who seemed to assume that the main task of Christian evangelists was simply to get people to '*hear* the message' of Jesus and/or to *read* the Bible. In contrast to this, the Catholic understanding of the mission of the church was much broader; it included getting people to join the church, receive the sacraments, etc.[3] So it was felt that there was need for the new word 'evangelization' even though it does not fit very easily into everyday English. In more recent years, however, the meaning of the two words has converged, though each of them still retains its own nuances.

The Human One

When we think of mission as evangelization we are thinking in terms of bringing good news. But what exactly is this 'news', this 'message'? Can it be summed up in a few sentences? Yes – at least to some extent. Already at the very beginning of this chapter I have given two different summaries of the 'message', both based on scripture. The first is the passage from Luke's gospel, in which Jesus quotes from Isaiah's prophecy about giving good news to the poor and in which Jesus goes on to claim that the prophecy is now being fulfilled. The second summary is the series of texts which I gave from the Pauline epistles, mainly from Colossians and Ephesians. In the gospel of Matthew (1:23) we find the most succinct formulation of the good news; it is expressed in the one word – 'Emmanuel' (which, the text adds, means 'God with us'). This word sums up the nature, the mission, and the message of Jesus.

These scriptural articulations of the good news are of enduring value for Christians of all ages. But it is well to remember that they are expressed in the language and idiom of the audience for whom they were originally written – people familiar with the Jewish and/or the Greek culture and religion of that time. Alongside these scriptural summaries of 'the message' we need also to express the good news in a way that allows it to be heard by Christians and non-Christians today.

Karl Rahner, one of the great theologians of our time, attempted to work out a summary of the basic Christian message, the good news. But most ordinary Christians would be mystified by the complex philosophical language he used. I venture here to give a much simpler version, inspired partly by Rahner, but mostly by the main title which Jesus in the gospels used of himself. On about 75 occasions in the gospels Jesus refers to himself in a phrase that is usually translated as 'the Son of Man'; but this is a misleading and sexist translation. A more accurate translation is 'the Human One'.[4]

The significance of this title is twofold. Firstly, it indicates that by living a fully human life, Jesus revealed to us the meaning and purpose of human existence. Secondly, it indicates that it was precisely in being fully human, in revealing the deepest meaning of what it is to be human, that Jesus opened up for us our relationship with God, our way to God, and even the very nature of God. His revelation of God was not something over and above, or different from, showing us what human life is about. This idea can be the basis for a summary of the good news in the language of today:

Jesus calls himself 'The Human One'; so we see him as fully human, one who shares our life, and as the perfect model of what it means to be human, drawing out all the potential that remains fallow in the rest of us.

Jesus is 'the Way' – he shows us what we can become and how to get there. He went before us to show us the way forward; he lived life to the full, then faced death and so came into new life. The ministry of Jesus was to share his life-energy with all who chose to follow him. This giving of life reached its culmination in his death and resurrection which empowered and inspired his first followers and all who have put their faith in him ever since. Jesus did not leave us orphans; he remains with us by his Spirit who guides us on every step of the way through our life and death into the fullness of life in God.

Every human person is made in the image of God; but Jesus is the perfect image – so perfect that in him we see God and experience God's presence. We believe that Jesus himself is divine because otherwise he could not be the perfect revelation of God, and also because, by the power of the Spirit, he evokes in us the same kind of unconditional faith and trust that we have in God.

The God revealed by Jesus is a God of love, a caring God, a God whom we can call 'Abba' (Daddy) as Jesus did. But the God revealed by Jesus becomes an angry God when people are exploited and nature is despoiled. This is a powerful God who chooses to be on the side of the poor and oppressed, and who calls and empowers us to follow Jesus in working for human liberation, and in creating truly human communities where people live in the presence of God, guided by the Spirit, with love for all people and with respect for the earth.

My hope is that this very inadequate attempt to summarise the good news will inspire readers to engage in the same kind of exercise – and to do it more successfully. It is well to remember that such summaries are bound to differ from one person to another – and even to change at different stages of each person's life. Furthermore, differences of culture are likely to give rise to quite different summaries of the good news.[5] The question of the inter-relationship between culture and the good news is one to which I shall return in the next chapter.

How Necessary is Jesus?

The 'summaries' of the good news which I have referred to all give a central role to Jesus. This raises questions about the uniqueness of Jesus and the possibility of salvation for the millions of people who have known little or nothing about him. That is an issue which is as old as Christianity. But it has come to the fore quite strongly in recent times, mainly because we now live in a very pluralist world where Christians have come to appreciate the value and richness of other religions.

Theologians became very polarised on this issue. Some insisted so strongly on salvation through Jesus that they offered little hope for those who do not know Jesus or do not accept him as the unique source of salvation. Others adopted a purely pluralist and relativist approach which effectively treats Christianity as one of many ways to find God. More recently, some theologians developed an 'inclusive' approach. Drawing on the more universalist strands in scripture and in the writings of the early Fathers, they hold that the Spirit works through non-Christian religions. But this still leaves them with questions about whether knowledge of Christ is necessary for salvation and whether Christ is the unique saviour of humankind. Few theologians now follow Karl Rahner in saying that a good Muslim or a good Hindu may be 'an anonymous Christian'.[6] But in effect the 'inclusivist' view remains quite close to that of Rahner. It sees the faith and commitment of good non-Christians as amounting to some kind of implicit Christian faith. Or it sees Christian belief as a more explicit development of a primal faith which may have been articulated in non-Christian terms or may not be verbalised at all.

Why Mission?
This leads on to the question: 'If people can be saved without explicit knowledge of Christ, why engage in mission at all?' This issue has agitated theologians for the past century – ever since they began to take seriously the fact that the dogma 'outside the Church there is no salvation' is not to be taken at its face value. Around the time of Vatican II many theologians settled for the idea that, even if it is not *essential* to become a Christian, at least being a Christian makes it much *easier* to be saved. More recently this idea has fallen out of favour.

An alternative approach was put forward by the missionary theologian Eugene Hillman.[7] He focused on the idea that the church is 'the sacrament of universal salvation'. He argued that the purpose of mission or evangelization is not that every *individual* should hear of Christ, but that the gospel be incarnated in every *culture*. There are many different 'peoples' in the world, each with its own culture. The aim of the church should be to ensure that the gospel is truly inculturated among each of these 'peoples'. In this way there will be a community of Christians in every culture, present as a sign and sacrament of God's saving will in relation to that particular segment of humanity.[8]

In recent years there has been a tendency to stress the notion that the purpose of the church is to serve the kingdom or reign of God. One very clear example of this is found in Pope John Paul's mission encyclical, *Redemptoris Missio*, no 20, which spells out three ways in which the church is at the service of the kingdom:

by preaching, by establishing Christian communities, and by spreading 'gospel values'. Similarly, the well-known theologian John Fuellenbach puts forward a definition of mission which takes the kingdom as its focus. For him the mission if the church is threefold: first, 'to *proclaim in word and sacrament* that the kingdom of God has come in the person of Jesus of Nazareth'; secondly, '*to offer its own life* as a test case that demonstrates that the kingdom is present and operative in the world today'; and thirdly, '*to challenge society as a whole* to transform itself along the basic principles of the kingdom now present: justice, peace, community, and human rights.'[9] This certainly provides an inspiring and integral vision of evangelization; but it still leaves us with some questions about the need for explicit knowledge of Jesus.[10]

This new emphasis on the reign of God can be a very liberating one for those who wish to share in the mission of Jesus. However, I think it must not be allowed to *replace* the emphasis on the founding of the church but should rather *supplement* it. I find it useful to distinguish between two partially overlapping but partially different purposes of evangelization: (a) the building up of the church both in its community and its institutional aspects; and (b) promoting the reign of God by giving witness to certain key Christian values. I shall have more to say about this distinction in Chapter 12 where I look at the purpose of 'mission to the nations'; and I shall return to it again in chapter 14 which deals with the relationship between missionaries and development workers.

Behind much of the debate about the need for mission lies an anxiety to *prove* that the work of missionaries is necessary or at least very useful. My own feeling is that this approach is not very fruitful. It is much better to hold that we engage in mission or evangelization because in this way we follow Jesus and are privileged to share in his mission and his life's work. At his baptism, Jesus had the wonderful experience of being called 'the Beloved'; this 'drove' him to share this experience with others. In so far as we share in his experience we, too, find ourselves led and driven by his Spirit to share his good news with others.

From this point of view we need not concern ourselves unduly with the question of whether or how God could save people without explicit faith in Christ. How anybody can be saved is always a mystery of God's grace. It seems best to leave that to God

while we get on with the exciting and challenging task of sharing with others our experience of Jesus and our faith in him,
while at the same time engaging in dialogue with them about
their own religious experiences.

Prior Presence of the Spirit

For Catholics today the word 'evangelization' has come to be the
most comprehensive word to describe the mission of Jesus
Christ and of the church. It is a very useful term, with a sound
base in scripture. It focuses attention on some very important aspects of the work of Christ and the church, aspects which might
easily be overlooked, e.g. that salvation is a *gift* from God, that it
brings *joy,* and that in some respects it has *already* taken place before any action of ours so that we need simply to become aware
of it.

Despite the fact that the term 'evangelization' is such a good
one, it does not highlight all aspects of the mission of Jesus and
the church. That is only to be expected, since what God offers to
humanity in Jesus is an infinitely rich reality, a mystery that we
cannot fully comprehend and cannot adequately express in one
word – even in such an expressive word as 'evangelization'. The
notion of 'good news' is a kind of metaphor or image which we
use to evoke some understanding of the salvation offered by
Jesus. As such it is limited and if we confine ourselves to this one
word we may overlook some important aspects of mission.

One big difficulty with the word 'evangelization' is that it
puts all the emphasis on *bringing* the good news, whereas many
reflective Christians today would prefer to stress the *prior presence* of spiritual values and of the Spirit of God in those who
have not yet heard the gospel. By choosing to devote the first
four chapters of this book to the question of inter-religious dialogue I have indicated that evangelization must not be seen as a
one-way communication.

Our first task as evangelizers is to be *present* to people, to
share their lives, to enter into their history. In learning a local
language or idiom our first aim should not be to preach or teach
or even to tell people the good news. Rather it should be simply
to listen to people, to be in solidarity with them and to endeavour to understand them. It is only when we recognise the presence of the Spirit at work among them that our evangelization
can find an effective entry-point into the lives of the people. If

we do not first of all acknowledge and rejoice in this presence then what we have to give will not really be good news at all. It will rather be a gross insult to these people, since our behaviour will contain an implicit message louder than our spoken words; we will be 'telling' people that God has not been with them up to now or that God's prior presence is of no real significance.

On the other hand, when we look for the ways in which God has been at work among the people, then there is an opening for a very rich two-way communication. At times we may be so moved by the richness of people's spiritual experience that we may wonder whether we have anything to offer. But at other times we may see how faith in Jesus Christ can enrich the lives of our partners in dialogue.

Undue Stress on Words

The words 'good news' and 'evangelization' evoke an image of somebody speaking to others, telling them news. This is a very apt image for *preaching* or *teaching*, and also for offering people the scriptures which we understand to be the word of God. But because the focus here is on *news* there is a danger that we might overlook the fact that the salvation which comes to us from Jesus is *a new way of life* as well as a new *power* or energy to do good. Furthermore, when we think in terms of *news*, we may fail to highlight the transformation of our personal lives, of our inter-personal relationships, and of the structures of the world we live in.

Many evangelical Christians – and evangelical missionaries especially – take the image of communicating good news so seriously and so literally that they run the risk of giving undue emphasis to the more verbal aspects of Christianity, as though the most important thing is to get a copy of the New Testament into every person's hands. The same tendency can be found in various official documents of the Catholic Church. The gospel is referred to as something to be *proclaimed*. So Christianity is con-ceived of as a *message*, as though that was the very essence of what it is about. This can lead to an undervaluing of other as-pects of Christian life and Christian mission.

One example of this can be found in the decree of Vatican II on missionary activity (*Ad Gentes*, 6). This document says that, where there is no possibility of preaching the gospel directly, missionaries ought at least to bear witness to the love and kind-ness of Christ; in this way they will prepare a way for the Lord and in some way make him present. This implies that bearing witness is only a second best – a preliminary approach which is to be used in preparation for the fully authentic way to make Christ present, namely, by preaching the good news. This style of thinking led theologians in the past to describe various kinds of Christian action as 'indirect evangelization' or 'pre-evangelization'.

A decade after the Vatican II decree, a more enlightened way of understanding the mission of the church was put forward by Pope Paul VI in his Apostolic Exhortation 'Evangelization in the Modern World' *(Evangelii Nuntiandi)*. That document insists that both words and witness are of fundamental importance. The words require the witness in order to give them credibility, while the witness requires the words in order to reveal explicitly its true meaning (EN 21-2 and 41-2). This is a great improvement on the earlier account of mission. However, even in this document the dominant image of mission still seems to be the verbal one of evangelization, the bringing of good news. The result is that when the text speaks of 'witness, ... presence, sharing of life, and solidarity' it uses the word 'proclamation', as though these activities have to be 'interpreted' in such verbal categories in order to show how important they are in the mission of the church.

A Complex Reality
In order to provide a corrective to this unduly verbal understanding of mission, I want here to explore a number of different aspects of what it means to be a Christian. Instead of thinking of Christianity as primarily *news* it is helpful to think of it as a *life lived out in a community*. Christians are a people who live by faith in Jesus Christ, who live according to his way. To become a Christian is to join a community of believers, a group who are trying to live their lives as followers of Jesus. This aspect of Christianity is very obvious in many of the 'young churches' where a significant number of adults become Christian each year. Prior to their baptism they normally have to go through a fairly long period of initiation. This includes religious instruction; but it is primarily a time when the convert is learning to take an active part in the life and worship of the Christian community.

If we want to describe what is involved in passing on the Christian life to others it is not sufficient to list out certain truths

which are to be communicated. Certainly, there are basic truths,
but they are only one aspect of Christianity. Our way of life is
embodied and passed on in a variety of ways. These can be
grouped into four major categories as illustrated in the accom-
panying diagram.

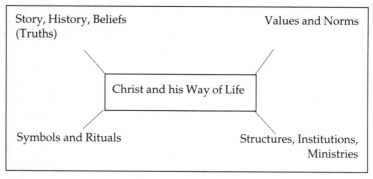

Firstly, there is a *history*, a *story* – the history of human salvation which, for Christians, finds its centre in the story of the life,
death, and resurrection of Jesus. His story follows on from the
earlier history of the Jewish people recounted in the Old
Testament. And the Acts of the Apostles begins the story of the
followers of Jesus after he had gone on before them. Certain key
elements of this history have been picked out and systematically
formulated as fundamental beliefs which can be put in a 'creed'
– e.g. 'we believe that Jesus died and rose again'. Other basic
truths listed in the creeds and expounded in books of theology
or catechisms are beliefs which Christians believe to be implicit
in the scriptural story (e.g. 'we believe that Jesus is true God
from true God', or 'we believe in the forgiveness of sins').

The truths of the faith can be communicated to others by
teaching and preaching – and this has been the preferred approach in the Catholic Church. They can also be transmitted by
making the Bible available to people – and, traditionally, the
Protestant churches have put the emphasis on this. Within the
past generation, missionaries influenced by liberation theology
have found an effective way of bringing together the best in
these two approaches. Bible study and social analysis of the
local situation have been linked together in a way that enables
the gospel message to come alive and to shed its light on the
daily life-situation of ordinary people. The truth of the gospel is

no longer locked up – neither in the formulas of the catechism nor in a fundamentalist understanding of the Bible – but is enabled to give a richer meaning to the pain, the joys, the struggles and the hopes of ordinary and extraordinary people in a variety of cultures and nations.

Secondly, Christianity offers not merely a belief system but also a *value* system. Christians seek to live on the basis of certain moral principles which are concerned with all the different aspects of life. For instance, we feel called to practice integrity in our personal lives, to be loving in our interpersonal relations, to act responsibly in the organisations in which we are involved, to promote justice, peace and reconciliation in the society and in the wider world in which we live, and to be concerned for the health of nature and of the earth itself.

Thirdly, the church has a large body of *symbols* and *rituals* employed by Christians to give expression to religious beliefs and attitudes, and used especially in public and personal prayer. The sacraments are obvious examples; so too are the use of holy water, blessed oil, statues, medals, holy pictures and scapulars. But there are other more taken-for-granted rituals such as kneeling, bowing, genuflecting, and joining one's hands or stretching them out in prayer. Christianity has many rich religious symbols – images which nourish the faith – of which the most central is the cross.

Finally, there are various *institutions, structures,* and *roles* which determine the way the Christian community is organised and how authority is exercised in it. For instance, bishops, priests, deacons, lay readers, ministers of the eucharist and choir members all have particular roles to play in ministering to the community. The Catholic Church also has many 'religious congregations', 'societies' and 'orders' whose members determine their specific purpose and charism, and whose structures are carefully defined by church laws. Furthermore, there is a whole variety of councils or commissions – ranging from parish councils to synods of bishops – each with its own purpose and constitutions.

If we see the task of evangelizing – or of Christian mission – as playing a part in the passing on of Christian life, then it includes all four of the above elements. One part of it is communicating to people the Christian story and the belief system which gathers together the fundamental *truths* of that story. Another aspect is

witnessing to Christian *values*. A third aspect is helping people
become familiar with, and draw fruit from, Christian *symbols
and rituals*. The fourth aspect is the setting up of some of the
more fundamental *institutions* such as vibrant Christian communities with ministries of worship and service – and some system
to ensure that these ministries continue.

The Task in Practice
What has to be done in practice by the person who wishes to
evangelize? I think many missionaries, and other committed
Christians, are sometimes inclined to imagine that they will find
some mission theologian to spell out for them what exactly they
ought to be doing when they set out to evangelize people. But
this is an illusion. One could make a long list of activities, ranging from prayer to education and from dialogue with other religions to helping to set up co-operatives. But the list would not
be exhaustive; to be complete it would have to include every
possible kind of authentically human behaviour. Furthermore,
the more detail it included the less help it would be, because it
would not enable one to set priorities.

Does this mean that we have to limit ourselves to vague gen-
eralities? Not quite. We can at least say that evangelization or
being in mission is concerned with the four elements outlined
above. This means that evangelization cannot be reduced to just
one category of actions such as preaching/teaching, or distribut-
ing the Bible, or celebrating the sacraments, or forming Christian
leaders and ministers, or working to promote human rights and
development.

The fifth chapter of the mission encyclical of Pope John Paul
II gives a very useful list of nine different 'paths' or ways in which
mission or evangelization is carried out.[11] They are: (1) witness,
(2) initial proclamation of Christ the Saviour, (3) conversion and
baptism, (4) founding and forming local churches, (5) forming
basic ecclesial communities, (6) incarnating the gospel in people's
cultures, (7) dialogue with people of other religions, (8) promoting human development by forming consciences and (9) charity
(in fact this final item refers mainly to the church being on the
side of the poor).

It is important to note that these 'paths' are not presented as
stages in evangelization. The order in which they are carried out
in practice will vary from one situation to another. Neither does

the encyclical suggest that some of the nine 'paths' are more central or important than others. The priority which is to be given to any one of these lines of action will depend on local circumstances. Individual evangelizers may specialise in one particular sphere of action, e.g. in working for peace, or in designing meaningful liturgies, or in building small communities. But none of us is entitled to act as though our own specialisation is the only element essential to evangelization. (Later I shall devote a chapter to looking at various 'vehicles of evangelization' which may be appropriate in different situations.)

In this book I have placed dialogue with other religions at the very beginning. This indicates that I give it a certain logical or psychological priority in the whole task of mission or evangelization. I think it somewhat misleading that the encyclical puts it as number six in its list of the 'paths of evangelization'. That may perhaps be a remnant of an older way of thinking about mission, in which dialogue would come after the establishment of Christian communities and the inculturation of the gospel.

How can we find a unity in such a wide variety of activity? What can give a focus to our approach as evangelizers or people in mission? It is helpful to approach this question from three different points of view: first, how it affects individuals and communities; secondly, how it affects the wider society; thirdly, how it affects the church itself. In the remainder of this chapter I shall consider the first of these aspects. Then in the following chapter, entitled 'Mission as Inculturation', I shall go on to examine how evangelization affects the wider society and the church; another aspect of the issue of evangelization in the wider society will be taken up in Chapter 7: 'Mission as Struggle for Liberation'.

The Personal-Community Dimension
The aim of evangelization from a personal and community point of view is to promote *conversion through an integral Christian spirituality*. What this means can be spelled out by looking more closely at each of the four key words in this phrase:
– We are committed to promoting an integral Christian *spirituality*. By choosing the word 'spirituality' rather than 'religion' I am indicating that evangelization is not confined to promoting a set of religious beliefs and practices. Spirituality is something which permeates all of life. To evangelize is to help people find a deeper meaning in the bits and pieces of their everyday lives, and to ensure that as far as possible all their activities are carried out in the presence of God.

– The spirituality which is our concern is an *integral* one. This means ensuring that spirituality is not confined to the personal or private aspect of people's lives. It must extend also to their relationships with their families and acquaintances, the communities they belong to, the wider society, and the earth itself. There is need for a balance between these different aspects. Some people are very caring of others but their spirituality is unbalanced because they do not take care of their own physical, psychological and spiritual health. Others devote great energy to acting justly in their interpersonal transactions while failing to work for structural justice in society. This, too, leaves their spirituality unbalanced and not integral.

– Our concern is to promote an integral *Christian* spirituality. The point here is that the one who evangelizes is not content to help people to discover a spiritual dimension in every part of life. The aim is to relate this to the vision of Jesus Christ and his way of living.

– This spirituality is one which calls each person to *conversion*. Anybody who adopts a spirituality centred on Jesus is invited to personal transformation. There will, of course, be a large measure of continuity with the past; but there is also a real disjunction, a letting go of previously held ideas and assumptions, of ideals and values. This is the 'new mind' (*metanoia,* e.g. Lk 5:32; Acts 13:24) to which the gospel invites each of us. We are called to a *different* way of life. As St Paul put it to his converts: 'Do not be conformed to this world, but be transformed by the renewing of your minds, so that you may discern what is the will of God – what is good and acceptable and perfect.' (Rom 12: 2)

QUESTIONS FOR REFLECTION

1. What would you include if you were asked to summarise the kernel of the Christian message in a few sentences?
2. Should the church be content to be a small highly committed minority in any given area? Should it go for quality rather than quantity?

CHAPTER 6

Mission as Inculturation

At the end of the previous chapter I looked at the aim of evangelization from a personal and community point of view. In this
chapter I propose to examine it from the viewpoint of the *wider
society*. Here there are two aspects of evangelization: on the one
hand, to bring about an *appreciation and enrichment* of what is
best in every human tradition and way of life; and, on the other
hand, to put before each of them a radical challenge and call to
transformation. Let us examine each of these two aspects.

Appreciation and Enrichment
The Spirit is at work among peoples, traditions, and in cultures
long before the good news of Jesus reaches them. This work of
the Spirit becomes embodied to a greater or lesser extent in people's cultures and ways of life. So when a formal process of
evangelization begins to take place the first task of the evangelizers is to recognise and celebrate this prior work of the Spirit.
Western Christians who come in contact with the people of
other cultures soon become aware (if they are open and sensitive) that in some respects these cultures are much closer to the
Christian ideal than the cultures of the West.

Among the rich values of many tribal peoples in Africa and
elsewhere are a great awareness of the presence and power of
God, a strong sense of community, a vivid experience of the
communion between the living and the dead, a sense of harmony
with nature, and a marvellous ability to celebrate; all of these are
very much in harmony with the Christian outlook. In the major
Asian cultures one may often find a deep mystical awareness
and a search for enlightenment. Mainstream Latin American
culture is also deeply religious, with a particularly strong sense
of the providence of God and an instinctive awareness of human
community and of the importance of celebration.

Faced with such cultural riches, Western Christians often

become more keenly aware of the inadequacies of their own culture. They look back wryly at the naïve enthusiasm with which
they wanted to evangelize others. Now they find that they are
being evangelized at least as much as they are evangelizing.
They lose some of the cultural arrogance which can so easily in-
fect Westerners in their relationships with the people of other
cultures. In this way they become more effective evangelizers.

The task of the evangelizer is not merely to acknowledge
such rich values and to name them as the work of the Spirit. It is
also to help these people to come into living contact with the
person of Jesus and his good news, and with the Christian tradition and traditions which have developed over the centuries.
This interaction can bring a wonderful growth and flowering of
the values of people's traditions and cultures. Furthermore,
those who are hearing the good news may come to see some of
their original values as 'seeds of the gospel' which will come to
full fruition when integrated with the truths and values of
Christianity.

Transformation
However, it is also very likely that in some respects the traditions
and cultures of non-Christian peoples may be quite at variance
with gospel values. So there is discontinuity as well as continuity between the good news and the different patterns of living
with which it comes into contact. The would-be evangelizer has
to learn to avoid making global judgements on one side or the
other – either dismissing a non-Christian way of life as totally
perverse or accepting uncritically every aspect of it. What is required is to facilitate these people in allowing gospel truths, values
and symbols to permeate their consciousness, so that gradually
the people themselves become aware not only of the enrichment
that can come through the gospel but also of the challenge posed
by the gospel to certain aspects of their existing society. At that
point the call to the *transformation* of society and of the world
begins to emerge.

Evangelization involves a commitment to working for major
changes in the social, economic, political, and cultural structures
of society. This *transformation* in the public sphere corresponds
to the *conversion* which evangelization looks for at the personal
level.

Over the past generation there has been a sharp polarisation

in the church around this question. Proponents of liberation theology put a lot of emphasis on the need for radical structural changes in society. This kind of talk frightens many of the more cautious church leaders. They see it as an attempt to politicise the church and to turn it into an agent of revolution. This tension was seen very clearly at the conferences of the Latin American bishops at Puebla in 1979 and in Santo Domingo in 1992. At these meetings the conservatives were fearful that too much attention would be given to political and economic changes. So they stressed the importance of cultural change instead. They felt that working for change in the culture is more in line with the nature of evangelization and does not 'reduce' the church to being an agent of political change.

It is a great pity that this polarisation occurred; and it is particularly unfortunate that cultural change came to be set over against political and economic changes, as though it were 'a soft option'. The truth is that all these changes are very closely interlinked. The economic and political structures of society can only be transformed successfully if there is a concomitant fundamental change in the culture, that is, in the structures of human thinking, feeling, and judging. Mao Tse Tung (Mao Zedong) realised this, and so he called for a 'cultural revolution', alongside the political and economic revolution in China, and in the wider world. In fact major cultural change is both a cause and an effect of economic and political transformation; and it is a serious mistake to focus unduly on one without the others. In some respects, cultural change is more fundamental, for culture underpins the social, economic, and political framework of society and provides the meaning and purpose which shape a people's corporate life. Here I shall focus mainly on cultural change and in the following chapter I shall take up the question of struggle for economic and political transformation and liberation.

What kind of transformation of culture and society does the good news call for? The best answer I know to this question comes in the document 'Evangelization in the Modern World' (Evangelii Nuntiandi), issued by Pope Paul VI in 1975:

> For the church, to evangelize is to bring the good news into all the strata of the human race so that by its power it may permeate the depths of humanity and make it new. ... The various strata of humanity are be transformed. This is not simply a matter of the church preaching the gospel in ever-

expanding geographical areas or to ever-increasing numbers.
It also means affecting the standards by which people make
judgements, their prevailing values, their interests and
thought-patterns, the things that move them to action, and
their models of human living; in so far as any or all of these
are inconsistent with the word of God and the plan of salvation they are to be in some sense turned upside down by the
power of the gospel. (E.N. 18-9; my translation; emphasis
added).

Inculturation
This passage brings out very well the fact that evangelization
has to do not just with handing on a body of beliefs or with promoting those values which affect people as individuals and
small communities; it is also concerned with human culture and
society in the broadest sense, that is, with the patterns which
mould our thinking, our feeling, our behaviour and even how
we experience life. The good news affects people's 'thought-
patterns', 'values', 'standards of judgement', 'incentives to action' and 'models of human living'. Just as Jesus took flesh in a
particular place and time, so the good news has to become 'embodied' or incarnated in the different cultures within which people live. This process has come to be called 'inculturation'. It is
not just a question of replacing or transforming each human
culture so that all become identical. The gospel is compatible
with many different cultures. It respects cultures. It is enriched
by them. It helps to draw out what is best in them. And it also
poses a challenge to each one of the cultures with which it comes
into contact.

It would be totally wrong to assume that the process of inculturation has already been completed in the Western world and to
imagine that Western culture has already been fully 'Christianised' and is now a Christian culture. Even more wrong is the
tacit assumption that Western culture is *the* Christian culture.
Western culture, like all other cultures, needs to be transformed
in the light of the gospel and by the power of the Holy Spirit.[1] I
have spelled out some aspects of this in more detail in the early
chapters of this book which deal with inter-religious dialogue.

Is the aim of evangelization to 'Christianise' the various cultures of the world? Yes and no. Yes, insofar as one hopes that the
thought-patterns, values and standards of each culture will be

transformed and come closer to those embodied in the gospel.
But the answer is 'no' if the word 'Christianise' is understood as
a once-for-all process which can be successfully accomplished to
a point where a particular culture can be designated as truly
Christian. The transformation of a culture through the gospel is
an on-going process which is never complete. One can never
point to any particular cultural pattern as a perfect embodiment
of gospel values. At best we have only approximations. And
even patterns of living that had seemed to come close to the
Christian ideal may gradually or suddenly be shown up as having some major weaknesses or some aspects in which they are
quite out of tune with Christian values.

Furthermore, the process of evangelization may at times go
into reverse gear. That seems to have happened in Europe over
the past couple of hundred years. However, I would want to
qualify that statement to some degree. Certainly, the churches
do not have the same influence in either Eastern or Western
Europe as they had in the past. So they no longer have as much
power as they used to have to insert their views and values into
the legal systems and into the general 'shape' of society. But this
decline of overt church influence may not be quite as much a re-
versal of the process of evangelization and inculturation as
many church leaders assume. For the mere fact that official
church teaching is reflected in a country's laws is no guarantee
that Christian values have become truly embodied in the culture
and living pattern of the people.

It is hard to find a balance between, on the one hand, the desirable position where Christians help to shape the thinking and
the values accepted in society and reflected in legislation, and,
on the other hand, an unacceptable degree of church pressure
which is experienced as an imposition on the freedom of citizens
who have different views. In this age of democracy and pluralism the balance between personal freedom and cultural shaping
must be quite different from that of the past.

Enrichment of the Church
A very interesting aspect of the process of inculturation is that it
brings about an *enrichment of the church itself*. The end result of
the process of evangelization is a new creation. It is an embodiment of the gospel in what had been a 'foreign' culture. This
other culture will enrich the church – and the world – by bringing

out aspects of the good news that were previously undiscovered or at least under-developed. As Pope John Paul says in his encyclical on the missions, by becoming inculturated in different areas the church 'comes to know and to express better the mystery of Christ'. (*Redemptoris Missio*, 52)

In this way the church becomes a mosaic of slightly different versions of Christianity. All will share the fundamental elements of the gospel, but in each case the gospel will be 'incarnated' in an uniquely original way. So the church does not just grow in numbers; it is enormously enriched in its understanding of the gospel and in the way it responds in faith. It develops its full potential when the good news becomes expressed and lived out in such a wonderful variety of human cultures. I shall return a little later to this topic.

Pluriformity in the Church?

Just at this point there arises a major theological controversy with serious practical implications. No less an authority than Cardinal Ratzinger maintains that we should no longer use the word 'inculturation' but should instead speak of 'inter-culturality'.[2] Why is he is uneasy about the use of such a widely accepted word as 'inculturation'?

In order to answer this question it is useful to go back to the late 1960s when an American missionary priest called Vincent Donovan was working with the Masai people who live in East Africa along the Tanzanian-Kenyan border. He came to the conclusion that a great deal of what was being presented to these nomadic people under the name of Christianity was quite unnecessary. He became convinced that missionaries were playing a crucial part in drawing the Masai into a model of Western so-called 'development' which was irrelevant to their present way of life and was in fact doing them enormous harm. The schools and health centres provided by a Westernised church were undermining the traditional pattern of life.

Donovan held that there was need for a radical re-appraisal of the missionary approach being used at that time in that area. He designed a way of presenting the good news which he believed to be appropriate to his situation. He visited the temporary settlements of these nomadic people, accepted their hospitality, listened to their religious stories. Then he told them part of the Judeo-Christian story, beginning with Abraham and with the nomadic people who lived with Moses for forty years in the desert. These stories were of great interest to the Masai, whose lifestyle was quite similar to that of the biblical characters they were hearing about. Donovan gradually introduced the story of Jesus and the new elements brought by his gospel, so that the New Testament followed on organically from the Old. But he insisted that there was no need to burden this nomadic people with all the 'baggage' that has accrued to Christianity over the centuries. The evangelization of the Masai would be quite similar to that described in the Acts of the Apostles. It would be like a new beginning which would lead to a genuine inculturation of the gospel in Masai culture – one that would respect all that is best in that culture and would not disrupt that traditional way of life.

Donovan wrote up his ideas first in a series of articles and later in a beautifully-written book called *Christianity Rediscovered*.[3] It was several years before this book became widely known. But then it really caught the imagination of very many people in the West. As he had intended, it appealed to people who knew little or nothing about the reality of nomadic life; and it inspired many Christians to wonder whether a similar approach would be possible on a much wider scale.[4] Among professional missionaries Donovan's idea of presenting 'the naked gospel',[5] 'the bare message of Christianity',[6] 'the unchanging, supracultural, uninterpreted gospel'[7] became 'a sign of contradiction'. Some were inspired to question their own approach – particularly the close association between the gospel and modern Western education and health-care. Particularly attractive was his view that the task of presenting the Christian faith could be completed within a year[8] and that the missionary, having planted the seed, could then move on, leaving behind a self-sufficient Christian community.[9] Others dismissed his whole approach as naïve romanticism. But I feel sure that Vincent Donovan's initiative with the Masai contributed in some degree to the new approach adopted by the African bishops at the Synod of Bishops held in Rome in 1974; there they took a strong stand in favour of what they called 'the theology of incarnation'. Coming to that Synod, they insisted on the need 'to foster the particular incarnation of Christianity in each country, in accordance with the genius and talents of each culture so that "a thousand flowers may bloom in God's garden".'[10]

A somewhat similar re-appraisal of the Western missionary approach began to take place in India and Sri Lanka. Some of the questions being asked there were as follows. Why can we not return to the original missionary strategy adopted three hundred years ago by the great pioneer missionaries, Matteo Ricci in China and Roberto de Nobili in India? Why do we present the Christian faith in such a foreign Western guise? Should we not show that we believe the Spirit has been at work in the local religions (Hinduism, Buddhism, etc) by incorporating their scriptures and their rituals into Christian worship? Should we not use rice rather than bread in celebrating the eucharist? Can we not have an Indian version of Christianity which is fully at home in this cultural milieu, rather than the very Western model of Christianity which people see as foreign?

These questions soon led on to even more fundamental theological questions: Is there not an Asian 'history of salvation' parallel to that which begins with Abraham? Is Christ unique as the definitive revelation of God – or in what sense? Why should it be necessary to visualise human salvation in terms of a *historical* paradigm centred on Jewish history; could we not see salvation in *cosmic* terms which would be more in line with non-Western religions?[11]

Inculturation' or 'Inter-Culturality'?
It is against this background that Cardinal Ratzinger expresses reservations about the word 'inculturation' and proposes that we use the word 'inter-culturality' instead. It is clear that he is trying to guard against two dangers. The first is a *syncretism* in which Christianity would be contaminated or 'diluted' with elements of non-Christian religions which are incompatible with the gospel. The second danger is a *relativism* where there would be several conflicting versions of Christianity, all of which would be seen as equally valid or true; this would involve what he calls a 'hindu-ising' of the faith.[12]

In the Cardinal's opinion the word 'inculturation' and the way it is understood have become associated with these errors. He appears to believe that those who speak of 'inculturation' have a wrong conception of the faith or the gospel – that they see it as quite independent of culture and therefore as something that can be inserted in a whole variety of different cultures. That would then be a basis for allowing the development of many variant versions of Christianity, each of which is 'right' for its own situation. This is the relativism to which Cardinal Ratzinger objects.

In his address to Asian bishops the Cardinal puts forward a very closely argued and impressive case for using the word 'inter-culturality' instead of the word 'inculturation'. The core of his argument can be expressed in a few sentences. Religion, he says, is the essential element, the determining core, of all known cultures. 'There is no such thing as naked faith.' Faith is embodied in culture. In fact, 'faith creates culture'; and 'faith is itself culture.' But despite this, one does not have to choose between being a Christian and being, say, a German, or an Indian, or an American. This is because with Christianity there comes, for the first time a 'doubling of cultures'. By this he means that every Christian now lives in two cultural worlds – his or her own 'historic culture' and 'the new one of faith'.[13]

Already in the New Testament, says the Cardinal, Christianity 'bears the fruit of an entire cultural history'.[14] Elsewhere he says that Christianity 'is the synthesis mediated in Jesus Christ between the faith of Israel and the Greek spirit.'[15] And this synthesis as it has developed in the West has been irrevocably influenced by its history. This history cannot be ignored or abandoned; even God, having entered human history is now bound to that history; and therefore those who enter the church know that they are 'entering a cultural subject'. We 'cannot repeat the event of the incarnation to suit ourselves in the sense of taking away Christ's flesh and offering him another body.'[16] All this leads to the conclusion that the historical contribution of Western culture to Christianity is not something which can be by-passed; it has become part of what Christianity is.

Cardinal Ratzinger's position is clear: the Christian faith cannot be disengaged from the historical form in which it has developed. So he rejects the kind of views espoused by Vincent Donovan, namely, that one can make a fresh start in relating the gospel to each culture. He is very strongly opposed to the idea that Christian faith transcends all cultures and that therefore one can let go of all the 'cultural baggage' of the past and develop a new embodiment of the faith in each new culture. He sees this as a misguided reaction against the imposition of a European version of Christianity.[17] The Cardinal holds that Christian thought as it has developed in the West has come to have a universal

significance.[18] So he insists that 'there can be no simple return to
the past'.[19]

An Alternative View

The well-known theologian and anthropologist, Aylward Shorter,
agrees with Cardinal Ratzinger on this one point, namely, in
being quite dismissive of a simple return to the past. He says:
'Vincent Donovan's picture of the newly evangelized Maasai
reinventing the Roman Catholic Church is attractive but ultimately unrealistic.'[20] But on other aspects of inculturation he
adopts a position which is a serious challenge to that put forward by the Cardinal. He holds that Christianity, being a historical religion, necessarily has its own 'cultural patrimony' which
he describes as 'an accumulation of meanings and images which
derive from a variety of cultural sources'. For him, this patrimony
is variable and changing; and it is not to be identified with sacred tradition (which cannot be abandoned though it may have to
be reformulated in other cultures). As the church moves forward in time and outward to other cultures, some elements of
the patrimony should be retained, some should be reformulated,
and some, having outlived their usefulness, should be sloughed
off.[21]

Shorter takes it for granted that Christians, like other humans,
are inserted in their own culture. When Christian missionaries
reach out to people of other cultures there are two phases in the
process. In the first phase of evangelization (which Shorter calls
acculturation) the flow is predominantly in a one-way direction –
from the culture of the missionaries to that of their followers.
But before too long the missionaries should 'become culturally
educated, and strive to present the person of Christ and his
teaching in terms of the new culture'. In this second phase
(which is *inculturation*) the missionaries 'begin to perceive new
insights into their Christian faith'; and some of the 'imported
cultural elements will fall away to be replaced by indigenous
ones'.[22] At this point the Christian patrimony brought in by the
missionaries has to be carefully re-evaluated. New culturally appropriate devotions may replace imported ones, indigenous
forms of liturgy may be developed and, for instance, an African
theology of Christ might be worked out in terms of Christ as
ancestor or as healer rather than in terms of Christ the King.[23]

In the process of inculturation 'everything depends on the

decision as to which of the imported cultural elements are essential and which are non-essential'.[24] The whole project of evangelization-inculturation can get blocked if there is a failure to recognise clearly which elements in the cultural patrimony are unchangeable and which can be adapted or dropped. Shorter believes such a blockage has occurred in the Catholic Church. He maintains that 'by and large the church has become immobilised in the acculturation phase'. The result is that '[t]he reality of the Roman Catholic Church today may well be that of a universal sub-culture ubiquitously present as a sub-system in the various cultures of humanity.'[25] It is clear that what Shorter has in mind when referring to a 'sub-culture' are such things as the imposition of Roman Canon Law and Western theology on churches in the non-Western world; and, in general, a strong emphasis by Rome on uniformity rather than pluriformity.

For Shorter the objections to such a 'universal sub-culture' are twofold. First, it 'does not seem to square ... with the human right to cultural self-determination'.[26] It is an obstacle to genuine inculturation and therefore to effective evangelization, because it causes Catholics to be 'somehow distanced from their own cultures'.[27] A second major objection to a 'universal sub-culture' is that it means that 'there is no genuine complementarity among particular churches'. This is because the church's patrimony is 'culturally top-heavy', 'accidentally weighted towards the culture of Europe'.[28] It is quite clear that Shorter's position is very much at odds with that of Cardinal Ratzinger and that he has put forward a formidable critique of present Roman policies. Further on in this chapter I shall note an even more trenchantly critical judgement made by Shorter on a closely related topic, namely, what he sees as an effective alliance between Western church leaders and those who are promoting the economic dominance of the West.

Centralisation or Pluriformity?

This discussion of the views of Donovan, Shorter, and Cardinal Ratzinger may, at times, have seemed rather abstract and theoretical. But it has very serious practical implications. The issue is what 'shape' the church of the future is to take. Should it be highly centralised and largely mono-cultural? Or, on the other hand, should it be pluriform and multi-cultural, with notable differences from one culture to another in the spheres of spirituality,

theology, liturgy, ritual, symbols, community life, legal framework, ministries, authority structures, and organisation?

It is easy to lay down the general parameters. Even the most
cautious Roman theologians and curial officials will allow for
some differences in church life and thinking between the West
and Africa, Asia, Latin America, or Oceania. And on the other
hand, few if any of even the most radical advocates of multiform
Christianity would claim that Asian or African Christians
should entirely ignore the contribution of Western Christianity.
But the crucial issue is *to what extent* has this Western Christian
history culminated in a version of the gospel which has now become normative for Christians of other cultures? What are the
limits of pluralism? How can one know whether a particular aspect of Western Christianity is now binding on all cultures? And
how can one know that what is claimed to be a new cultural
expression of the gospel is not a distortion of it? How can we decide that such a new embodiment remains faithful not only to
the original revelation but also to the historical reality of the
gospel today?

Various criteria have been put forward as a basis on which
these crucial judgements can be made. They include fidelity to
Christ, to the scriptures, and to the creeds. There is also a role for
the teaching authority of the church, for continuity with the
past, and for the *sensus fidelium,* that is, the Spirit-guided instinct
of the believing church as a whole as to what is true to the
faith.[29] But these criteria are very general. They can be invoked
by Rome to justify an extremely cautious and centralising policy.
But they can also be invoked by those who favour a great lot of
cultural 'experimentation' and who hope that what will emerge
will be a great flowering of different forms of Christianity – with
variations at least as great as those between the Western, the
Byzantine, and the Ethiopian versions of Christianity.

Facing the Future

I have tried to present both sides of the argument as fairly as
possible. But now I want to make some suggestions about a way
forward. I begin by acknowledging that the case put forward by
Vincent Donovan is attractive and very persuasively presented.
It remains as a very valuable challenge to much of the modern
approach to mission. I think it would be helpful for everybody
who takes on the task of evangelization to read his book every

couple of years. But I do not accept his arguments entirely. There is one fundamental reason for not starting with what Donovan calls 'the bare gospel' in each new culture and situation. It is that the good news embodied in the Christian faith cannot be reduced entirely to the stories of the Old Testament and the story of Jesus. The Spirit has also been at work in the church, and in the wider world, since the time of Jesus; and at least some of that work of the Spirit is relevant for all humankind; and so it has become part of 'the gospel'. In other words, revelation did not stop once the New Testament had been written. Aspects of revelation have come more clearly into the light during the intervening period of history between then and the present day. We are not entitled to eliminate these from the gospel we share with people who have not previously been evangelized.

In regard to the case put forward by Cardinal Ratzinger, I begin with the old Latin adage: *contra factum non datur argumentum,* which may be loosely translated as 'no argument is strong enough to disprove a fact'. The fact in this case is that there already is a remarkable degree of pluriformity within Christianity. There is the enormously deep and rich tradition of the Eastern churches, with its own rich theology and spirituality, and a liturgical tradition that is quite different from that of the West. Then there is the Maronite rite, and that of the 'St Thomas Christians' in India,[30] as well as the Coptic Church, the Chaldeans, and the Ethiopian Christians.[31] Even within the West, the church tends to develop a different complexion from one country to another – not to mention the differences between the Catholic Church and the various Protestant and Pentecostal Churches. Furthermore, over the past century hundreds of indigenous churches have emerged in many parts of Africa, Asia, Oceania, and Latin America. Looking at all these different ways of being Christian one can only say: what an enrichment it is for the church – and for the world – that the Western model of Christianity is not the only one.

It would be a very serious error to imagine that the differences between all these churches is due solely to failure by many of them to grasp the kernel of the good news or to respond adequately to it. Of course there are aberrations and failures and these play a notable part in the differences between the churches and even within individual churches. But the variety of forms taken by Christianity should be seen mainly in a positive light – as an indication that the gospel is so rich that no single culture can adequately embody it. The sheer pluriformity of Christianity helps us to realise that we are dealing with a mystery rather than a system. The different versions of the faith can be seen as facets through which the light of the mystery shines forth in our world.

The best way forward would seem to be for church authorities and the general church membership to encourage the flourishing and expansion of all of the Christian traditions which have been accepted as authentic and in communion with the rest of the church. Each of these church traditions would grow and blossom first of all through dialogue with other branches of the church and with the people of other religions, ideologies, or ways of life. Each would also be expected and encouraged to engage in active evangelizing and other missionary activities and to give vigorous witness to its own embodiment of the gospel.

I have referred to *branches* of the church. This indicates that my image is of the church as a tree. A tree has many branches. All the branches sprout buds which produce other branches, each of which has its own originality. Nobody can deny that a tree has unity – but it is an *organic* unity, which is very different from the unity of an institution or of a bureaucratic system. In the gospels Jesus tells us that a good tree brings forth good fruit (Mt 7: 18). If we see the Eastern and Western churches as two major branches of the tree that is Christianity in the world, then we can rejoice when each of them expands and branches out further. The same applies to the other branches which are much less developed at present.

The gospels also teach us that even fruitful branches may need to be pruned in order to help them bear more fruit. (Jn 15: 2) The pruning can be done primarily through an honest sharing and dialogue between the different branches of the church. But there is need, also, for some authority structure which will co-ordinate this process and monitor its effectiveness. The Catholic and Anglican Churches have much to learn from each other in this regard – by comparing the advantages and disadvantages of the very loose Anglican structures with the very tight Vatican structures.

The crucial point in relation to the issue of inculturation is that however important the Western church may have become over the past thousand years, it is not in fact the only authentic version of Christianity. Cardinal Ratzinger is quite correct in saying that we must not ignore the insertion of the gospel into Western culture. But we need to remember that the gospel has also been inserted into the cultures of Eastern Europe and Greece; this contribution, too, is fundamental to the life of the church as it has developed through history. Each of these two traditions is greatly impoverished insofar as it fails to take serious account of the other and acts as though it were the *only* branch or the *main* branch of the embodied gospel today.

We in the West need to nourish ourselves by drawing on the rich spirituality of the Eastern Church.[32] And it is even more important that we Western Christians keep in touch with this spirituality when we reach out to evangelize other cultures or situations where the gospel is absent. We should follow the example of the great missionary Cardinal Charles Lavigerie, founder of the Society of Missionaries of Africa ('White Fathers') and of the Missionary Sisters of Our Lady of Africa ('White Sisters'). Not only was he insistent that missionaries should respect African cultures and use local languages, but he also had a particular interest in the Greek-Melkite Church of the Middle East. In order to help these Eastern Christians to find a more equal place *vis-à-vis* the church of the West, he had his missionaries open an 'apostolic school' for them – one in which they would not be forced to adopt the Latin Rite.[33]

When we set out to evangelize non-Western peoples we should ensure that those to whom we go are put in touch with *both* of the great traditions of Christianity, and that they are also aware of the other less well-known strands in the Christian tradition. I am very aware that this poses a big challenge to today's missionaries who, for the most part, have little knowledge of the spirituality of the Eastern Church. But if we can accept this challenge the rewards will be great. Familiarity with the existing pluriformity of the church will give the emergent 'young churches' the spiritual freedom to choose the aspects that are most in tune with their own culture. They will also be inspired to move on from there, under the guidance of the Spirit, to become truly indigenous and truly authentic embodiments of the gospel in organic unity with the worldwide Christian community of local churches.

Western Technological Dominance

Cardinal Ratzinger rejects the religious relativism which holds that each culture finds its own way to God. He does not agree that the spread of Christianity is an aspect of Western colonialism. It is in this context that he insists, as I mentioned earlier, that 'there can be no simple return to the past'. I agree. But I feel uneasy about one part of his argument on this score. He maintains that 'the diffusion of technological civilisation is irrevocable'.[34] My own experience leads me to doubt the 'unstoppableness' of technological progress. I lived for a year in an area in Africa which had a functioning phone system in the 1960s but where the phones have not worked for the past thirty years. And my contact with Africa makes me very aware that there is now an almost total breakdown not only of technology but even of modern government in Somalia, the former Zaire, Sierra Leone, Liberia and most of the south of Sudan. Can we any longer presume that these are temporary reverses in the 'irrevocable' advance of technological civilisation? Perhaps, instead, they are portents of the future – at least of the future in many of the poorer areas of our world?

There was a time when the Roman Empire brought advances of technology and civilisation which must have seemed irreversible – aqueducts, a major road system, a highly developed legal system, a very sophisticated military technology, and a relatively efficient system of government, stretching across much of Europe and the Middle East. But it all collapsed; and nearly a thousand years passed before an advanced technology emerged again. This pattern may repeat itself. Our present technological world may collapse as a result of war or ecological despoliation; and in the world of the future the West may no longer maintain its present dominance. But the gospel still flourished in the West even when Roman technology failed. Similarly, the importance of the Western embodiment of the gospel now and in the future is not dependent on the spread and dominance of Western technological civilisation.

Aylward Shorter goes further. He sees the technological dominance of the West as a serious hindrance to the gospel. He suggests that there is an alliance between those who promote 'the secular Europeanisation of the world' and Western church leaders who wilfully 'refuse to distinguish between unity and uniformity'.[35] He believes that 'the socio-economic hegemony of the West' results in the manipulation of local churches in poor parts of the world, because they are economically dependent on the West.[36] In this way the religious values of indigenous cultures are not respected and are not incorporated in the local embodiment of the gospel.

A Time for Humility and Trust

It is salutary to remember that the present 'shape' of the Western church did not develop solely on the basis of a careful discernment by wise church leaders led by the Spirit. Much of it was the product of power-struggles and abuses of power. If church leaders in the West keep that in mind they may not be so defensive of all aspects of this legacy of the past. Furthermore, we can look back now and see how often church leaders in the past confused their own selfish interests with the wider good of the church, and how often they invoked the Spirit of God in support of their own limited vision. Awareness of this may help today's leaders to be more hesitant in insisting on their own interpretation of orthodoxy, and more willing to trust that the Spirit may be at work even beyond the limits of their own horizon.

I am not at all suggesting that the developments of Western Christianity can be by-passed as though they were an aberration or a passing phase. What I am saying is that we should not exaggerate their importance. We should not use the Western version of the gospel as the only or main criterion for the insertion of the gospel in other cultures. Cardinal Ratzinger is quite right in saying that 'there can be no simple return to the past'. But equally we must insist that there should be no simple extension of the present highly centralised and almost mono-cultural Western church into the future and into other cultures. We must regain our organic contact with the different strands or branches of Christianity in the past and present.

Anchored in that pluriform tradition we can confidently engage in dialogue with the major world religions, with primal religion, and with the Western world of today, along the lines outlined in the early chapters of this book. The road to inculturation is through religious dialogue. There is a notional distinction between the two but in practice they are the two sides of one coin. The excitement and challenge for Christians at this time is to engage in dialogue and to commit ourselves to inculturation, confident of the on-going guidance of the Spirit leading the church into a future that we cannot predict or control.

QUESTIONS FOR REFLECTION

1. What elements in the tradition of Western Christianity would you consider to be 'cultural baggage' which could be discarded without undermining the integrity of the gospel?
2. Name some fundamental truths and values which are not explicitly present in the Bible but which have emerged more clearly over the centuries and which you consider to be now an integral part of the gospel or of Christian faith.
3. How would you go about inculturating the gospel in the more secularised parts of the Western world today?

CHAPTER 7

Mission as Struggle for Liberation

Mission is such a complex reality that we need many different approaches or entry-points to convey its different aspects. If we look at it as 'evangelism' or 'evangelization' then our entry-point is 'the good news' as a message which is to be passed on in words, or perhaps by good example. But if our basic paradigm of mission is one of liberation then we are putting the emphasis on struggle. These two approaches, and several others as well, all have a basis in scripture and no one of them should be taken as the one correct or primordial way. I want here to look at the model which emphasises liberation and struggle, while insisting that it is by no means exclusive.

I have written elsewhere about different aspects of oppression and liberation.[1] So here I simply note that the struggle for liberation has to take place at several levels:

– At the *economic* level, countries and individuals find themselves oppressed by the unjust terms of international trade which cause their primary products and their labour to be grossly undervalued; poor countries are also weighed down by the heavy burden of international debts which should have been cancelled long ago.

– At the *political* level, the need for liberation arises in two different situations: within countries, dictatorial governments often impose frightful oppression on their own citizens, depriving them of basic human rights; and, in the relationship between countries, the weaker ones are often oppressed by stronger neighbours or major powers.

– At the *cultural-religious* level, minority groups are frequently treated as second-class citizens: not allowed to follow their traditions, to practice their religion, or to learn their own language in school. This in turn causes them to suffer from internalised oppression: they have been taught to be ashamed of their accents and customs and to undervalue their own abilities; and so they

have a poor self-image. The struggle for liberation often begins
at this cultural-psychological level. It is from a re-discovery of
the value of their own heritage that people get the inspiration
and energy which enable them to endure the long-drawn-out
battle for political and economic liberation.

A Struggle against 'the Powers'

In looking here at mission as struggle I want to emphasise the
fact that work for liberation ultimately involves a *spiritual* battle,
even though it is necessarily carried out at the political, economic and cultural levels. From this perspective we can see it as a
struggle against 'The Dominating Powers'. I am putting that
phrase in capital letters to indicate that it is a technical term
which I shall now go on to explain.

There is a well-known scriptural text which tells us that our
struggle is not just against flesh and blood but against 'the principalities and the powers' (Eph 6:12; cf. Col 2:15). Many scripture
scholars have assumed that St Paul is referring here to evil spirits,
that is, to spiritual beings which are irremediably evil. This
would mean that our mission is to struggle tirelessly against
these evil powers and that success in our mission means driving
these 'Powers' out of our world and back to hell. But the text
does not have to be interpreted in this way. I propose here to
borrow from the scripture scholar Walter Wink[2] the understanding he has of these 'Powers', because his approach provides a
helpful basis for understanding the struggle for liberation.

If we follow Wink we can see 'the Powers' not as angels or
demons in the traditional 'extra-terrestrial' sense. We will instead
think of them as agencies or movements or philosophies which
exercise a compelling quasi-spiritual power in our everyday
world. These can be socio-political entities such as empires.
They can be political-cultural realities such as ideologies (e.g.
communism or capitalism). They can be mindsets (such as patriarchy or racism). All of these 'Powers' are ultimately spiritual.
There is an inner spirituality which shapes the various institutions
and movements of our world. This is the outlook and tradition
which holds them together; and it is this inner 'spiritual' aspect
which entitles us to call them 'Powers'.

Take, for example, 'the Roman Empire'. Behind the visible
reality of the Emperor, the Senate, the Forum and the whole
body of Roman law and the rights of citizenship, there was the

inner meaning of the empire which was partly embodied in each
of these institutions. Belonging to the empire was so much a part
of the identity of its people – especially of those who were entitled to call themselves *citizens* of the empire – that it seemed like
the end of the world when the empire collapsed.

It is not an exaggeration or a metaphor to say that the Roman
Empire was a spiritual 'Power'. When it came into conflict with
other 'Powers' (e.g. with the Carthaginian Empire or with the
nation of Israel) what took place was not merely a clash of
armies but also a clash of 'Powers'. Similarly when the British
Empire clashed with Spain or France or Germany – or with the
Irish, or the newly-emergent United States – what took place
was a struggle which had a spiritual dimension as well as a
purely military aspect.

If we follow this line of thinking then 'The Soviet Bloc' was
not merely one of the *political* 'Great Powers' of its time; it was
also one of 'the Powers' in the *scriptural* sense. So too are China
and the USA and, presumably the European Union (as well as
the individual nations of which it is composed).

If we understand 'the Powers' in this sense then it is evident
that they are not totally evil. Rather they have within them elements that are good and grace-filled as well as aspects that are
corrupted or evil. The British Crown is a good example of a
'Power' which can be an embodiment both of sin and of grace in
our world. In the past, British Christians tended to see the crown
as basically an agent of good – of enlightenment for less civilised
peoples. On the other hand, many Christians from Asia, from
Africa, and nationalists in Ireland, Scotland and Wales would be
inclined to take a more jaundiced view. *Both* views are partly
correct. The task of the authentic Christian is to transcend national
prejudice on one side or the other and to discern, on the one
hand, the ways in which, and the extent to which, the crown is
and has been an embodiment of divine grace and redemption;
and to discern, on the other hand, the ways and extent to which
evil has contaminated it and made it be an evil 'Power', a symbol and an agent of oppression.

Other examples of what Wink means by 'Powers' might be
'the West' or 'Socialism' or Amnesty International or Green-
peace or the Women's Movement. Each of them is obviously an
important instrument of the Spirit in many ways. Yet, despite
this, each of them could become contaminated or even corrupted

to some degree. Or take such deeply religious realities as The
Covenant and The Law. For the Jewish people, and for Christians too, they were obviously an embodiment of divine grace –
and they still are. Yet Jesus showed how such legal and religious
traditions and systems could over many years gradually become
tainted, and infected with evil. The gospels suggest that by the
time of Jesus they were being used by the Scribes and Pharisees
as instruments of oppression for the common people.

Mission as Struggle

All this is very relevant to our understanding of 'mission as
struggle'. The key point is that though 'Powers' such as empires
and ideologies are generally evil in practice, they are *not evil by
their very nature.* So they are not beyond redemption. Most of
these 'Powers' have become corrupted in some degree and to
that extent they have become forces for evil. Nevertheless, they
can still be redeemed, be made subject to the power of Jesus
Christ. If they were redeemed they would become forces for
good. The task of those who struggle for liberation is to resist the
evil and eventually to rescue these 'Powers' and enable them to
become agents of healing and growth.

It follows that it is no longer an adequate description of the
missionary task to say that it involves a struggle *against* 'the
Principalities and Powers'. That could mislead us in two ways:
– Firstly, it could suggest that 'the Powers' are themselves wholly
evil, whereas if we interpret 'Powers' in the way I have just done
(following Wink) they can be seen as a having a mixture of good
and evil.
– Secondly, to say our task is to struggle against 'the Powers'
describes only the more negative or dismantling aspect of our
missionary work. It does not give any clue about the positive or
constructive aspect. This is the challenge of transforming even
'the Powers' themselves to become embodiments of saving
grace. The extent to which we succeed in this is the extent to
which we help to bring about the reign of God within the very
fabric of our world.

The *dismantling* part of our mission is to share in the work of
Jesus in challenging and unmasking the evil in our world. This
evil is twofold. There is the personal wickedness that lurks in the
heart of each human person. And there is the sinfulness that has
become embodied in most of the traditions and institutions of

our nations and our world, that is, in what Wink calls 'the Powers'.

Although I make this distinction between personal sinfulness and the sinfulness of 'the Powers', in fact these two aspects are very closely related to each other. The relationship is rather like that between the chicken and the egg – each of them is both the cause and the consequence of the other. On the one hand, the personal sin of each of us – and particularly of those in a leadership role in society or in the churches – tends to corrupt the agencies and communities to which we belong. We might say that the personal sin of many individuals congeals into institutional and cultural sin. In this way 'the Powers' come tainted, contaminated, corrupted. They become evil powers which bring oppression and domination into people's lives. This way of describing what happens gives priority to personal sin. But, on the other hand, the same reality can be described in a way that gives more prominence to the evil social reality which pre-dates the personal sinfulness of any individual alive today. There is an evil embodied in 'the Powers' – a sinfulness which tends to contaminate each individual who is affected by any of them. So the corporate sinfulness of 'the Powers' is not only an *effect* but also a *cause* of the personal sinfulness of the leaders and of the ordinary people who are subject to these 'Powers'.

The *constructive* aspect of our mission is to share in the redemptive work of Jesus by helping *to transform 'the Powers' themselves.* An authentic struggle for liberation is one where the aim is not merely to bring about the personal conversion of individuals but also to bring about changes in the very fabric of society. Our aim is to bring conversion and liberation to traditions and institutions – to the social, economic, political and (perhaps above all) the cultural and religious structures which shape the way people feel and think and live. For these are the 'Powers' which provide meaning and order in our world.

This is an on-going work. It has already been partly achieved, yet there is very much more to be done. And when grace has become embodied in any particular institution or tradition this achievement is not only partial but also provisional. This means it is always in danger of being lost or corrupted again, so there is need for constant conversion.

A crucial first stage of mission is a prayerful discerning of 'the signs of the times'. The purpose of this discernment is to identify the aspects of sin and the aspects of grace within the 'Powers' which affect people's lives. Only when this is done are we in a position to move on to the task of challenging the sinful aspects and making common cause with others in the work of welcoming and co-operating with the grace-filled aspects of the 'Powers'.

Liberation within the Churches

The struggle for liberation is not just against political and economic 'Powers'. We also have to face the fact that we may at times be called to struggle against agencies which are specifically religious and which engage in an overtly spiritual oppression. The different church organisations to which Christians belong – and even the churches themselves – can be seen as instances of 'Powers'. This means that, while partly remaining instruments of God's saving grace in our world, they can become tainted and even corrupted in varying degrees. Evil can coagulate around them and within their very fabric, not only in their institutional aspects but even in the inner spiritual traditions which animate them.

Churches and church agencies can be oppressive in their own internal organisation. For instance, church authorities and clergy may fail to respect the right of lay Christians to participate in decision-making. They may hinder lay people – and especially women – in responding to their fundamental Christian call to share in the ministry of Jesus. Churches can also be oppressive by colluding with oppressive governments or failing to denounce evils and to encourage those who struggle for justice in society. The struggle against these abuses of spiritual power is a key element in the attainment of liberation. This means that the struggle for liberation has at times to take place within the church itself. Wherever we find within it an element of domination or corruption, we are called to engage with the church authorities in a manner which combines a spiritual struggle with respectful spiritual dialogue.

Down through the ages some of the most painful struggles for liberation have been within the churches themselves. In the struggle against spiritual oppression, as in the overall struggle for liberation, the poor and the powerless are the specially chosen instruments of God. We think of Catherine of Siena taking on the spiritual power of the Pope. And before her were Francis

and Clare whose long struggle against rich and powerful clergy-
men brought into the church a renewed understanding of the
liberating power of the gospel. We can all make up our own lists
of apparently powerless people who were inspired to raise their
prophetic challenge against abuses of spiritual power and who,
by the grace of God, succeeded against all the odds.

The realisation that each of us is called to partake in the
struggle for liberation even within the church itself can make us
scared or at least uncomfortable. It is probably good for us as
Christians to have a little of this discomfort mixed in with the
fundamental peace and assurance which is the gift of the Spirit.
As Isaiah says: 'Woe is me; I am a person of unclean lips, and I
dwell among a people of unclean lips.' (Is 6:5) Faced with this
fear we can respond in three ways:

– We may run away from the discomfort by refusing to let in the
possibility that our churches and church agencies could have
become tainted.

—We may allow ourselves to be crippled by a vague sense of
guilt.

—Or we may face up to the challenge through a process of on-
going discernment and social analysis in relation not only to the
world around us but more particularly to our own church institutions and traditions. This discernment and social analysis must
be followed by a struggle to take action on the basis of what they
reveal.

In referring here to *social analysis* I am thinking of a careful,
rational examination in which we employ the wisdom of experience and the scholarship of the human sciences. When I speak
of *discernment,* on the other hand, I have in mind an approach
which relies more obviously and directly on the power of the
Spirit, and on the intuitive part of our own spirit where the Holy
Spirit is often able to get through to us more effectively than in
the rational part of us.

Struggle and Dialogue
There are some very practical implications of all this for our missionary call to engage 'the Powers'. The first is that, although
our faith is not a 'Power', our churches, as I have said, are
'Powers' and as such they may sometimes need to be challenged
and transformed. The same applies to other institutionalised religions such as Islam. This means that our encounter with these

overtly spiritual 'Powers' should have a very particular character. We are called to engage with them in a manner which combines a spiritual *struggle* with a spiritual *dialogue*.

For instance, in our relationship with Islamic fundamental- ism or Hindu fundamentalism we need to hold together both the dialogue and the challenge, despite the tension between them. We have to be realistic enough not to ignore the gross in- sensitivity and lack of respect for basic human rights which often characterise the fundamentalists. But at the same time we have to be open enough to engage in dialogue even with agen- cies (or 'Powers') which at times engage in oppressive practices which horrify us.

A Spiritual Struggle

Furthermore, it is important to understand what it means in practice to engage in a struggle that is spiritual. We are not really engaging 'the Powers' at all if we see the spiritual struggle in pietistic, dualistic terms. A genuinely spiritual struggle does not take place in some disembodied other-worldly realm but in and through our engagement in the social, economic, political, and cultural structures which shape the way people live.

On the other hand, it is vital that church leaders realise that they have already lost the authentically spiritual aspect of the struggle if they cause the church to use the usual weapons of 'the Powers', namely, economic pressure, political control, and cultural domination. This is illustrated by the history of the churches in Ireland, north and south, over the past 70 years. In the Republic of Ireland the Catholic Church made the mistake of trying to win the spiritual struggle for the hearts and minds of people by exercising undue control over the educational and medical systems. In Northern Ireland the Protestant Churches tended to collude in a situation where the state educational sys- tem became, in large measure, a Protestant system.

Clearly, the issues are very complex. I do not think we can ex- pect to find a *blueprint* for how we can be both committed and respectful in the way we go about challenging and seeking to transform the different 'Powers'. But we can find numerous in- spiring *examples* of people who show us some of the ways in which the work can be done. We find such people within our churches – for instance, Martin Luther King, St Joan of Arc and Helder Camara. And we can also find them in other religious traditions and in secular society – for instance, in Aung San Suu Kyi, Nelson Mandela, and Mahatma Gandhi. We see the spiritual power these leaders have exercised and how they have engaged 'the Powers' of their time and place. In doing so we must also notice the high price they paid – just as Jesus paid a high price for his redeeming work.

The Kernel of the Struggle

In 1982 I was invited to go to South Africa as part of a team whose task was to train community activists engaged in the liberation struggle. Working with this group made me aware of the totally oppressive nature of the apartheid regime and how pervasive was its control over every aspect of the lives of the people. At that time it was very difficult to have any real hope that liberation could be achieved without massive military intervention from outside. Seven years later, in 1989, I was back again in South Africa working with several of the same people and with others engaged in the struggle. This was some time before Nelson Mandela was released from prison and it was a period when political oppression was in some ways worse than ever. But the whole atmosphere had changed; the spirit of the people and of the place was completely different. Even though all the political and military machinery of the regime was still in place, those who had struggled for liberation were now assured of victory. It was clear to all that it was just a matter of time until the oppressive government would give up and the 'New South Africa' would come into being.

This experience helped me to realise that behind the political and economic struggle for liberation lies a more fundamental psychological-spiritual struggle. If the powers of domination succeed in breaking the spirit of the people then no real liberation can take place. On the other hand, if those who are struggling against oppression are able to win the psychological-spiritual struggle, then the other aspects will soon fall into place. It is not just in South Africa that this pattern is played out. It was very evident in the long struggle led by Gandhi in India against British colonialism. It was the spiritual struggle animated by Gandhi which led to the defeat of the Empire and the independence of India. And the same applied in my own country, Ireland, in its struggle for independence eighty years ago.

The Spirit of the Crab

When I refer to a psychological-spiritual struggle it might be assumed that I am thinking about a struggle to avoid sin or to act
virtuously. But I mean something much more elemental than
that: a kind of struggle which we can see even among animals.
To illustrate what I mean let me recall a time some years ago
when I was working as a missionary in Lagos, Nigeria.
Occasionally we went to a remote beach to swim. The beach was
home to hundreds of little crabs and we had great fun chasing
these crabs. Occasionally I managed to chase a crab to a part of
the beach where there was no hole in the sand down which it
could escape. I noticed that whenever a crab found itself cor-
nered in this way it stopped running and turned to confront me.
Even though it was tiny – smaller than my hand – it braced itself,
seemed to look me in the eye, put up its claws just like a boxer
ready to fight and dared me to take it on.

The significant thing was that at that point I always found
myself stopping and getting afraid of this little crab. Despite its
weakness and vulnerability it prevailed over me by its courage
and defiance. It showed so much *spirit* that it intimidated me
and caused me to back off and leave it alone. It is no accident
that I can speak of the crab showing such *spirit*. What happened
was that the crab, when really desperate, turned the chase into a
struggle of the spirit and won the battle by instilling into me a
fear of the crab and a healthy respect for it.

When I claim that behind the political and economic struggles for liberation lies a more fundamental struggle *of the spirit*,
that is the kind of thing I have in mind. In India, Gandhi succeeded in generating among millions of ordinary people a spirit
of resistance to colonial oppression; and that was how the struggle for liberation was won.

In the life of Nelson Mandela we see a particularly clear instance of this kind of spiritual struggle. In jail and totally at the
mercy of the warders, how could he give expression to his resistance? At first, the only effective way he could do so was by
refusing to run when the warders shouted at him to run. He suffered cruelly for his dignified passive resistance. His example inspired the other prisoners; and eventually even the warders and
prison authorities came to respect him. Over a period of years he
grew in stature as a symbol of resistance. His spirit of resistance
gave *inspiration* to millions. He became a focus for the energy of

a whole nation struggling for liberation. By the time Mandela was released, the spiritual struggle had largely been won because the people were now convinced that the day of freedom was at hand.

As I write, Aung San Sui Kyi in Burma is engaged in the same kind of struggle of the human spirit. Although she has no army and no weapons she is willing to pit herself against the overwhelming military power of the ruling junta. By the steely courage of her non-violent resistance she has become a far more effective threat to them than if she had engaged in terrorism.

Stages in the Liberation Process

There is a pattern in the struggle for liberation. It goes through a succession of stages. This can be seen very clearly in the life of Nelson Mandela. As I have already noted, an early stage was in those first years in prison when the only options open to him were either to allow his spirit to be broken by the cruelty of the prison regime or to offer a brave and dignified *resistance* to oppression. He choose to resist and he paid the price. This crucial first step on the road to liberation gave increased spiritual power to this apparently powerless man.

As his authority expanded he began to have a wider range of choices in the liberation struggle and he made his choices shrewdly and wisely. He inspired and led his followers towards the creation of a *mass movement* of committed people, with comparatively little reliance on military action. This was the next stage of the process of authentic liberation.

A further stage in the process of liberation was the period of *negotiation* with the enemy. It came when the apartheid regime eventually admitted that they would have to talk with the ANC – and with Mandela as its leader. Here again he showed the extraordinary strength of his spirit. He was utterly steadfast in his insistence on majority rule and in resisting the pressure to allow the Whites to have their own separate state. But at the same time he had the breadth of vision and the strength of spirit to resist the temptation to seek revenge or the annihilation of those who had treated him so cruelly. Without his towering spiritual presence it seems certain that the transition to the 'New South Africa' would have been much more difficult and violent.

During his years as president of his country he opened up new stages of the struggle for liberation. One of the most striking moments was when he went to the World Rugby Championship in 1995 and put on the Springbok jersey. Through this generous gesture he transformed that hated symbol of White dominance into a symbol of national reconciliation. This reminds us that liberation remains incomplete until it leads on to *reconciliation*.

President Mandela also channelled the energy of liberation into a programme for the *development* of his country. This reminds us that liberation and development are not necessarily opposed to each other, as Latin American liberation theologians have been inclined to assume. Liberation is opposed only to a version of development which betrays the struggle by widening the gap between the rich and the poor. But authentic development is an integral part of true liberation.

A further stage in the struggle for liberation is the stage of *global leadership*. It came when President Mandela took up his role as an African leader and a world statesman. He sided with those who cried out against the oppressive regime in Nigeria and he was willing to put his extraordinary moral authority on the line in seeking peaceful solutions to conflict in other troubled parts of Africa. Furthermore, he played a significant part in promoting peace and genuine liberation for the people of Northern Ireland. In fact he became a beacon of inspiration to the whole world.

Jesus

It is interesting to compare and contrast these different stages of the liberation struggle as manifested in Mandela with different stages and aspects of the liberating life and death of Jesus. At its heart was the unbounded love of Jesus for the people to whom God had sent him. This love first found expression in the respect and *care* with which he reached out to bring healing and liberation of spirit to 'the common people' and especially to those who had been left on the margins of society.

The next stage was the careful *formation* of a group of disciples, drawn from these ordinary poor people. These followers were people whom he taught and coached to share his vision and his liberating mission so that they could bring fresh hope and new life to those who could not see or hear him in person.

When those in power reacted to his message with incomprehension and opposition, he firmly *challenged* their oppressive use of religious and political power. This led to a tussle of wills with the religious power-brokers of his country, namely, the scribes and Pharisees. This was a spiritual struggle in which Jesus battled for the liberation of his people against spiritual and religious oppression. The struggle reached its climax when Jesus endured his shameful trial and death not only with uncompromising dignity but even with a generous prayer for forgiveness for those who were torturing him to death.

Underpinning all of this was the unconditional trust of Jesus in the One who had sent him, a faith that remained true when his followers let him down, a faith that even survived the dark of apparent abandonment by God. The final stage was what we may call 'the unveiling of his victory'. The clearest example of this is in the story of the disciples on the road to Emmaus to whom Jesus showed how all that had happened was part of God's plan of salvation.

Prayer and Struggle

I want now to note the importance of prayer in the struggle for liberation. If we do not pray we are in danger of losing our conviction and our energy. In prayer we discover our own inadequacy and poverty – and we learn that God is our only hope. So prayer teaches us *why* the poor are primary agents of liberation: it is because they have to rely on God rather than on human power.

When we find ourselves becoming dismayed by the difficulty and complexity of the struggle for liberation, we can find nourishment of spirit in prayer. We see then the inner connection between the nights Jesus spent in prayer and the days he spent bringing healing, empowerment and liberation to his world. We realise that it was his agonised prayer in the Garden of Gethsemane which enabled him to face his death next day with courage, dignity and freedom of spirit.

As I noted earlier, liberation includes two aspects: a struggle *against* the 'Powers' and a commitment to *transform* the 'Powers' from within. Prayer helps us to become more authentic in our attempts to combine struggle with a real commitment to dialogue. Through prayer we find the courage and strength to engage in the struggle. And in prayer we are given the openness and humility to engage in a truly listening dialogue with 'the Powers', so that they can be transformed. Furthermore, it is only through prayer that we learn the wisdom which enables us to avoid deceiving ourselves both in the dialogue and in the struggle.

Violence

Up to this point I have been stressing the underlying spiritual dimension of any authentic struggle for liberation. I want now to move to the opposite end of the spectrum by facing up to the issue of whether violence can ever be a legitimate part of that struggle. The very first point to make here is that those who struggle against oppression are not just faced with a simple choice between violent or non-violent action. The struggle for political liberation can take many forms, ranging from guerrilla warfare to strikes, mass protests, and passive resistance.

History teaches us that it is a fatal mistake to think that genuine liberation can by brought about by adopting the oppressive methods of the 'Powers' against which we are struggling. It is an illusion to imagine that a purely military takeover is a way of transforming the world. For, if a grossly unjust regime is overthrown by violence, the new government is itself quite likely to become authoritarian. People quickly find that a new set of oppressors have taken over from the old ones. There are no easy short-cuts. Those who struggle for an authentic political liberation must begin the slow task of building participatory structures at every level of society, even while the struggle against the oppressive regime is going on.

However, these provisos should not be used as a way of dodging the question whether there are any circumstances in which violent action can be justified as one element in an overall struggle for liberation. Some years ago the Philippino theologian, Ed de la Torre, posed that question in an interesting way: what should the Good Samaritan have done if he had arrived on the scene about an hour earlier than he did – at the time when the robbers were still attacking their victim? Should he have fought against the robbers? This raises the basic issue of whether the victims of injustice (and those who wish to help them) are ever entitled to use physical force or military means to resist oppression.

A Just War?

Only a small minority of Christians have adopted a stance of total pacifism. There is a long Christian tradition which says that there is such a thing as a just war. But in applying this teaching nowadays there are three difficulties:

– First, modern weapons are so indiscriminately destructive that it is hard to see how they could be used without killing large numbers of non-combatants. (This became very clear in the bombing of Iraq and Serbia.)

– Second, modern warfare is so intimately dependent on a highly developed technological and economic base that it is difficult to claim that the war (or 'the war effort') is being conducted only by the soldiers; the military scientists and those who manufacture the weapons are just as involved as those who use the weapons. And where does one stop? It is difficult to make a clear distinction between combatants and non-combatants.

– Third, despite every effort of theologians to lay down objective criteria about a just war, it is almost impossible to make unbiased judgements. The reality tends to be quite 'fuzzy' – at least as it is perceived on the one hand by those who see themselves as victims of oppression and on the other hand by those who are accused of being the oppressors. Down through history, in practically every war, the protagonists on *both* sides have had the support of prominent theologians and church leaders who were convinced that their own side was engaged in a justified war. As a result the 'moral voice' of those proclaiming that one side is justified was 'cancelled out' by similar declarations made by church people on the other side.

My own view is that that it is not possible to conceive of how *in practice* a just war could be waged between modern states. This is partly because of the type of weapons being used or likely to be used, and partly because there are other far more effective and less damaging ways of resolving disputes and enforcing judgement. I am thinking here of embargoes and other sanctions of various kinds.

Just Revolution?
The previous paragraphs refer to the issue of war between sovereign states. But what about situations where oppressed peoples are struggling against ruthlessly oppressive governments? It seems to me that the 'just war theory' may have more relevance in such cases than in cases where two countries are pitted against each other. The main reason for this is a very practical one: it is less likely that those who rebel against oppressive governments will use weapons of mass destruction such as nuclear or biological weapons; and even the most oppressive government is unlikely to use such weapons within its own territory.

So it is useful to adapt the theology of the just war to address the question of whether there can be a just revolution.

Such a theology of revolution can help to sharpen up our moral evaluation of situations of struggle. But situations are so complex – and people tend to be so one-sided in the way they perceive and interpret the facts – that theology scarcely ever offers us an easy and clear-cut answer to the moral dilemmas which arise in such situations. When the question comes up in a particular situation whether a government is so oppressive that armed insurrection is justified, we must start off with the acting assumption that such violence is *not* justified. It is only in the most extreme cases, where all other options have failed, that it is possible to think that we might be dealing with a very rare exception to the general rule.

Examples which come to mind are the struggles in the late 1970s of the peoples of Nicaragua and Zimbabwe against very oppressive regimes. There are good arguments for saying that those who fought against the governments in these countries were engaged in a struggle that was justified in principle (while also acknowledging the fact that some of the means they used were morally unacceptable). The main reason for saying this is that it seemed that their armed struggle was in practice the only way the unjust governments could be overthrown. In theory, of course, the community of nations could have imposed effective sanctions on the offending governments; but in practice this was not done and there was no real likelihood that it would be done within the foreseeable future.

Zimbabwe is a particularly interesting case because the moral issues were very well articulated at the time. The well-known moral theologian, Enda McDonagh, was invited by some of the local church authorities to go out there in the middle of the liberation war. His task was two-fold. First, he was to help church people in Zimbabwe come to a truly Christian moral evaluation of the situation in which they found themselves. Secondly, he was invited to make his own moral judgement about the morality of the liberation struggle in that country. I have no doubt that the first aspect of this assignment was very successful. His workshops with the church people on the ground helped them in their own moral assessment of what was going on. In regard to the second aspect, his conclusion was that the Zimbabwe situation was, concretely, one where the struggle for liberation was justified (even though he could not condone all of the actions of the freedom fighters). But, ironically, by the time this conclusion of his was published[3] the struggle for liberation had been successfully concluded!

'Theological Hijacking'
It is very likely that church authorities and missionaries 'in the field' are likely in the future to confront the same kind of practical dilemmas which arose during the Zimbabwean liberation struggle. The issues faced by church people on the ground were not so much the overall question of whether or not the struggle was justified but the day-to-day question of giving practical help to 'freedom fighters'. Should they obey the government decree which made it a crime to provide elementary medical treatment for those who were wounded and could not go to government-controlled hospitals? Should they obey the law which demanded that they report the presence of 'terrorists' in their area? How far should they go in refusing to obey the directives of an oppressive government on the one hand or violent revolutionaries on the other?

Even though theology may not always provide us with clear-cut answers about such specific issues or about the overall morality of any particular liberation struggle, it would be a serious mistake to underestimate the importance of knowing the theological principles and engaging in a serious attempt to apply them in specific situations. If we fail to do so, the protagonists on one side or the other may succeed in their attempt to gain religious support for their cause through a kind of 'theological hijacking'.

On the one hand, oppressive regimes and their supporters frequently try to 'hijack' the churches or other religions into giving them ideological support. An obvious example is the concerted campaign against liberation theology which was waged not only in Latin American and South Africa but also in the Western media: it served their interests to suggest that liberation theology was mainly about inciting people to rebel violently against legitimate authority. We can also find instances of what I am calling 'theological hijacking' by those engaged in a revolution against state authorities. A very striking way in which this happens is in the teaching of Islamic fundamentalist leaders that those who engage in suicide bombing are assured of going directly to heaven. Christian and Jewish revolutionaries are also inspired by their long tradition of martyrdom and by their conviction that God is on the side of the oppressed. In my own country, because of our history, those who go on hunger-strike in support of a liberation struggle are able to evoke in many people a quasi-religious belief that their cause is justified (even when church leaders refuse to sanction their cause).

Conclusion

In this chapter I have tried to situate the issue of violent resistance to oppression within the wider context of a struggle against 'Powers' which are corrupt or partly corrupt. It may be useful to insist again that violent action is only one of many ways in which one can resist. In many situations armed resistance is likely, in the long run, to be one of the least effective forms of struggle. In making this claim I am thinking, for instance, of the role played by 'The Kairos Document' in the South African liberation struggle.[4] This document, signed by about 150 South African theologians from the various churches, roundly condemned the 'state theology' of the apartheid regime; and it also condemned a type of church theology which effectively failed to challenge the regime. I believe that this document was a far more effective 'weapon' in the struggle against oppression than any number of guns or bombs. It was a practical proof that, at its core, the struggle against 'the Powers' is a battle of the spirit, and that the mission of the church is to play a key role in this struggle.

I have pointed out that the struggle *against* oppression is only the negative aspect of the work of liberation. The positive aspect is the struggle *for* transformation. I have already dealt with some aspects of this transformation in Chapter 6 on inculturation. I shall have more to say about this positive side in later chapters entitled 'Vehicles of Evangelization' and 'Missionaries and Development Workers'. But first I want to move on to another aspect of the church's mission, one that is the other side of the coin to the present treatment of mission as struggle. It is 'mission as reconciliation', which is the subject of the next chapter.

QUESTIONS FOR REFLECTION

1. Recall a situation where you stood up against one of 'the Powers'. How did you do so? What made it more difficult? What helped you at that time? Having learned from that experience, what would you do differently now in such a situation?

2. Suppose some friends of yours are engaged in what seems to them to be a 'life-or-death' struggle against injustice. How would you advise them to nourish and strengthen their spirit for the struggle? And how would you help them to remain open to dialogue and to the possibility that they might be at least partly wrong?

CHAPTER 8

Mission as Reconciliation

'Evangelization is the simultaneous proclamation of a liberating justice and of reconciliation.'[1] This remark of the Latin American writer, Segundo Galilea, brings out the point that liberation and reconciliation are complementary. So, having in the previous chapter looked at mission from the point of view of liberation, it is appropriate and even necessary to go on now to look at our call to share in the reconciling mission of Jesus.

As Galilea points out, the re-establishment of justice is a condition for Christian reconciliation, but justice alone is not enough, for it cannot heal old wounds and wipe out past offences. Without forgiveness, resentments will continue to rankle. So Jesus, the merciful liberator, calls us not just to struggle for justice but to love our enemies. It is hard to get the balance right, to know when to emphasise the struggle for justice and when to emphasise forgiveness and reconciliation.[2]

From the Start
Galilea makes the helpful point that reconciliation is a demand that should accompany conflict from the start. Furthermore, it should be present not just as a vague aspiration but in very practical ways. There is one good test of whether or not a realistic commitment to reconciliation is present. It is whether those who struggle for justice show a respect for human rights *during* their struggle. Do they avoid atrocities during the conflict, rather than waiting until victory has been won?[3] If we can resist the temptation to win at all costs, this indicates that the germ of reconciliation is already present in the midst of our struggle. This applies whether our struggle is a political one conducted against an oppressive government or an interpersonal struggle against an individual who is treating us unjustly.

Oppressors and Victims

Reconciliation is a process in which there is a restoration of good relationships between individuals, groups or nations. The need for reconciliation arises in two different situations:

– Firstly, where enmity and hatred has arisen between two more or less equal parties – e.g. between family members or friends, or between neighbouring communities or nations.

– Secondly, where one of the parties is an oppressor and the other is the victim. (The oppressor may be an individual, or a whole group, or a nation, or even a whole group of nations; and the same applies to the victim.)

However, it may not always be easy to distinguish between these two situations in practice. The reason is that, when the victims of tyranny begin to struggle to overcome their oppression, the struggle frequently leads on to horrible acts on *both* sides. (This happens both when the oppression is at the personal level and when it is at the political level.) So both sides become wounded and resentful. Each has a deep sense of grievance and each focuses on the wrongs inflicted by the other. When the struggle drags on and becomes more intractable it may seem that there is a kind of 'equality of grievance', where the wrongs of one side balance those on the other side.

It is important to realise that such an 'equality of grievance' is not at all the same thing as an 'equality of power or of fundamental injustice'. The fact that victims of oppression sometimes do terrible things (e.g. terrorist bombs or murders) does not mean that both sides are equally to blame for the injustice and hatred which marks the relationship. This is not to suggest that we should overlook the excesses of those who struggle against oppression either at the personal or at the political level. But there is need for a clear-sighted analysis which goes back to the *root causes*. Such an analysis should show whether we are dealing with a struggle arising from a tit-for-tat escalation of a dispute between two more or less equal parties; or whether, on the other hand, the struggle is fundamentally that of a victim against an oppressor. This analysis is necessary because there is a notable difference between the kind of reconciliation that is called for in the two different situations.

Naming the Evil

Reconciliation between two more-or-less equal parties requires a willingness by those on either side to forgive and to reach out in understanding to the other. Reconciliation between oppressor and victim is more complex. Undoubtedly it calls for forgiveness and understanding on both sides. But there must also be a clear recognition by both sides that there has been a fundamental inequality and oppressiveness in the relationship. In situations where there has been such an imbalance and a serious one-sided oppression it is important to see reconciliation not just as the resolution of a quarrel. It has two stages: first, the recognition of the injustice; and, following that, the restoration of a good relationship between the former victim and the former oppressor.

The oppression may have been only partially conscious. Indeed it may at times have been almost entirely unconscious. For instance, the patriarchal world in which most of us lived until quite recently meant that men were largely unaware of the many ways in which women were oppressed. Similarly 'white' people who grew up in a thoroughly racist society often remained almost blind to the gross inequalities all around them. They were more or less oblivious of the oppressive and unjust character of the laws which enforced these inequalities. Furthermore, we have to take account of the reality of *internalised oppression,* which caused women to be largely unaware of their own oppression and which made it difficult for the victims of racism to really see themselves as the equals of those who oppressed them.

For this reason the first step towards real reconciliation may have to be a 'raising of consciousness' on the part of the victims of oppression so that they can clearly see and name the injustice under which they have been suffering. Such 'consciousness-raising' can easily look like trouble-making – especially to those who are benefiting from the oppressive situation. It is clear, then, that to engage in genuine reconciliation work one must avoid taking 'the easy option'. Reconciliation between oppressor and victim is not authentic if it glosses over the oppressiveness, the injustice, and the inequality of power which characterised the relationship between the two sides in the past. We remember the words of the prophet condemning the false prophets 'who say "peace, peace" where there is no peace' (Jer 6:14).

Reconciliation can be looked at from three points of view – the religious, the psychological and the political. In this chapter

I propose to look at each of these in turn – and to show how they are linked together.

Reconciliation is a grace. The initiative comes first of all from God. God calls the oppressor to repentance and calls the victim to forgiveness. The process can begin at either end – with repentance by the oppressor or with forgiveness by the victim. I recall a situation many years ago where I was working as part of a facilitation team in an intense week-long workshop. At one point some of the participants 'ganged up' on one of the other participants. When one of our facilitation team defended the 'victim', they 'ganged up' on this team member also and complained bitterly about him, behind his back, to another member of the facilitating team. At our planning meeting next day this second member of the team told us that, under the pressure of that situation, she had colluded with those who were complaining. She had failed to maintain the solidarity of the team and had joined in the criticism of her fellow team member. She now acknowledged what she had done and said she was sorry. Our colleague whom she had let down so badly looked at her aghast and said, 'I can hardly believe you did that to me.' Then, after a long moment of silence, he added in a tone of utter compassion, 'but I forgive you.' For me, that was a moment of pure grace. It taught me more about the nature of forgiveness and reconciliation than all the books I have read.

I do not think that forgiveness is authentic unless the injustice that has been perpetrated is named and acknowledged—at least by the victim. So, in working with those who have been victimised, it is important not to gloss over the wrong that has been done. If we try to move on too quickly to forgiveness, the victim is left with a kind of spiritual and psychological ambivalence about the whole affair and the process of healing cannot take place. I shall return to this point a little later, when dealing with the psychological aspects of reconciliation.

Forgiveness by the victim is greatly helped when the perpetrator acknowledges the injustice. Then it can lead on to full reconciliation. But forgiveness is not dependent on repentance by the oppressor. Quite the contrary: forgiveness on the part of the victim often comes *prior* to repentance by the oppressor, for the ability to forgive and to be open to reconciliation is a grace from God. But it is one thing to say that *forgiveness* by the victim can come before *repentance* by the oppressor; it is quite a different thing to hold that *reconciliation* can take place without *acknowledgement* of the injustice. It is a serious mistake to fail to distinguish these two situations. If a genuine reconciliation is to take place both victim and perpetrator must acknowledge the evil that has occurred. Only then can they reach out to each other in complete honesty and openness to be reconciled.

It is a mistake to think of reconciliation mainly in legal terms such as 'making satisfaction'. Such concepts were over-emphasised in both Catholic and Protestant theology in the past. As Robert Schreiter points out, where Western theology emphasised legal metaphors and satisfaction, Eastern theology put the emphasis instead on medical metaphors and healing.[4] It is important, then, that a theology of reconciliation incorporate the psychology of healing (see Section II below) as much as the political aspects (see Section III below).

A New Reality
Reconciliation is not the restoration of the state that existed prior to the oppression; so we cannot know what shape it will take. It is a new reality for both victim and for the former oppressor.[5] Victims cannot be as they were before; they will still bear the scars of the oppression they have endured; but they may become powerful instruments of God's saving power as 'wounded healers'. Converted oppressors cannot regain the innocence they have thrown away; but their repentance and the experience of reconciliation opens them up to become powerful instruments of God's grace.

The power released through reconciliation is neither of the two kinds of power which are normally at our disposal, namely, the power to dominate others and the power to enable or empower others. It is, rather, a mysterious power which God uses to draw good out of evil. For Christians, the new life brought forth from the torture and death of Jesus is, of course, the primary 'proof' that healing and hope can come out of injustice and evil. So Christians are entitled to give the title 'the power of the cross' to the mysterious power which is at work in such situations. But it is not limited to the cross of Jesus, nor is it confined to Christians. All those who are spiritually awakened, whether they be Christian or non-Christian, can find in their lives, or in history, similar instances of a creative and reconciling transcendent power drawing new and deeper life out of suffering and evil. Indeed, such experiences may be a more effective 'proof' of the existence of God than any purely rational argument.

Reconciliation with God
Where does reconciliation with God come into all of this? To be reconciled with God has some elements that are similar to being reconciled with other people. It involves an experience of repentance and of being forgiven. But in other respects reconciliation with God is quite different. It is not appropriate to think of having a quarrel with God in the way we quarrel with other humans. Nor can we imagine either being oppressed by God or oppressing God. We have to think rather of being loved by God with an endlessly forgiving love and being brought back into a living relationship with God. In other words, reconciliation with God does not involve the two-way relinquishment of hatred and strife which characterises reconciliation between humans. This means that the word 'reconciliation' has a different meaning when it is applied to the relationship between God and us than when it is applied to the restoration of peace between individuals or groups in our world.

Reconciliation with God and with people lies at the heart of the biblical view. St Paul writes that 'God was in Christ reconciling the world to God ... and entrusting to us the message of reconciliation' (2 Cor 5:19). One of the main messages of the Old Testament is that there can be no question of being reconciled with God unless we are willing to be reconciled with those around us. This theme is taken up again in the New Testament (especially in 1 John). The words attributed to Jesus on this point are very explicit and striking: 'If you are offering your gift at the altar, and there remember that your brother or sister has something against you, leave your gift there before the altar and go first to be reconciled to your brother or sister, and then come and offer your gift.' (Mt 5:23-4) This suggests that reconciliation with others is the only convincing evidence that we are reconciled with God. But the other crucial point in the New Testament vision is that God is the One who enables us to be reconciled to others. Reconciliation with our brothers and sisters is experienced as a gift from God, a pure grace.

SECTION II: PSYCHOLOGICAL ASPECTS

Reconciliation cannot be reduced to a purely psychological process since it is ultimately a gift of God's grace which takes place in the deepest spiritual depths of a person, a group or a whole people. But in order to be authentic it must include some measure of psychological healing of the wounds left by the hatred and strife between the parties. This is especially the case where the reconciliation is to take place between oppressors and victims; for oppression almost always damages the humanity both of the victim and the oppressor. It is a great mistake to imagine that that there can be a purely *spiritual* reconciliation which takes little or no account of these psychological wounds. It is also a mistake to assume that an effective and lasting *political* reconciliation can be achieved (in places like South Africa, Guatemala or Northern Ireland) without seriously addressing the personal pain, suspicion and bitterness which are the legacy of past oppression.

Where there has been widespread and public oppression the healing which is part of reconciliation has to be worked for at the individual level and also in a more public way. In this section I propose to focus mainly on the more individual or personal level. But most of what I say here applies also where there is a more public dimension to the reconciliation. (In the following section I will go on to consider the somewhat different issue of political reconciliation.)

Personal Healing
It is very valuable to help the victim to bring the pain and the anger into the light. This may require psychological counselling since it is likely that the hurt and anger will be at least partly re-pressed, and therefore not immediately accessible to the person. If the oppression took place while the victim was young, these feelings may have been so thoroughly buried that the victim has no direct memory of them. So long as these memories remain 'buried' they have a very damaging effect on the person's behav-iour and self-image. In such cases a lot of therapy may be required before these 'lost' memories come back into consciousness.

Wounded Societies
Nowadays we tend to assume that it is only through formal

counselling or therapy that the healing of such deep wounds can take place. But what can we do when faced with a situation where whole societies – millions of people – have been wounded by racism? Or by sexism and patriarchy? In such a situation there is an urgent need to find ways of making psychological healing techniques available on a far more widespread basis than at present. A combination of two fairly simple approaches could go quite some way towards meeting the need – or at least opening up the situation for more elaborate further steps. The first is a training for convenors of support groups and the second is a training in co-counselling techniques.

The training of convenors of support groups could be quite short – provided the people being trained are carefully chosen for their sensitivity and listening skills. The main thing would be to establish some basic 'groundrules' to ensure that people taking part in such groups feel safe, and are able to tell their stories and really feel *heard* by others. The simplest and perhaps most effective 'groundrule' may be that people who have been oppressed or victimised be allowed to tell their own story in their own way, without interruption and without having to put up with unasked for advice from others.

Co-counselling goes one step further. It is an arrangement by which two or more people take on the role of being amateur (i.e. unpaid) therapists to each other. There are organisations which offer short intense training programmes in the skills required. The training provides people with skills in what might be called 'deep listening'. They are taught to listen not only to the words but also to the other person's body language. This helps to create an atmosphere in which those who are telling their stories can get in touch with their feelings of deep hurt, anger, inadequacy or fear. There can at times be a helpful discharge of these strong emotions, leading to greater inner freedom and wholeness.

The process is called *co*-counselling because two people take turns to play two different roles. First one person takes, say, 30 or 60 minutes to share their story and be the 'client', while the other person plays the role of the listener and encourager. Then the roles are reversed and the same length of time is given to the other person to be the 'client'. This means that a lot of valuable healing work can be done without having to pay a counsellor.

The training also teaches people how to establish some clear guidelines. An important guideline is that those who are telling their story must remain in charge of the whole process; they do not 'hand themselves over' in complete trust to the 'listener' as they would to a professional therapist. Another guideline is that those who are playing the role of 'listener' must not intervene in the process except when the 'client' explicitly requests it; they must learn to avoid acting as though they were professional therapists. Perhaps the most crucial guideline of all is that the time-boundaries must be maintained, so that it is always quite clear who is in which role – and when they are to come out of these roles. (Otherwise the whole process is likely to get 'fuzzy' and people could easily get hurt.)

A co-counselling programme can be particularly helpful in situations where there are many poor people who have no access to professional therapy or no money to pay for it. It can be a very useful 'tool' for missionaries or other church people trying to respond to the needs of large numbers of people who have been traumatised by war or oppression. A small support group or one-to-one co-counselling can provide an opportunity for people to tell their story (perhaps over and over again) to one or more willing, compassionate and attentive listeners. The victim needs to have a sense of the story being *heard* and really believed. In cases where the memories had been partly repressed, the victim may require a lot of reassurance of being believed since part of the oppression may be a destruction of the victim's trust in her/his own feelings and memories.

Deeper Work

In formal therapy or counselling – and perhaps also where those who have trained in co-counselling have become more experienced and skilled – the person seeking healing may find it helpful to do 'body-work'. This means that one is no longer confined to the story as told in *words*. Instead, the person may be encouraged to find in his or her *body* the location and effect of the wounds of the past and especially repressed memories. This can be a very potent way of bringing memories back into consciousness and of promoting healing.

In all of this it is particularly important that people be helped to become aware of the ways in which oppression has become *internalised*. This means that victims begin to see how they had been blaming themselves for the damage that was being done to them. This is an important step towards shaking off internalised oppression and attaining true inner freedom.

Forgiveness
Forgiveness is crucial to the whole process of reconciliation. When people have oppressed others in the past and are now acknowledging the evil, it brings a great healing into the situation if they can know that they have been forgiven. The same applies if the oppression has been perpetrated by a whole ethnic group or nation. If forgiveness is important for the oppressors it is perhaps even more important for the victims of the oppression. Refusal to forgive, or inability to forgive, imposes a block on a person's growth. Healing and recovery of full humanity takes place only when one is able to forgive.

However, people who are working for reconciliation, either for themselves or by acting as formal or informal counsellors for others, must always keep in mind that forgiveness cannot be rushed. It is wrong – because it is futile – to pressure oneself or others into trying to forgive before the time is ripe.

Confrontation
One way of moving towards reconciliation is to create a situation in which the victim of past oppression is able to *confront* the oppressor and tell him/her/them what they have done and what have been the consequences. If those who have been guilty in the past of oppression are genuine in their search for forgiveness and reconciliation then they should be willing to hear the stories of the victims. Of course this can only take place in a situation where the former victim feels that it is really *safe* to do so. But if that is achieved then the confrontation can be very empowering for the person who has been victimised. It can help to establish a greater equality between the parties and make a genuine reconciliation more likely.

It is also important for oppressors to be made aware of the ways in which they may have projected their own unwanted feelings on to the victim. This is a kind of escape mechanism which oppressors use to justify the wrongs they inflict on others: They try to escape from acknowledging (to themselves and others) the evil of what they have done, by *blaming* or even *demonising* the victim. When former victims engage in dialogue with those who have oppressed them in the past, this process of projection can be brought into the light. The dialogue often helps those who have been guilty of oppression to see how, even in seeking reconciliation, they may still be inclined to *patronise* their former victims.

Ritual

In the process of psychological healing, and in the reconciliation to which it is linked, *ritual* can play an important part. Rituals can be very effective in giving expression in a solemn and formal way to feelings and values which may be too deep or too complex to express in words. They offer the former victim and the repentant oppressor a way of acknowledging,

– the evil which has been perpetrated,

– the suffering and righteous anger felt by the victim,

– the experience of repentance and desire for forgiveness on the part of the oppressor,

– and, hopefully, the willingness of the victim to forgive and of both parties to let go of their grievances and be truly reconciled with each other.

A ritual is a very effective way of 'sealing' and giving formal expression to reconciliation. It is particularly important in situations where there has been a more widespread and public form of oppression, such as racism or discrimination against a whole group. The ritual then meets the need for a publicly visible expression of reconciliation. Furthermore, the ritual plays an important part in making the reconciliation a truly memorable event. It may then be recalled, celebrated and renewed at regular intervals, e.g. on an annual remembrance day or after, say, a five-year interval.

The ritual may be a traditional one such as a solemn and ancient religious ceremony. On the other hand, it may be a specially designed event, emphasising the newness of the situation and the new hope it brings. Best of all, perhaps, is a ritual which combines the ancient and the new. For instance, where both parties are Christian there could be a celebration of a solemn eucharist incorporating a specially designed ritual and formula of reconciliation.

Truth and Reconciliation Commission

The 'Truth and Reconciliation Commission' set up in South Africa shortly after the apartheid regime came to an end represented a very serious effort to promote genuine reconciliation and healing in a society that had been grievously wounded by the evils of the past. Some people criticised it on the grounds that it was 'raking up past grievances' and re-opening old wounds. But critics who said these things failed to understand that some wounds need to be lanced, in order to release the poison. And where the evil was a public one it is helpful – and sometimes even essential – that the acknowledgement of the evil also take a public form.

On the other hand, the work of the Commission was criticised by others on the grounds that 'it only touched the problem' and that very many terrible stories remained untold. This is, of course, true; but it is not a valid criticism of the work of the Commission. It fails to take account of the ritual and symbolic value of the public sessions. The terrible stories which were told in public, the public acknowledgement of the evils that were done, and the public requests for amnesty had (and still have) a value that may be called 'sacramental'.

The stories told in public were representative of many other similar situations. The (partial) closure and resolution which they brought to particular horror stories will, hopefully, have a wider cleansing effect in the society as a whole. They are 'outward signs' of a healing and reconciling grace which is available far more widely than these particular instances. Not every story needs to be told in public; but those which were brought before the public gaze through the work of the Commission acted as a catalyst for the personal healing of many other people who were wounded by similar situations in the past. So the Commission had a significance which is effectively religious, standing on the boundary between the personal-psychological aspect of reconciliation and the more political dimension.

For me, all this was encapsulated in a remark made by the mother of a young freedom fighter who had been captured, tortured and killed by under-cover security forces, who then went on to place his body on a landmine and blow it to pieces. The mother of that murdered boy came to a public session of the Commission where she listened in silence to the story of the death of her son as told by those who killed him. Then she walked out of the hall and said simply: 'Now, I can pray.'

The Commission was chaired by Archbishop Desmond Tutu who played a crucial role in steering it through very difficult moments. His work was an excellent example of how a church-person can exercise a mission of real service to civil society. He worked hand-in-hand with lawyers and other professional people. But at the same time his presence added an extra dimension of sacredness to what was already a deeply spiritual project. His status as an archbishop would have meant little on its own; but when combined with his personal integrity, courage, and commitment it gave an added power and dignity to his role and to the Commission itself. In this work the archbishop gave a shining example of what the reconciling mission of the church is all about.

SECTION III: POLITICAL ASPECTS

Politics is more an art than a science. So we cannot expect to have a set of ready-made rules to govern how reconciliation is to be achieved in the political sphere. However, some general principles and guidelines can be worked out.

First of all, it must be insisted that reconciliation is *not an alternative to liberation.* The desire for reconciliation is not authentic if the oppressor wants the victim to ignore or forget about the injustices of the past and wants to build a relationship purely on the basis of the present situation. There must be an acknowledgement of the injustices of the past, together with some commitment to undo the consequences of former injustices.[6]

This commitment will include an assurance that there will be a determined effort to overcome the structural injustices that have become built in to the society as a result of the unequal relationships of the past. For instance, the very wide gap between the rich and the poor in South Africa today is largely the legacy of the racialism of the past. Therefore a genuine reconciliation ought to include a commitment to bringing about a far more equitable society. However, the extent of such social and political changes, and the speed and manner in which they take place, is a matter for on-going negotiated agreement between the parties.

Realism
It is wrong – because it is quite unrealistic – to take *interpersonal* reconciliation as a model for *political* reconciliation. Reconciliation between two individuals may involve an unconditional apology by the former aggressor and a submission in complete trust to the injured party. But this may be neither possible nor necessary in a political situation.

Of course we may occasionally find a very high level of political reconciliation which includes, or leads on to, warm interpersonal relationships of friendship between the reconciled

parties. However, there is a much lower level of political reconciliation which is nevertheless genuine. Frequently this may be
the best that can be expected, at least in the short term. It is well
to remember the remark of Izaak Rabin in relation to his meetings with Yassar Arafat: 'It is not with our friends but with our
enemies that we negotiate and make peace.'

This lower level of political reconciliation involves a minimum measure of mutual respect, which should include at least a
tacit recognition of past oppression. The test of this mutual respect is whether the parties are willing *to abide by the agreements
they have negotiated and by the general norms of the democratic political process.* (An example might be the way in which, in South
Africa, de Klerk and the National Party reluctantly agreed to universal voting rights and very reluctantly handed over power.)

Negotiation and diplomacy are essential to the achievement
of a genuine political reconciliation. In normal circumstances it
is quite unrealistic to look for an unconditional apology by the
former aggressor and a submission in complete trust to the former victim. If the political representatives of the former oppressors were to abase themselves completely and to put themselves
entirely at the mercy of those who have been oppressed, it is
very likely that they would be repudiated by the people they
represent; they would be replaced by more 'hardline' representatives. In these circumstances it does not make sense to look for
some solution which is theoretically just but is unrealistic in
practice.

The 'right' solution will be the one which is freely accepted
by a consensus of the people on both sides, in the light of all the
concrete circumstances of the situation. However, as I have
noted earlier, where there is a legacy of past oppression there
should be at least a tacit recognition of this evil and a commitment to undo its legacy, at least on a gradual basis.

South Africa

As an example of a realistic approach to reconciliation we might
look at the case of South Africa today. Strict justice would require an immediate massive transfer of ownership of land and
property from the Whites to the Africans, the Asians, and the
people of mixed race. But the present leadership knows that if
they were to insist on such radical changes at once, the country
might well be plunged back into a civil war which would cause

even greater hardship than people have to put up with at present; alternatively, there might be a flight of capital and skilled labour on such a large scale that the economy could collapse.

In these circumstances, in order to preserve the peace and ensure a realistic possibility of genuine reconciliation over time, those who represent the victims have to scale down their demands. The aim should be to ensure some *immediate* redress for past injustices, coupled with realistic policies for *on-going* action. An approach which combines justice with realism would include:
– arrangements to tackle at once the more urgent manifestations of poverty and marginalisation (e.g. squatter camps);
– some assurance that a more equitable society will be brought about in the medium term, and especially that the *apartheid* based on race will not be simply transposed into a grossly unjust social stratification based on wealth.

'Win-Win'

In the dialogue which leads to political reconciliation, the most essential skill that is required of the negotiators is the ability to find ways of avoiding a situation where one side's gain is the other side's loss. The aim will be to work for agreements which replace 'win-lose' with 'win-win'. By 'win-win' is meant a situation where both sides have the sense that a reasonably fair balance has been worked out, and where each side can see that both their own side and the society as a whole benefits from the agreement.

There is an exercise called 'Win-Lose' (also called 'Prisoner's Dilemma') which is sometimes used in programmes devoted to the training of community leaders.[7] It is a simulation where two groups have the opportunity to negotiate with each other in circumstances where each group is tempted to take advantage of the other. It mirrors the situation in which we often find ourselves in real life; and it is particularly relevant to those who find themselves negotiating for reconciliation with an opposing group whom they find it difficult to trust.

By taking part in this simulation people may come to appreciate more clearly that in the real world it does not pay in the long run to seek short-term advantage at the expense of others. It is possible to find ways in which all sides can gradually make progress. But this requires a gradual build-up of mutual trust;

and this in turn will only take place if all parties resist the temptation to grab a quick advantage.

There is a further aspect to reconciliation which I have not yet dealt with. That is the question of different styles and models of negotiation which can be used. I shall return to this question under the heading 'Making Room for the Excluded' in my treatment of 'option for the poor' which is the subject of the next chapter. There I shall describe an approach which has been called 'deep democracy' – an approach which should be of keen interest to anybody interested in the church's mission of reconciliation.

In the present chapter I have looked at reconciliation from a religious point of view, from a psychological point of view and from a political point of view. In my opinion it is important for missionaries and other church people to have some familiarity with all of these different aspects of reconciliation if they are to engage effectively in the mission of the church today. I have suggested a number of practical ways in which they can become involved in a ministry of reconciliation and in this way share in the mission of Jesus.

QUESTIONS FOR REFLECTION

1. Do you find yourself personally drawn more to the notion of mission as liberation or to mission as reconciliation? To what extent is your attitude determined by your own temperament and to what extent by the social and political situation in which you are living?

2. What part could you play at local or national level in promoting reconciliation? Can you think of any situation in which you are involved where some agency like the South African Truth and Reconciliation Commission is needed?

3. Do you feel you are sufficiently qualified to be a really effective listener? How could you improve your listening skills?

CHAPTER 9

Mission as Option for the Poor

Mission involves reaching out. Obviously, then, no treatment of
mission would be complete without some consideration of what
it means to reach out to those on the margins of society. That is
what 'option for the poor' is all about. The first section of this
chapter sets out to clarify what is involved in being poor and to
explore the main causes of poverty. In the second section I shall
clarify and refine the meaning of an *option* for the poor. The third
section is an account of why such an option is so controversial –
and so unacceptable to some church authorities. In the final section I shall suggest a more extended and richer understanding
an option for the poor as a key missionary attitude and activity.

SECTION I : THE NATURE AND CAUSES OF POVERTY

Indicators
I begin by noting that poverty has a very wide range of meaning.
So in order to avoid ambiguity and confusion the social scientists try to specify more accurately what it means to be poor by
using various 'indicators' as ways of measuring the degree to
which an individual, or community, or nation is poor or
wealthy.[1]

Perhaps the most obvious indicator is the amount of regular
or occasional *income* which a person has and the extent of the
person's *capital resources* (such as land or other property) which
can generate income or can be sold to provide income. Another
indicator is whether or not a person has *work* which brings in
income, either by being self-employed or by having a job where
the person is paid by somebody else for the work done.

The amount and quality of food, clean water, unpolluted air,
clothing and housing are all useful indicators of the degree to
which a person is rich or poor. So too is availability of energy for
heating, lighting and power. Again, there is the degree of access

144

which people have to services such as transport, sanitation, schooling, post, telephone, media, recreational and sporting facilities, and cultural institutions (e.g. theatres and libraries).

Health is a major indicator of one's degree of wealth or poverty. This includes not only day-to-day health but also more general factors such as average life-expectancy, the level of infant mortality, the prevalence of endemic diseases, the availability of health services and of helps to overcome bodily or mental disabilities, and treatment and care of those who suffer from mental illness.

Another indicator of poverty is the extent to which people do not have efficient and non-corrupt governmental services available to them; for instance in some places it costs a fortune just to get a passport or a driving licence. Insecurity and fear of violence, abuse and crime are also important indicators of poverty. Closely related to this is the availability of a reliable and non-corrupt police service.

A further important indicator of poverty is the level and quality of a person's general education and of training in various specialist skills which are in demand in the society where a person lives. 'Education' in this context does not refer simply to schooling. It is more a matter of learning to make use of the available resources. So it includes practical and technical skills such as ability to drive a car or engage in farming. It also extends to ability to read and write and to communicate effectively. Furthermore, it includes such social skills as knowledge of the accepted norms and good manners of the society where one is living. Those who are lacking in the ability to get on well with others and to work with others are 'poor' in some degree. The fact that they do not fit easily into the society around them means that they are at a disadvantage not just socially but also in the economic and political spheres.

None of the above indicators are fully 'objective' in the sense that they cannot be applied in the abstract. One has to take into account the situation in which the person is living. For instance, to have no heating in one's home is a clear sign of poverty in a cold climate, but not if one lives in the tropics. Again, to be unable to read and write puts people at a disadvantage and so makes them 'poor' in our modern world; whereas in traditional societies in the past it wasn't necessarily a serious disadvantage. Furthermore, if refugees who happen to be doctors or lawyers are not allowed to take up employment in the country to which they have fled, then their training will not enable them to avoid poverty.

It is very difficult to find some fully objective way of measuring the degree to which a person or group or nation is poor. This is because poverty is almost always a matter of having a whole complex of 'symptoms' (i.e. many of the above 'indicators'); and the combination is different in each case. A person may have a high income and own lots of property; but if this person becomes sick and does not have access to medical services then he or she becomes disadvantaged and therefore 'poor'. On the other hand, a healthy person living in a privileged area may suddenly become poor simply by losing his or her job and not having prospects of alternative work. But in general, poor people are likely to score low on most of the above list of 'indicators'. In other words, it is very likely that a poor person will be disadvantaged in terms of income, property, health services, life-expectancy, recreational facilities; and the poor person is also likely to suffer the kind of ill-health which stems from inadequate diet and stressful living conditions. This brings out the point that the different indicators of poverty are usually linked to each other.

Qualitative Indicators
The indicators of poverty which I have mentioned up to now can be measured – at least to some extent. But in addition to these 'quantifiable' indicators there are others which are called 'qualitative' indicators, because they have to do with the quality of people's lives. To understand what is in question here we need to take account of *psychological* and *cultural* issues.

It is a well-known psychological fact that people who are poor very often suffer from low self-esteem. This poor image which they have of themselves is not merely an *effect* of poverty but can also be seen as itself a significant *component or aspect* of poverty. The very fact that a person is lacking in self-confidence and self-respect makes the person's life very uncomfortable and miserable. Furthermore, people who do not value themselves are generally looked down upon by others. They are treated disrespectfully because they are not able to stand up for themselves. We may not have any objective way of calculating just how miserable their lives are, but we can hardly doubt that their lack of self-esteem and of the esteem of others is a genuine form of poverty.

Something similar applies in the case of whole races or cultures. Racism and cultural oppression are very common in our world. Some ethnic groups are looked down upon and despised by more dominant groups. This means that there is a kind of poverty which comes simply from belonging to a despised race or culture. Furthermore, it very frequently happens that those who belong to such despised cultures or racial groups suffer from what is called 'internalised oppression'. This means that they accept unthinkingly the judgements of others and come to believe that they are somehow inferior. It is bad enough to have others assuming that a person belongs to an inferior race or group; but the situation is much more serious when that person does not question this assumption of inferiority; that is a particularly damaging form of poverty.

What I have just said about belonging to a despised race or culture can apply also in the sphere of *gender*. In many parts of the world today women are seen as inferior to men and quite frequently they themselves accept that they are second-class citizens. Even in those areas where people have begun to reject such obvious sexism there is a long heritage of patriarchy which leaves most women at a serious disadvantage compared to men living in similar circumstances. They have to contend with lingering half-conscious prejudices against women, with traditions and practices which were designed with men in mind rather than women, and with the remnants of the internalised oppression which is the effect of thousands of years of patriarchy. This long tradition made it appear 'normal' that women should see themselves as less important than men.

Most of what I have just said about women applies also in the case of people of a homosexual orientation. Indeed in some ways their oppression can be worse. In many societies there is a common assumption that there is 'something wrong with them'; and sometimes they are seen as sinful. They pick up these notions when they are very young; and so they generally internalise this prejudice and come to think of themselves as flawed or evil.

Causes of Poverty
There are many different causes of poverty. But perhaps the most striking thing is that each kind of poverty tends to be the

cause of other kinds of poverty. For instance, the person with a low income does not have enough money to buy good food and good health-care; so this person is more likely to become ill; and this in turn causes further poverty. Again, the carpenter or dress-maker who cannot afford to buy expensive tools or equipment is not in a position to break out of the cycle of poverty. Another obvious example is that those who have a poor education or are lacking in technical or social skills are most likely to remain unemployed or to have poorly paid jobs. Furthermore, people are often discriminated against for no other reason than the fact that they are poor. For instance, people who live in a so-called 'undesirable' area generally find it much more difficult to get 'respectable' employment. So, paradoxically, poverty itself is one of the most serious causes of poverty!

Discrimination is a very significant cause of poverty. People who are seen as inferior because of their gender, race, culture, or sexual orientation are very likely to be discriminated against in getting good jobs and therefore their income is smaller. So racism and sexism are major causes of poverty. More recently 'ageism' has to be added to that list: older people find it very hard to get jobs even when they are very well qualified.

Corruption can be a serious cause of poverty. In many countries those who have influence and power often refuse to give people their due unless they are given a bribe. This means, of course, that those who can afford to pay larger bribes are in a position to get access to further sources of wealth. So the cycle continues: the rich get richer and the poor get even poorer.

It suits better-off people to assume that poor people are largely responsible for their own poverty: if they worked harder or had more initiative they could 'get on in the world'. It is of course true that some people succeed in breaking out of the cycle of poverty through a combination of hard work, dedication, initiative and luck. But the odds are stacked against poor people. The reality is that the great majority of poor people in the world are poor because they were born into a family which was poor. This helps us to realise that poverty is transmitted from one generation to the next. That is how the whole class system develops. Traditionally, the children of peasant parents found themselves stuck in a cycle of poverty. More recently, poverty in the cities has become a huge issue: there are vast areas around most great cities where poverty is endemic and is transmitted from one generation to the next. The people who live in these areas have little chance of 'getting on in the world' except through crime.

In recent centuries the world has become more unified in economic and political terms. The result is that poverty has become a geographical reality in way that was not true in the past. We now have whole continents which can be classified as 'wealthy' (even though there may be many poor people living in them) and continents which are 'poor' (even though a small proportion of the people there may be very rich indeed). The fundamental reason why poverty now takes this *geographical* shape is not because of a shortage of natural resources in the 'poor' continents but because of the *history* of the interaction between the different nations.

It cannot be seriously denied that the colonial expansion of six or seven imperial nations of Europe between the 15th and 19th centuries laid the foundation for the present very unequal distribution of wealth in our world. The colonialism of the past led to the build-up of enormous wealth and power by some nations and by Western banking institutions.

Of course we must not over-simplify the complexity of history. Not all the countries which have a colonial past are now wealthy. The power-struggles between the imperial nations left some as winners and others as losers. Furthermore, Japan and some Arab countries have succeeded in becoming part of 'the West' from an economic point of view, even though their wealth is not directly linked to colonialism. But the fundamental point here is that the present pattern of the distribution of wealth and poverty in the world cannot be explained without taking account of the history of past exploitation and past power-struggles.

Debt and the International Monetary Fund
The wealth and power of 'the West' is the foundation for the tyrannical control exercised nowadays by the International Monetary Fund (IMF) over the economy and politics of poorer countries. The IMF, and the wealthy countries who largely control it, have been very reluctant to cancel the crushing burden of international debt; the conditions they set for debt remission have been so difficult that few if any indebted countries have had any significant amount of their debt remitted. Poor countries are forced to spend a very high proportion of their available

resources in paying interest on their debts; and this undermines all their efforts to escape from their poverty.

Furthermore the IMF imposes on indebted countries a very harsh regime of 'structural adjustment' which greatly exacerbates the problems of the poor in these poor countries. Western bankers, economists and politicians rightly identify corruption and inefficiency in poor countries as a major cause of poverty. But it must be added at once that the greatest and most shocking cause of widespread poverty in our world today is the intransigence of 'the West' and of its banking institutions on the issue of international debt.

Poverty as Powerlessness

In the light of what I have said about the indicators of poverty and the causes of poverty, there is one conclusion that emerges very clearly for me. It is that poverty is above all about *powerlessness*. It is clear that lack of power of one kind or another is both an essential *part* of being poor and is also the key *cause* of poverty.

This leads on to a second conclusion, namely, that the overcoming of poverty is at least as much a *political* issue as an *economic* one. It would be very convenient for those of us who live a comfortable lifestyle to imagine that poor people can escape poverty by working hard and accumulating savings. But history teaches us that the only really effective way for the poor to get out of poverty is for them to gain some power. They can then use that power to 'level the playing field' between themselves and those who are keeping them poor. In other words, it is almost inevitable that the poor have to engage in a political *struggle* against those who are rich and powerful in order to overcome their poverty or relative powerlessness. For wealthy and powerful individuals and nations, however generous they may be, are seldom willing to relinquish freely the power which would allow poorer people or nations to be real equals in the on-going negotiations which determine how resources are distributed in the world. (The Marshall Aid given by the United States to European countries after World War II *may* be an exception to this general rule; but that, too, can be disputed since the USA has remained the dominant power in the world.)

The Poor in the Bible

In the Old Testament the term 'the poor' is not confined strictly to those who have little or no money. The term refers to those groups of people who are economically deprived, who have no social status, and who are treated unjustly by foreign rulers or by the authorities in their own land. These people are oppressed because they are poor, and are therefore at the mercy of the unscrupulous. Furthermore, they are poor because they are oppressed: they have been further impoverished by being cheated and deprived of their rights. Some groups of 'the poor' are doubly oppressed. They are the people who are at risk not only because they are economically poor but also because they happen to be widows, orphans, or resident aliens – categories of people who have nobody to defend them against exploitation.

Jesus should be seen as one of 'the poor'. Having 'emptied himself' to share our humanity (Phil 2:7), he became a native of a despised village (Jn 1:46) in a remote part of a great empire. He did not belong to any privileged group but was known as a carpenter's son (Mt 13:55). So he did not have to pretend in order to be in solidarity with ordinary poor people.

SECTION II: OPTION FOR THE POOR

Biblical option versus Marxist option

It is hardly a coincidence that the phrase 'option for the poor' was adopted by liberation theologians at a time when the more adventurous of them were engaged in a serious dialogue with Marxism. But that does not mean that the theological phrase 'option for the poor' should be understood as more or less the same thing as a Marxist-inspired 'class option'.

The liberation theologians have undoubtedly borrowed important elements from Marxism. I think there is a good case for claiming that liberation theology's emphasis on solidarity with the poor springs at least in part from a Marxist influence, and so too does its willingness to take account of the reality of the class structures of society.

On the other hand, there are major differences between the two approaches. By far the most important of these is that liberation theology draws its inspiration not from a class analysis of society but directly from biblical sources. And what the Bible reveals is very different indeed from what Marxism teaches. The

Marxist position makes sound political sense; and that is why it was seen as such a threat by those who held power in the West. The Italian Marxist philosopher and activist, Antonio Gramsci, called middle-class people to make a 'class option', that is, to make common cause with the poorer classes. He argued very convincingly that, if a significant number of educated and privileged people were to do so, then they could provide the masses with the analytical and organisational skills required to mount a successful revolution.

When we come to the Bible I think it is useful to make a distinction between an option for *justice* and a specific option for the *poor*. In much of the Bible there is an emphasis on social justice. We see the outrage of God, expressed by the prophets (and also by Jesus) about the mistreatment of the poor and the hardheartedness and arrogance of the rich. This is the option for *justice*. Option specifically for the *poor* is located within this wider context, but the emphasis is different.

When I speak of option for the poor in a biblical sense I have in mind a spirituality inspired by the belief that God chooses the weak to confound the strong, and chooses the foolish to show up the wisdom of the wise (1 Cor 1:27-8). Again and again in the Bible we see the weak ones, the unlikely ones, being chosen by God in order to show that what matters is not human power but trust in God and reliance on divine initiative and power. We think of the letting go of most of the army of Gideon when they faced the forces of Midian (Jud 7:3-7), or of the choice of Moses who was a poor speaker (Ex 4:10-12). Similarly, the selection of Israel as God's own special people was not intended to make political sense but rather to undermine conventional political wisdom. And in the New Testament it is no accident that Jesus comes from a despised village in a 'backward' province: 'can anything good come out of Nazareth?' (Jn 1:46)

By contrast with the Marxist concept of a class option, a biblically-inspired 'option for the poor' is not at all a shrewd political choice to take the side of an oppressed but potentially powerful working-class. It is rather a matter of taking the side of those who are the most marginalised and weakest people in society. There is no serious likelihood that the widows, the orphans, the 'strangers' (that is, the refugees), the prostitutes or the tax-collectors will ever become major political powers in society. To opt for the poor is not to make a carefully calculated political gamble but to throw oneself on the mercy of God. It is to re-nounce any likelihood of political success in the conventional sense, and even to re-define radically the very notion of success. It is a decision to find joy and fulfillment in ways that are incomprehensible in conventional terms.

Relationship to Practical Politics

Some people ask how 'option for the poor' relates to 'the Third Way' proposed by Anthony Giddens[2] who is said to have inspired much of the 'New Labour' policies in Britain. I think it is legitimate to ask to what extent 'the Third Way' embodies an 'option for justice'; but if one asks how it relates to an 'option for the poor' (in the sense outlined above), this comes quite close to making what philosophers call 'a category mistake'. It is rather like asking how 'the Third Way' relates to the beatitudes.

'The Third Way' is intended to be a practical political programme which can be adopted by a government. 'Option for the poor', on the other hand, is an ideal, which is in line with the beatitudes and carries the same kind of moral weight. It is a serious moral invitation put before all Christians. None of us is entitled to dismiss it as not applicable to our own situation. But the manner and the degree in which each of us lives it out varies very much from person to person; and we should not be too quick to judge others on the way they respond to this call, this invitation, this Christian ideal.

The institutional church has a serious duty to promote such an option for the poor and to give witness to it in its own life and organisation. Religious Orders and Congregations have a duty to take it particularly seriously since their members take a vow of poverty. What about the government of a country? Should it make an option of the poor? I would say that we can and must demand that it show particular *concern* for the poor and for all categories of people who have been left on the margins of society. We can go further and demand that governments show a kind of *preference* for the poor, since they do not have the power to protect their own interests. But that does not quite amount to an *option* for the poor in the strict sense – the kind of option which the church as a whole, and religious congregations, and individual Christians are invited to make.

Realistic or Idealistic?

Catholic social teaching proposes a wide spectrum of moral values and ideals. At one end of this spectrum there are several important moral values which are 'realistic' in the sense that they are immediately relevant to practical politics today. The most obvious example of these is *subsidiarity* which has become such a 'buzz-word' in the European Community in recent years. At this 'realistic' end of the spectrum we might also include such values as social justice, participation, respect, and human dignity. At the other end of the spectrum of Catholic social teaching are moral values and ideals which seem less obviously 'realistic' in terms of practical politics. 'Option for the poor' is located in the more idealistic part of this spectrum.

Recently, I was invited to take part in a dialogue in Cambridge between theologians, economists and other social scientists to explore some practical implications of Catholic social teaching. The main focus of the discussion was on the moral values and ideals which are at the more 'realistic' end of the spectrum. This is normal and healthy; and I found the conference stimulating and valuable. But I came away with the conviction that we must not to lose sight of the whole range of Catholic social teaching, including values or ideals such as option for the poor, which seem less 'realistic' from a political point of view. If we focus only on what seems politically realistic at any given time we are failing to give the church its prophetic role and voice. A major purpose of the church is to stand for, and give witness to, a *different* and better future which is bound to seem unrealistic in present-day terms.

Effective prophetic witness and prophetic action can change a whole people's attitude. It can bring into the sphere of practical politics values that previously seemed quite unrealistic. Gender equality is one obvious example; so too is the very idea of democracy. It is salutary to recall the mistakes of church leaders and teachers in the past. They allowed themselves to become wedded to patriarchal assumptions and to an autocratic non-participatory concept of state authority. So they failed to promote the ideal of effective gender equality; and they dismissed the concept of democracy as unrealistic and even as evil. In doing so they betrayed the prophetic dimension of the Christian vision. We must aim to avoid a repetition of such mistakes. That is one good reason for continuing to hold on to the ideal of an option for the poor as an integral part of Catholic social teaching – a part which is especially relevant from a missionary point of view.

Solidarity with the Poor and Option for the Poor
An authentic option for the poor has two equally important aspects – a 'solidarity' aspect, which is about lifestyle, and a political or quasi-political aspect, which has to do with analysis and action.[3] The solidarity aspect involves a deliberate choice to enter in some degree into the world of those who have been left on the margins of society – to share in a significant way in their experience of being mistreated, by-passed, or left helpless. This choice of a different lifestyle springs from compassion – a word which means, literally, suffering with others. It involves a choice to deepen this compassion by sharing, to some extent, in the suffering of the poor. By entering the world of deprived people one extends and deepens this experience of 'suffering with' those on the margins. And, by doing so, one comes to share not only their pain and struggle but also their hopes and their joys.

Solidarity is a gift which those who are poor or marginalised may freely offer to the person who opts to share their life in some degree. It is a gift which cannot be presumed or demanded from them. They give it in their own time and in their own degree, and only to one who comes to them with no air of superiority or paternalism. Despite differences of skin colour, or accent, or background, the group may choose to accept this person as 'one of us' – or at least 'one *with* us' – one who shares their interests (in both senses of that word).

The *virtue* of solidarity emerges and flourishes within the matrix of *experience* of solidarity. This virtue is a habitual attitude and style of being and of relating which inclines one to be sensitive to the needs and feelings of others in the group and to devote oneself generously to the common welfare. In order to nurture this virtue one must be open to be challenged by other members of the group and to challenge them in turn.

It is time now to move on from solidarity, which is the first aspect of option for the poor, to the second aspect which has to do which analysis and political or quasi-political action. There are several stages in this process:
– The first is a careful *discernment* and *analysis* of the situation. This is needed in order to ensure that one understands the core

of the issue, that is, the fundamental reasons why this group of people have been left 'on the margins', and the depth of the pain this inflicts on them. This calls not only for political insight but also for psychological insight into what it means to be marginalised.

– The second stage is to ensure that one is not unconsciously *colluding* in this process of marginalisation. Sometimes it takes a sharp challenge from members of the group to make one aware of such unconscious collusion.

– The third stage is joint action to *challenge* the marginalisation. It is not enough that a protest be made *on behalf of* those who have been marginalised; the protest must come *from the group themselves*. Marginalised groups who begin to stand up for themselves are profoundly changed by their action. This inner change is probably more important than any changes in behaviour and attitude in those who are being challenged.

– The fourth and final stage is to convince people that there are realistic *alternatives* to the present state of marginalisation; and then to devise and promote these alternatives. This may involve a life-time of work with no guarantee of short-term success. What spurs one on is not a naïve optimism but a hope based on trust in the power and promises of God.

At each stage of this process, those who have made an option for the poor must not assume that they know the answers or even that it is for them to set the agenda. The people who have been marginalised should be empowered to speak and act on their own behalf, so as to overcome their sense of helplessness. This means that those who have opted to be in solidarity with them often have to 'hold back'. And when they do intervene it should be to encourage or facilitate the disadvantaged people themselves in articulating their own experience and in planning realistic action.

SECTION III: THE OPTION AND CHURCH AUTHORITIES

Option for the poor is solidly rooted in scripture. The concept is also in continuity to some extent with the organic tradition of Catholic social teaching.[4] Furthermore, it appeals to our highest ideals; who could deny that it is a truly Christian thing to make a commitment to solidarity with marginalised people and to effective action for and with them, along the lines I have outlined above? Nevertheless, there are aspects of this option which are distinctly new. I think here first of the strong emphasis on challenge to the rich and powerful – even when they happen to be prominent members of the church. Secondly, I have in mind the shift from a consensus model of politics to a more confrontational approach.

It seems clear that if the concept of option for the poor is authentically Christian, then it applies not only to individual Christians but also to communities (including local churches and religious congregations), and even to the church as a whole. So the general thinking behind this option has gradually come to be accepted more and more widely in the church – mainly, but not exclusively, in the revised constitutions and programmes for renewal of religious congregations and missionary societies. The concept has gradually come to be seen as part of the mainline thrust of a renewed church, and in this sense it has become more 'respectable'. So it is not surprising to find that in the 1980s Pope John Paul II began to include occasional references to a preferential option for the poor into some of his addresses in Latin America. Such references are also found elsewhere in his writings and talks, for instance in his 1994 Apostolic Letter 'the Jubilee of the Year 2000' (*Tertio Millennio Adveniente*, No 51); so much so that preferential option for the poor became a significant but not major emphasis of his pontificate.

Resistance

But, on the other hand, there is major on-going resistance to the notion of an option for the poor, at least when taken in its full sense. The basic reason seems to be that there are many church leaders and theologians who are quite reluctant to face up to the kind of radical challenges which it involves. And of course theologians and church leaders are the very people who have what we may call 'theological power', that is, the power to articulate on behalf of the community the meaning and implications of the call to be Christian. So, if some of them are themselves unwilling to face the challenge of making an option for the poor, there is a strong temptation for them to avoid or evade it by toning down or even distorting their articulation of what it means to be a Christian. Like other temptations this one disguises itself. So those who yield to the temptation may scarcely be aware that they are distorting a crucial aspect of the faith they profess.

The problem gets much more serious when the institutional life of the church comes into the question, as it usually does. As part of its evangelizing mission, the church sees itself as called to insert Christian values and, perhaps, some elements of 'a Christian ethos' into the community in different countries, and even into international relations. In recent centuries church leaders have operated on the assumption that one of the most effective ways to do this is to own or control some of the major 'instruments of culture' such as schools, hospitals, newspapers and other media. So the institutional church frequently becomes quite a powerful agent in society.

This means that the official church generally becomes part of 'the establishment' and its leadership has a 'respectable' position in society. This, in turn, means that church leaders often have a certain vested interest in preserving the main structures of the society in which they live, even while they seek to bring about certain changes for the better.

Furthermore, the fact that 'the church' in many countries is part of 'the establishment' means that most church leaders and many theologians there belong to a rather privileged class of people in society. At the social level they are not likely to have many close friends among those who are on the margins of society. And they can scarcely avoid being influenced in their opinions and values by those with whom they mix.

The new emphasis on option for the poor calls into question this whole model of church influence and the corresponding status of church leaders and theologians in society. For instance, the Jesuits and many other religious congregations in much of Latin America made a deliberate *option* to move out of many of their elite schools. They deliberately and publicly re-deployed their resources of personnel and money to serve poorer people. Furthermore, they made it quite clear that they were doing so in the belief that this is what the gospel and their faith called them to do. Naturally enough this angered and alienated the ruling classes who had relied on them to give a good education to their children.

The reaction of some church leaders was incomprehension and anger at the abandonment by influential church people of their power to 'mould' the future leaders of their countries. This led to a serious polarisation within the institutional church, with each faction developing its own theology and spirituality as an ideological justification and support for its stance and option.

By and large, the Vatican has held on to the older model. This helps to explain the strong resistance put up by Rome to many practical applications of option for the poor undertaken by local churches or religious congregations. This counter-offensive has taken place in several different ways. Firstly, Roman documents and teaching have included repeated warnings against Marxism and have tended to give the impression that liberation theology as a whole, including its emphasis on option for the poor, is tainted by Marxist thinking. Related to this is a consistent effort to 'tone down' the language. The most obvious instance of this is the use of the cumbersome phrase 'a preferential but not exclusive option for the poor' – a phrase which has irritated or infuriated some liberation theologians.[5] Even the Pope's references to a preferential option for the poor are hedged around with provisos and warnings. He seems to be somewhat hesitant or cautious about using the phrase, often choosing different words when he speaks out against injustice and in favour of the poor.

A second way of playing down the importance of an option for the poor was by putting other options alongside it. For instance, the Puebla documents speak of an 'option for youth' alongside the option for the poor. But the liberation theologians felt that this was just a way of playing down the special character of the option for the poor.

A third stratagem for playing down the significance of an option for the poor is a blurring of the difference between it and *special care* for the poor. The church has a long and honourable tradition of providing loving care for those on the margins of society, ranging from the Lazar-houses of the Middle Ages to Jean Vanier's L'Arche communities and Mother Teresa's care for the destitute. Down through the ages many committed Christians have made a truly radical choice to devote their lives to such people. An option for the poor is not necessarily more or less radical than this; but there is a distinct difference between the two. Special care for the poor fits admirably with the older model of church influence in society, whereas option for the poor presupposes a fundamentally different approach. Its basic challenge to the present structures of society does not sit easily with present Vatican policy and style.

A fourth way in which the Vatican has resisted the option for the poor is in the manner in which it has used its power and authority. Most of the bishops appointed by Rome in areas where liberation theology was influential have been very conservative; and it is widely believed that part of their mandate has been to undermine and dismantle the efforts that had been made to embody the new approach in everyday church life. Furthermore, the Vatican has intervened to exercise very tight control over CELAM (the Conference of Latin American Bishops), over CLAR (the Conference of Religious of Latin America), over religious congregations which were thought to be taking an unduly radical stance, and over the more 'adventurous' seminaries in various parts of the world. There has also been an unrelenting pressure on leading liberation theologians, which has severely hindered them in their work.

Finally, there is a more subtle way in which Rome may have, perhaps unconsciously, undermined the attempts by local bishops or national conferences of bishops to take a strong stand against oppressive governments. During his visits abroad, Pope John Paul has frequently spoken out very strongly against oppression and injustice – most notably in Haiti and Brazil. But it has been noted that in Kenya and Malawi the Pope did not seem to give strong backing to the protests of local bishops against government injustice. Some commentators have suggested that the Pope prefers that it be left to him and to the Vatican to decide when such condemnations are called for. Whatever the reason behind it, the result was that the oppressive governments were able to dismiss the protests of the local church leaders on the ground that the highest church authority in Rome does not agree with them.

The cumulative effect of these various policies and actions is to leave a disparity between the official teaching and the practical action of the Roman authorities. There is little or no practical support from the Vatican for any really radical option for the poor, taking that term in the rather technical sense I have outlined here. Concern for the poor, yes; 'option' for the poor, not yet …

SECTION IV: MAKING ROOM FOR THE EXCLUDED

In this section I want to propose a development of the notion of option for the poor – an extension of its meaning beyond the way it has been understood up to the present. This broadening and deepening of the concept is particularly relevant from a missionary point of view, since it concerns issues such as reconciliation in the world – issues which lie at the very heart of the notion of mission.

The Excluded in Interpersonal Relationships

David, the young son who had been left out in the cold, was the one chosen to become Israel's greatest king (1 Sam 16:11). Similarly, Jesus went against the general prejudice against tax-collectors in calling Matthew – and this ensured that we have four gospels rather than just three. Again, Mary the unmarried mother from a despised village was chosen to play a special role in the plan of God. These instances – and many others – indicate that not only has God special care for people on the margins of society but that God often chooses to use such people as special instruments of divine providence, going against all the odds to make them channels of grace.

Each of us is called to make an act of faith that today, just as in biblical times, the excluded and 'the unlikely people' play a vital role in human salvation. The distinctive feature of a biblically-inspired option for the poor – the point at which it goes beyond Christian kindness and charity – is the belief that, despite all the appearances, those who are on the margins are privileged instruments of God's providence, and have a special gift to bring to the rest of us. In practice, this calls us to give time and attention to people who are looked down in social life, to find ways of drawing them into the inner circle of those who feel they 'belong'.

Consequently, we should go out of our way at meetings to give a voice to the silent ones who would normally be left on the margins of the dialogue. Doing so is not only more Christian but also 'pays off' in practical terms. I recall several situations where, quite unexpectedly, the whole atmosphere of a meeting was changed by a quiet intervention from somebody who had been sitting silently on the margins of the group. This 'unlikely' person offered a word of wisdom which touched the participants in their hearts. The group could see that the 'word' which God was speaking to this group – that is, the fundamental truth which they most needed to hear – was coming through this person whose gifts and contribution had previously been overlooked or undervalued.

A more difficult situation arises when we have to deal with

one or two 'awkward' individuals whose views seem quite out of harmony with those of the rest of the group. It stretches one's faith to the limit to extend an option for the poor to include such truly intransigent people. It is almost impossible to believe that they may be special instruments of God for the rest of the group. But this is one of those places where as Christians – and even as human beings – we may find ourselves called to be wildly generous, to 'go the extra mile', and then some more. This kind of extravagant generosity does not make sense in terms of the normal procedures of discussion and decision-making. But it can serve a purpose if we switch over to a very different model of dialogue, one where we devote our energy to making a space in ourselves to really hear the dissonant voices.

Option for the Excluded in Society

I want to put a case for applying the notion of option for the poor not merely to the awkward or excluded ones in a group or community meeting but also to finding space for those who are often seen as 'the untouchables' in the *public* world, the global society in which we live out our lives. This involves extending the concept to include ways of addressing the most fundamental issues of exclusion in our world – such issues as racism, ethnic hatred, terrorism, sexism, abuse, ageism, fundamentalist extremism and homophobia. Any serious attempt to address such intractable issues puts one 'on the frontiers' and is therefore of particular significance and interest for anybody who feels a call to mission.

Of course, such issues are matters of concern for all liberal people. But my emphasis here is on reaching out not just to the *victims* of racism, sexism, etc., but also to the *perpetrators* of these evils. The aim is to promote dialogue across the widest chasms which split our world today.

Needless to say, it is extremely difficult to imagine how there could be effective communication between terrorists and their victims, or between abused women and macho men. One is tempted to cry out: 'How could we dare to take on such an apparently impossible task?' The answer, of course, must be: 'As Christians, can we refuse to believe that God loves those who are commonly labelled as "sinners" (and who may well *be* sinners); can we deny that God wants us, too, to make a space for them?' Surely God wants us to play some part in bringing reconciliation and healing to this broken world? Why should we assume that God's grace is confined mainly to the personal and interpersonal sphere and that God's option for the excluded is itself exclusive – that it does not extend to male chauvinists, or racists, or terrorists?

Let's take the highly sensitive issue of dialogue with terrorists. The Quakers and the Mennonites are well known for their commitment to peace-work of all kinds. For many years they have been involved in finding ways to initiate and promote dialogue between warring parties, even when some of those involved in the struggle are seen as terrorists. More recently members of the San Egidio Community in Rome have been notably successful in this kind of peace-making diplomacy. And in Northern Ireland a few priests and ministers played a key role in bringing paramilitary groups into dialogue with mainstream politicians and government representatives at a time when 'the accepted wisdom' was that respectable politicians 'should never talk to terrorists'.

In dialogue of this kind, 'the terrorists' are frequently represented for much of the time not by the 'activists' themselves but by people who have a high level of credibility with them – for instance, by former paramilitary leaders who have now moved nearer to mainstream politics. The reason is that the dialogue is usually conducted in a low-key diplomatic mode where passion is muted and reason prevails. In this model of dialogue the participants have to refrain most of the time from giving immediate impassioned expression to the burning anger, pain, or hatred which they feel. So the activists allow themselves to be represented by people who have drawn back a little from 'the front line' of the struggle and may have 'cooler heads' and a more long-term vision. This is useful, but it also poses the danger that the negotiators may lose their credibility with the people they are representing. For that reason we should consider the possibility of a different style of dialogue, one that is less 'diplomatic' and rational and that allows more room for the expression of emotion and even of passion.

'Worldwork'

The psychotherapist, Arnold Mindell, and his associates, have developed a model for dialogue of this kind. Mindell uses the term 'deep democracy' to express the notion that all the voices in a society or group need to be heard. He allows this to happen not only in small groups but in meetings of as many as three hundred people at times. These are groups who have come together to do what he calls 'worldwork' – that is, facing up to burning issues such as racism or sexism or various other issues where one group feels oppressed or excluded by another.

Those who take part in a 'worldwork' conference are not asked to come as negotiators or even as formal representatives of the groups or factions from which they come; but they are people who will give voice with courage and passion to their own beliefs and values. They are not expected to be able to articulate their position with perfect clarity and compelling logic. For in this kind of dialogue personal authenticity may be more effective than cold logic. It is left to the group themselves to decide which issue or issues to focus on and where they want to go with them. The role of the facilitators of the dialogue is to help the participants to address the issues that are important in this particular gathering.

Changing the Rules
A key element in this model of dialogue is the abandonment of the conventional norms of debate or rational discussion. Those who engage in it find at times that they have to put up with people who interrupt them, or who cry, or shout, or even scream. Mindell says: 'The Western world, especially, needs … multicultural forums where feelings can be expressed, people can weep, people can rage …'[6] Those who are accustomed to the more conventional kind of discussion will almost certainly find this very emotional behaviour quite shocking and difficult to put up with. But the 'new rules' can be a very effective way of giving a voice to the voiceless. There is less dominance of those whose forte is rational debate – and these are more likely to be the people who have had a lot of formal education. Furthermore, this alternative style is often found more congenial by people who do not belong to the dominant Western middleclass culture. The ones who command attention in the new situation may well be individuals or groups who previously had little or no chance of having their voice heard or heeded.

The result is a dialogue which is more inclusive and more effective. More inclusive: because there is room for alienated or disaffected people and the interaction is not weighted from the start in favour of those with a lot of formal education. More effective: because this alternative approach leaves more room for the expression of emotions and this can lead to more profound changes than are usually attained when burning issues are discussed at a purely rational level.

There are special skills required for this kind of facilitation over and above the facilitation skills employed in a more conventional group discussion. The facilitators must not remain aloof from the movement and struggles of the group; for the process is not one which can be steered from the outside. They have to be in touch with their own feelings of compassion, or anger, or frustration and resistance to really hearing the views of those with whom they feel out of sympathy. The facilitators must be able to express their feelings authentically and 'cleanly' when that is appropriate – and they need to sense when it is appropriate to do so.

These are not 'skills' in the usual sense of strategies for managing other people. They are more like gifts than techniques. But if they are gifts they are not ones which come easily to many people. They have to be honed and perfected – and this is an ongoing work which is never completed. In that sense these 'skills' are really *virtues,* that is, fundamental spiritual attitudes which have become characteristic of a person's being.

During the dialogue the facilitators must be able to move between opposing positions and in this way play a mediating role. This mediation is not, however, a purely rational one – an effort to find a synthesis of two points of view or a compromise between them. Mindell insists that what he has in mind is quite different from the more conventional forms of negotiation, arbitration, conciliation or dispute-resolution.[7] It is not just viewpoints which have to be brought together but real people – people who are torn apart or brought together much more by their strong feelings than by their ideas. Mindell sees this role as akin to that of the elders in a tribal society – wise people who can resonate with the different stances that have been put forward and can find creative ways of fostering community in the group while honouring its diversity.

A serious commitment to this kind of 'deep democracy' is, in my opinion, a way of making a very effective option for the poor as an integral aspect of being in mission.

QUESTIONS FOR REFLECTION

1. Do you think some sectors of the church have been influenced by Marxism? If so, what have been the good effects, if any? What have been the bad effects, if any?
2. Can you envisage ways in which you personally could be involved in dialogue with people who are marginalised or despised in society?

CHAPTER 10

Mission as Power from the Spirit

As the title of this chapter indicates, I am concerned here with the role of the Holy Spirit in the life and approach of those who share in the mission of Jesus and the church. Missionaries, and other church people who work 'on the frontiers', exercise many different ministries, ranging from preaching or celebrating sacraments to community-building, and from promoting health, or adult education, to saving the rain-forests or work in the media. But the diversity in mission work does not depend solely on this variety of ministries. Cutting across the diversity of *activities* is an even more significant variety in the *mode* or *style* in which people engage in their ministries. For instance, some of those who work on the frontiers have a very high profile in their work while the ministry of others is carried out in a low-key and almost invisible manner. I could give this chapter the sub-title 'Styles of Mission' because I intend to present five different styles or modes of activity in which mission may be exercised. I believe that each of these modes involves the exercise of a specific kind of prophetic power which comes from the Spirit of God. Furthermore, each of these different styles reveals a particular aspect or modality of the prophetic *call* of the Spirit.

Before going on to consider these various types of prophetic power, it is important to make a preliminary clarification. There are kinds of power and uses of power which are oppressive, dominating, abusive or manipulative. Obviously, these are in no way prophetic and so I do not propose to consider them here. But it is important to be aware of the danger of such misuses of power – to be on our guard lest we allow the prophetic powers which are gifts of the Spirit to become contaminated and corrupted.

Inspiring Power
The first type of power from the Spirit can be called 'inspiring power'. I came across a prime example of it recently when I

worked with a young man who had met Mother Teresa some years ago. He told me that she looked into his eyes and said: 'You are called to be a saint.' Ever since that time he has lived on the basis of that encounter. It was clear to me that her inspiring power was so great that it made her prophecy come true. In speaking about 'inspiring power' I have in mind the wonderful ability which some people have to convince, inspire and even to 'enchant' others. It is evident from the gospels that Jesus had this power to an amazing extent – 'they left their nets and followed him' (Mt 4:20).

The inspiring of others can be done by powerful preaching or teaching. It can also occur simply through the way some people touch others by the quality of their presence. This kind of power was possessed in high degree not only by Mother Teresa but also by almost all the founders of charitable agencies, religious congregations, and missionary societies. Some of the names which come to my mind are Teresa of Avila, Vincent de Paul, Mother Kevin, Bishop Shanahan, Mother Mary Martin, Bishop Galvin, Catherine Macauley, Nano Nagle, Mother Mary Aikenhead, Edmund Ignatius Rice, and Jean Vanier; I hope this list will encourage readers to make their own lists of such inspiring people. In the more secular world this 'inspiring power' was exercised by the great leaders whom I named in Chapter 7 when dealing with the struggle for liberation – Gandhi, Aung San Suu Kyi, and Nelson Mandela – as well as by Florence Nightingale and a host of others whom each of us could name.

We see this power at work in the rare teacher or lecturer who is able to hold listeners or students spellbound. It accounts for the ability of some people to persuade their friends to do things they hadn't had a notion of doing, for instance, to join them in a wild adventure. It is at work in the public sphere when very occasionally a really persuasive politician succeeds in getting whole masses of people to adopt a particular programme. We see it when a religious leader gathers a totally devoted following of hundreds or thousands of willing disciples.

The power I am speaking of is a gift which some rare individuals have in an exceptionally high degree and which most of us have in a lesser degree. The spellbinding and magnetic quality of this power can at times give one a sense that there is something uncanny and almost 'magical' about it. This spiritual quality suggests that we are dealing with a power which derives from the prophetic Spirit who has the function of inspiring and moving us. It is a share in a particular aspect of divine energy, namely, the power to touch people's hearts, inspire their minds, and move them to action. It is a wonderful gift which we all need and which is particularly important for religious leaders – and perhaps above all for those who wish to share in the mission of Jesus.

Even though inspiring power comes from God's prophetic Spirit, it is still very much a *human* power which integrates and perfects our natural intelligence and persuasiveness. It arises from the fact that we are made in the image and likeness of God, and therefore share in the divine mystery which people find inherently fascinating and attractive. Furthermore, it is an ability which can grow and become ever more powerful within us. The creative Spirit moulds us more and more deeply into the image of God so that it becomes progressively more difficult to distinguish those actions and qualities which are purely human and those where we are sharing in God's own life. There is no competition between God's grace and our humanity. So I don't think it is useful or even possible to draw a clear line between the part that is purely human and the part that is a share in the power of the Spirit of God. The more the Spirit moves in and through us, the more human we become.

I have been emphasising the *prophetic* (Spirit-given) aspect and now it is time to return to the fact that what is in question here is a real *power*. In giving us this ability to touch and inspire others, God is enabling us to carry out a vital ministry, namely, that of leading people beyond their everyday experiences or concerns and opening them up to the beautiful, marvellous and mysterious aspects of life. We can think of the way in which people were drawn to follow Jesus; and, a thousand years later, to join Francis of Assisi and Clare; and, more recently, to join Edwina Gately in her Volunteer Missionary Movement.

Most of us can probably locate moments when we were enthralled by the words or the very presence of some outstanding person. And most of us can probably recall some occasions when we, in turn, were able to inspire others. Of course it is embarrassing to say in public that one has sometimes inspired and enthused people, but I think it is important for each of us to acknowledge that we have at times exercised this kind of power. For myself, I can say I have experienced the thrill and fulfillment of giving a talk or making an intervention in a workshop which people found inspiring. I say this to encourage those who read this book to recall something they have said or done which inspired awe and wonder in others.

There is no guarantee that those who have this power will always use it wisely or even morally. The legend of the Pied Piper of Hamelin is about an extreme abuse of this kind of power. The legend reflects reality, for some of the religious gurus of our time have been guilty of leading people to destruction. We may think of the mad extremes to which people were led by Jim Jones (in the killing of over 900 people in Guyana in 1978), or by the leaders of the cults in Waco (Texas), in Switzerland, in Japan and in northern Uganda. There are many instances of the abuse of such power by political leaders such as Hitler. In everyday life it would seem that some spectacularly persuasive door-to-door sales-persons of encyclopædias or vacuum-cleaners are using a debased version of this power.

Even though the exercise of this kind of power can be a genuine gift of the Spirit and can be enormously satisfying, I think it is very important for people working on the frontiers to be willing to *let it go*. (I am not saying they should never use this kind of power but only that they should not always rely on it, and should be aware of alternative approaches.) In relinquishing it we are following the example of Jesus. Obviously, he was a most inspiring person, since people were willing to leave their homes and their work to follow him devotedly. Yet the gospel accounts of his 'temptations' indicate that Jesus refused to base his ministry on the exercise of this kind of captivating power over people. The gospels make it clear that he did not set out to impress people as a magician does. The miracles he worked were almost like a by-product of the 'wonder' that he himself was.[1] He resisted the temptation to enthral people in a way that would deprive them of their spiritual freedom. He chose instead a less compelling style, one which put far more emphasis on the personal freedom and responsibility of those who wished to follow him.

A major reason for being willing to relinquish this kind of power is that there is a constant temptation to misuse it by dominating or manipulating others. It is all too easy to get accustomed to having people hanging on one's words. And one can come to take the unquestioning obedience of others for granted. So the longer a person exercises 'inspiring power' the greater the temptation for that person to become unconsciously autocratic. There is a more positive reason, too, for letting go this 'inspiring power'. It is that we can move on to exercise other types of prophetic power which may well be even more helpful to others and a more effective way of answering the call to mission.

'Empowering Power'

The second type of prophetic power I want to look at is the ability to *empower* others. Like inspiring power, it too comes as part of the call to mission; and I believe that in many cases it may be even more valuable than the power to inspire and captivate people. This means that we may be called to let go of, or give less emphasis to, our power to inspire people and to respond more generously to the call to empower the people we work with. One reason why I feel this is because of what happened in my own life.

Twenty-five years ago I became very disillusioned with my role as a theology lecturer, where my main focus had been on what I wanted to teach rather than on what my students were learning. I spent two or three years searching for an alternative approach where there could be a genuine dialogue between me and my students. But I didn't have the skills needed to foster this dialogue. I look back now on that time as the first stage of a process of conversion, the stage where one is repentant for the past but has not yet found a better way forward. Then, in the most unlikely of places (the desert area of Northern Kenya), I came in touch with Anne Hope and Sally Timmel[2] – two women who were using what they called 'the psycho-social method'. This method is an approach to adult education inspired by the great Brazilian educator, Paulo Freire, whose own life was a wonderful witness to the use of this second kind of prophetic power. There in the desert I discovered for the first time how to use what I am calling empowering or enabling power; and I experienced the satisfaction and joy which comes from exercising it.

Empowering power is a facility in helping other people to get in touch with their own strengths, their own gifts, their own creativity. It is a gift which seems to come naturally to some people, as though they had been born with it. The rest of us have to work hard to learn how to work fruitfully with others by going through exercises of listening, of co-operation and of joint planning and evaluation. Being a good listener involves not just listening to people's words but also to their 'body-language', that is, the signals and messages which they unconsciously send out by their facial expressions or by the way they sit or move. We have to learn how to send out signals of affirmation and encouragement; and to know when to nudge people forward and when to hold back.

Even more important than these skills are the *attitudes* with which we approach others. We need to be really interested in them, respectful, patient and non-judgemental. Otherwise our skills are in danger of becoming just techniques for 'managing' or manipulating people.

Empowerment of others can take place on a one-to-one basis (e.g. in spiritual direction or counselling or in personal dialogue). Perhaps more common in work on the frontiers is the empowering which takes place in groups, committees and teams of all kinds. It is a matter of developing the leadership and animating skills of the committed people who are willing to serve their communities and the wider society. In this way we use 'empowering power' to create truly respectful and participatory communities. For me, 'the honours course' in this kind of work comes when we can engage with other people in a process of faith-sharing. There is a great enrichment in sharing our own faith at a deep level and having the privilege of listening to the hopes and dreams, the pain and the struggles of companions on the journey.

I find the experience of empowerment in a group particularly rewarding when I am working as part of a facilitating team of two or three people in co-facilitating a community. At its best this becomes a kind of dance where each facilitator inspires and empowers the other team members as well as the wider group. At its worst this co-facilitation can be a painful struggle. Quite frequently it is both struggle and dance, inextricably mixed together. I find it helpful to think that I am co-facilitating not only with a human colleague but also with the prophetic Spirit of God who ensures that the whole process is enlivened with creativity, challenge and mystery.

'Inspiring power' and 'empowering power' tend to pull us in opposite directions. Suppose I am invited to give a lecture; then I have to access my ability to *inspire* others. In that situation I tend to focus my attention on those members of the audience who show interest in what I am saying. I'm inclined to address myself

more and more to them, while becoming progressively insensitive to the rest of the audience – particularly to those who have
little or no interest in what I am saying! It is as though I protect
myself from the disinterest of those who are 'switched off' by di-
verting my attention from them. On the other hand, if my task is
to facilitate a group, I try to access my capacity for *empowerment*.
Then my antennae are out to pick up signals from those who
seem disinterested or who are on the margins of the group.

The danger of relying on 'inspiring power' is that it tends to
set up a closed circle which excludes those who are not inspired
by what I have to say or what I am interested in. Suppose I have
given a lecture and this has 'switched on' whatever ability I have
to inspire the audience. Then comes the time for a question-and-
answer session after the lecture. I have noticed that what takes
place may not be an equal two-way dialogue between me and
the interested listeners. Rather, I may allow their questions to
spur me on to a further development of *my own* ideas without
creating a space in which I am fully open to be inspired by *their*
ideas. My short-hand phrase to describe this situation is to say
that I have got locked into 'transmit mode'.

Now that I have come to be aware of this pattern, I endeavour
to switch over as quickly as possible to 'receiving mode'. This
means that I have to 'change hats', that is, to make a conscious
effort to disengage from using 'inspiring power' and deliberately
move into a facilitating role. It is not easy to switch roles in this
way because when I am in 'transmit mode' I myself become enthralled by the ideas that are bubbling up inside me! So in practice I find it helpful to define beforehand quite clearly which role
I am being asked to play. If I am asked to be 'an ideas person' or
'a resource-person on content', then it is better to work in conjunction with a facilitator whose task is to take care of the
process in the group and who will 'rein me in' if I lose contact
with many of the group.

Since I discovered the value of operating in a facilitative
mode I have spent endless hours learning, honing and practising the skills it requires. Furthermore, I have found it necessary
to undergo a lot of counselling – and do a lot of praying – in
order to overcome the things that block me from being a good
facilitator. I have to find ways to lessen the self-absorption and the
hunger for approval which limit my ability to really be attentive to
what others are saying and to be truly open to their questions and

their interests. As time goes on I find that these tasks are on-going and perhaps endless, with new dimensions opening up all the time. For instance, at first I found it very difficult to give my fully focussed attention to one person in a group without being distracted by my efforts to meet the needs of others at the same time. Now that I have learned to focus on one person at a time, I am discovering that it is equally important to retain a peripheral awareness of where the energy is flowing in the group as a whole. There is always more to learn ...

Despite all the effort I have put into learning to be an effect-ive facilitator, I have become more and more convinced that the ability to empower others is above all else *a gift from God*. One needs to be inspired by the Spirit to find just the right response to the pain or joy of an individual or a group, to know how best to deepen their searching or strengthen their self-confidence. So the facilitator must above all else have an openness to the Spirit (though it may not be expressed in these words). This openness expresses itself mainly in trust – trust in oneself, in the other person, in the group, and in the divine prophetic Spirit.

'Fulcrum Power'

Those who work on the frontiers can become quite exhausted if they are using one or both of the above types of power a lot of the time. So it may be a relief to discover that the Spirit can also work though us in a different way – using us as a kind of *ful-crum*, to bring about important changes with the expenditure of relatively little energy.

It was only about three years ago that I discovered that 'em-powering power' can be supplemented or sometimes even re-placed by this other kind of prophetic power which I am calling 'fulcrum power'. I was in a workshop looking at issues about power. As part of the exploration we were asked to find ways of taking away a person's power. My way of doing this was to or-ganise a walk-out which would leave the 'powerful' one with nobody to lord over. However, the co-ordinator of the exercise intervened to say that we were not allowed to talk or plan to-gether. I then found myself disempowered, unable to make use of my long experience of facilitating and organising others. I sat in silence, watching while other members of the group tried out various ways of reducing the dominant person's power. After a while I noticed that new power-centres had emerged in the group. There was one sub-group who were blocking off the former dominant person; and another sub-group had formed at the far end of the room. I realised that at that moment I had the power to tip the scales in favour of one or the other by adding my 'weight' to it.

This may seem like a rather trivial learning, but for me it became a catalyst for a lot of new light. I have come to realise that in many situations there is the possibility of making a key intervention which may have a major effect on the outcome of the whole process. The intervention may be an action or a few words which in other circumstances would have no great significance; but which, in the given situation, can make all the difference. That is why I speak of 'fulcrum power' – because the person who is using it has located a key turning-point in the process. An outstanding example is the decision of Pope John XXIII to convene the Second Vatican Council which brought about such momentous changes in the Catholic Church. A more recent example is the 'fulcrum' role played by my colleague Pádraig Ó Máille in the overthrow of the tyrannical regime of Hastings Banda in Malawi.[3]

But how is one to identify the exact point at which such a key strategic intervention can be made? Some people seem to have an intuitive sense of where a remark or action by them will be most effective. For them, it appears to be an innate gift. For most of us, on the other hand, this sense of where to intervene does not come so spontaneously. We can, however, develop and nurture this specialised kind of discernment by engaging in what I venture to call 'prophetic contemplation'.

In using the phrase 'prophetic contemplation' I have in mind the fact that the first task of the biblical prophets, before ever they were ready to challenge or comfort people, was to read 'the signs of the times'. There is 'a time to break down, and a time to build up … a time for war and a time for peace'(Eccles 3:3, 8); and the prophets were the ones who were taught by the Spirit to know which time was which. They were able to interpret the great movements of history, to give guidance on what God wanted of the chosen people at each stage of the process.

Similarly, Jesus spent long nights in prayer. During those quiet hours he was led by the Spirit to read 'the signs of the times'. In this way he engaged in what might be called 'divinely inspired strategising'. There are indications in the gospel that he sometimes changed his approach. We may presume that these changes of missionary strategy were the fruit of his long periods of prayer, where he was inspired to see what key interventions on his part would be most effective for his followers and for his wider mission.

The reason why Jesus and the prophets knew what kind of action was called for at any given time was because they were inspired by the Spirit of God. This inspiration is not confined to the publicly recognised prophets. Nor is it limited to situations where world-shattering events are taking place. Each of us can confidently ask for and expect the assistance of the Spirit in knowing what we ought to do in the various situations where we find ourselves, since in the eyes of God all are truly important.

The Bible sometimes gives the impression that inspiration came to the prophets in a blinding flash. But it is clear that the prophets were people of prayer and that it was the time they spent in prayer which opened them up to let in the inspirations of the Spirit. It is a reasonable assumption that they spent many hours and days in contemplation and that their insight was the fruit of this prayer. I visualise their contemplation as a process in which they brought into conjunction the mystery of God's love and the reality of the world around them.

This suggests that if we wish to develop within us the ability to exercise 'fulcrum power' then what we need above all is to take time for contemplation. Not, however, a type of contemplation which would cut us off from everyday reality. What we need is a *'prophetic* contemplation' in which we hold up to God in prayer the situation in which we find ourselves, and look at our situation in the light of God's love and God's will. Out of this contemplation comes *insight* into what is really going on and *guidance* on how God would like us to respond – whether by intervening or by waiting.

I do not think we should expect 'fulcrum power' to replace 'empowering power' entirely in the life and work of those who are on mission. But I find a great freedom in knowing that organising people for action is not the only authentic response to every unsatisfactory situation. As I grow older I am coming to see that an organising-empowering initiative on my part is *one* possible response to a particular state of affairs. But it is not necessarily the most appropriate one. Sometimes it is preferable – and much less burdensome – to wait and pray and look for more light. As Christians we can ask for inspiration and guidance about some relatively minor intervention we might make which could be of strategic importance in bringing a situation into harmony with God's will.

Flowing Power
A fourth kind of prophetic power comes from the Spirit as part of the call to mission. It is the ability to *flow* with life, to be so in tune with nature, with people, and with the world around us that things fall into place in a very easy and organic way. It is only very recently that I have begun to make a clear distinction between this 'flowing power' and the 'fulcrum power' which I covered in the previous paragraphs. The difference between them is that 'fulcrum power' focuses on a particular action or word through which we deliberately intervene at a specific point in an on-going process, whereas 'flowing power' is a matter of letting the whole process of life unfold in its own time.

Perhaps the best way to understand what is involved is to recall times when we experienced the *opposite* of this 'flowing' – times when we found ourselves 'out of sync' with the flow of life, times when everything went wrong for us. This negative experience may help us to advert to and appreciate the contrasting experience which we sometimes have as well – times when everything goes just right. We may even, occasionally, have a sense that there is a mysteriously benevolent quality in the way all the bits of the jigsaw of our lives seem to flow together – a sense of being gifted in a way that almost overwhelms us. That experience is a peak example of what I am referring to when I use the phrase 'flowing power'.

When this takes place, we become extremely powerful and effective in an effortless way. Without pushing or manipulating others we can have a major influence on the people around us and even in the public arena. It is as though we were in *continuous* touch with the 'fulcrum power' which I described in the previous section – as if we have become fulcrums not just at special moments but all the time, being powerful instruments of God in the world. The powerful effect we have on others arises not so much from anything we say or do, but simply from the quality of our presence to them. Francis of Assisi seems to me to be a person who exercised this kind of power; and my fantasy is that the present Dalai Lama is also somebody who has a powerful effect on the world through being able to flow with life in this way.

Some social activists might interpret this concept of 'flowing with life' as the adoption of a passive attitude, a giving up on the struggle for justice in the world. But when we are fully in touch with this 'flowing' prophetic power we do not lose our concern for social justice. Rather, we become more trusting of God and more aware that even our passion for justice is itself a gift of God, playing its part in the providence of God which unfolds in the world.

Getting in touch with 'flowing power' helps us to distinguish between two very different ways of 'stepping back' and allowing things to happen. The wrong way is a shirking of, or shrinking from, responsibility – a futile attempt to dissociate ourselves from the events that are unfolding around us. The right way is the precise opposite; it is a *tuning in* to the process to such an extent that we do not have to push or pull or fuss people in order to get the right things to happen. Rather we simply have a sense of things falling into place, a feeling for our own assigned role in the process, and a willingness to do what needs to be done and to leave the rest to happen in its own good time.

This reference to 'an assigned role' implies that there is some kind of overall design behind everything that happens. Some such idea is contained at least implicitly in the very notion of 'flowing power'. Christians who have a strong explicit faith in providence and the will of God should have no difficulty at all with this. But many people of our time, Christian and non-Christian, are inclined to react against the idea that God has a blueprint for the world and for our lives and that we are bound to conform to it. They are uneasy with the deterministic overtones of such a concept – the assumption that the universe is like a clockwork mechanism constructed and controlled by a clockmaker God. They also react against the way in which 'the will of God' was used in the past to impose on religious people a blind obedience to arbitrary authorities.

My hope is that people who have difficulties with the notion of a 'divine plan' will come to feel more positively about it when it no longer comes to them as an idea *imposed* by teachers of religion but arises from their own personal experience of 'flowing power'. Their sense of being in tune with the flow of life – with what Eastern spiritual leaders call the 'Tao' or the 'Way' – may lead them to have some inkling of a mysterious divine design revealed in the quasi-organic growth of our world. It is not a static blueprint imposed from outside but a flowing and emergent design which presupposes our freedom and utterly respects it. In other words, a growing awareness of 'flowing power' may lead people to recover their faith in providence – or discover it for the first time.

The lived-out experience of providence – whether it comes in a very explicit form or remains somewhat amorphous and unarticulated – requires a particular sensitivity of spirit which is itself a gift of the Holy Spirit. So we cannot simply decide to experience 'flowing power' when it suits us; we have to wait for the gift to be given. Furthermore, we may expect that the experience will vary in intensity. Occasionally it may feel as though the whole world were playing a symphony just for our benefit; while at other times we barely manage to cling on to our faith in providence – a faith which invites us to trust that we may eventually discover some meaning in what is happening to us.

We cannot just 'switch on' the experience of 'flowing power'. We cannot make things flow; but we can learn to *let* things flow. We can *dispose ourselves* to be open to 'flowing power' and we can nourish it when we are in touch with it. In order to cultivate the ability to flow with life we need to find ways of lessening the anxiety which often spoils the flow. We do so by developing an inner peace and a sense of 'attunement' with God and with life. We learn to trust in the providence of God, recalling the prayer of Julian of Norwich: 'All shall be well, all shall be well, and all manner of thing shall be well.' Taking quiet time, meditating, praying, walking in the countryside, sailing, climbing the hills – these are some of the ways in which we become centred and 'grounded' and nourish this power within us.

Perhaps the most important way to make use of 'flowing power' is to allow it to provide a *focus* in our lives at each moment. This focusing comes about when we are able to *live in the present*. Most of us are inclined to spread our attention too widely and too thinly. This happens because we are preoccupied with the past or with the future instead of paying full attention to what is happening in 'the here and now'. We often try to control the future by planning beforehand how we will cope with various scenarios. We 'double-guess' others – deciding how to respond if so-and-so says one thing or another person says something else. So our energy is no longer focused. We are not savouring the richness of the present moment, not in touch with the wonder of our surroundings and the excitement of the process that is unfolding moment by moment. We are not engaging fully with the passion of the people around us. Then our encounter with others and with life becomes uninteresting and we ourselves become rather dull. Our sense of 'flowing power' has become scattered and dissipated.

On the other hand, if we can stay focused in the present, there is an exciting exchange of interest between us and those around us. We begin to share in the energy they put into and draw out of their lives; and we in turn share with them our own passion for life. Then we make use of 'flowing power' quite spontaneously and very effectively. In this way we play a significant role in the shaping of our own lives and the lives of those around us – and we can have a real impact on our world. There is a certain paradox here: we become attuned to the overall flow of life, not by trying to anticipate various future possibilities or scenarios, but by focusing on the present moment that is unfolding. Life becomes an exciting adventure, because we are in touch with its ebb and flow from moment to moment. We are allowing ourselves to be carried by the currents of energy which are sweeping through us and through the world at every instant of our lives.

Yielding Power
The fifth and final type of prophetic power associated with the call to mission is what may be called 'yielding power'. It can be seen as 'the flip side' of the 'flowing power' which I have just been describing. If 'flowing power' is the ability to be in touch with life in all its richness, then 'yielding power' means being able to let go with dignity. It means knowing when the time is right to give up the struggle. It means sensing when this particular dance has been completed, being aware when the tide of life is ebbing without any prospect of flowing back again. 'Yielding power' is the ability to surrender to failure, to weakness, or to death when that is the only authentic way forward.

As the writer of the book of Ecclesiastes says, there is a time for giving birth and a time for dying, a time for laughing and a time for mourning (Eccles 3: 2, 4). By our own light, we cannot distinguish between them. It is not for us to decide on our own when is the time to yield. We need the guidance of the Spirit to know when to face death, or to accept the various 'little deaths' of failure or rejection that are part of life.

'Yielding power' is very different from the other four kinds of power – but it is a real power nonetheless. The clearest example of how it can be a power – rather than just an absence of power – is the death of Jesus on the cross. Throughout his public ministry he had struggled valiantly against his enemies and had never given up on his friends. But then came what St John's gospel calls 'his hour' (Jn 7:30, 8:20), and he knew that what remained for him was to find the right way to stop struggling and to allow his life's journey draw to its pre-destined end.

In his agony in the garden, Jesus came to accept that he had failed from a purely human point of view. All he could now do was let himself go into the loving hands of the One who had given him his mission in the first place. So far as anybody could see from outside, here was a man in the prime of life being forced to give up and accept failure. But when, on the cross, Jesus addressed the one he called 'Abba' and said, 'into your hands I commit my spirit', he was actuating or evoking another kind of power, one that was a total surprise for his friends as well as for his enemies. According to John's gospel 'his hour' was not only the time of letting go to failure and death but was also the moment of his glorification. Because he was able to go into his death in the right mode it brought forth new life for him – and became an immensely powerful source of new life for humankind and the world. Clearly, then, Jesus is the supreme example for us of the use of 'yielding power'. But we can also, perhaps, see it at work in the lives and death of Joan of Arc and of Damien the Leper.

The story of the death of Jesus indicates that 'yielding power' comes not from within us but from a transcendent source that is beyond us. Our role is not to exercise this power directly but simply to be its catalyst at the appropriate moment. We have to open ourselves to the ultimate wisdom which lets us know when 'the hour' has come for us to let go. This 'yielding' may be just a minor matter like knowing when to stop persuading a friend to do something. Or it may the acceptance of our death in the literal sense. (Missionaries who work among tribal people living close to nature are amazed at how the older ones among them generally know when the time has come for them to die; such tribal people have much to teach us both about 'flowing power' and about 'yielding power'.)

Long before the time comes for us to let go into death, the

'hour' for yielding arises when we find ourselves baffled by the mystery of the apparently pointless suffering or tragic death of a friend who had everything to live for. More seriously still, it arises when we are faced with the mystery of sin – implacable hatred, or perverted cruelty or blind insensitivity. When the flow of life has been definitively blocked, and we find that our sense of a pattern in life seems utterly undermined and confounded, that is when we know that it is the time to yield and to follow the example of Jesus by committing ourselves into the loving hands of a higher power.

If we do not appreciate the place of 'yielding power' then the other four kinds of Spirit-given power are subtly undermined. For this power is a last resort; and it is crucially important that we recognise the existence of this last recourse. Otherwise we will be unable to entrust ourselves fully to the Spirit in any of the other four kinds of power. Once we know that the Spirit is with us to the very end – even in what seems like moments of ultimate failure – then we can entrust ourselves fully to the Spirit in living life to the full. Only then can we follow our prophetic call in all its manifestations right to the end.

Conclusion

Trust is the common theme which runs through all five of the prophetic powers. To become agents of 'inspiring power' we have to trust the Spirit working within us and not allow the inspiration to get blocked by our fear that we won't know what to say or do. In order to allow 'empowering power' to work in and through us we have to trust others and trust the group. 'Fulcrum power' calls for trust in the guidance of the Spirit and trust in our own inner wisdom to know when and how to intervene. 'Flowing power' is essentially an exercise of entrusting ourselves courageously into the flow of life.

But, sooner or later, we learn that, despite all their energy and effectiveness, each of these four kinds of power may ultimately be blocked by the sheer intractability and ruthlessness of evil. This tempts us to put limits to our trust. Then, once these limits have been reached, we are tempted to fall back on our own efforts to control situations and manipulate people. In the Bible, Judith brings out very clearly that trust which is measured out in this way is not really trust at all. As Judith says, we cannot put time-limits on God but must wait patiently for the divine intervention (Jdt 8: 12-17). That is where 'yielding power' comes in.

The prophetic powers of the Spirit play a crucial role in the life of all who feel called to work on the frontiers. To respond successfully to this call it is not necessary to bring about visible results. What is essential is a wise use of the powers of the Spirit. And we must understand that the power of the Spirit is not confined to enabling us to *do* things, no matter how wonderful these actions may be. We are mortal and finite – and we often find ourselves at the mercy of evil. So the 'final' intervention of the Spirit must come in the form of enabling us to know when to *stop* 'doing things', when to let go and surrender ourselves in ultimate trust to providence. This means that like Job we put our trust in God to vindicate us (Job 19:25-27). The ultimate foundation of our hope, as of all Christian hope, is the belief that God can draw unlimited good out of what seems like utter failure. The core of our faith is that the divine power which brought new life and hope out of the 'failure' and death of Jesus is still at work today in our lives and in our call to mission.

QUESTIONS FOR REFLECTION

1. Name some people whom you know who use each of the different kinds of power dealt with in this chapter.
2. Which kind of power do you personally exercise most frequently and most naturally? Has this changed over the years?
3. Where is 'the growing edge' for you in this area – which kind of power do you feel called to develop or grow into?

PART THREE

Re-Visioning 'Mission to the Nations'
(Ad Gentes)

CHAPTER 11

New Models, New Images, New Attitudes

I am now moving on to the third part of this book, the part which deals with the specific issues which arise for those who see themselves as engaged in 'mission to the nations' *(ad gentes)* or 'mission on the frontiers'. In this chapter I propose to focus on the new attitudes which animate and motivate those who engage in such missionary action today. I begin by contrasting different 'models' of mission, that is, different sets of assumptions about what mission involves. Each model of mission has its own distinctive style, approach and strategy.

The Crusader Model

When I was about eighteen years old, a Columban missionary came to our school to tell us about the missions. He recited for us a stirring poem which included the following lines:

Who has a blade for a splendid cause,
a cause that is good and true?
To live and to die for the grandest thing,
that man could say or singer sing,
or ever soldier knew ...
Then flash out your blade for a splendid cause,
a cause that is good and true ...
As Louis did in the old crusade,
take up his cross and go ...

These verses were written by Father Paddy O'Conner who had worked as a missionary in Vietnam. They convey very well the way missionaries were seen, and the way they presented themselves, half a century ago – as inspiring, almost swash-buckling, adventurers who ventured forth to bring souls to Christ. The model of mission which lies behind the poem can be called 'the crusader model' or 'the commando model' of mission.

During the period from about 1850 to 1960 this model was

dominant. The vision behind it was that of the church militant. Unbelievers were to be converted, to be 'conquered for Christ' through spiritual weapons. The church was to be 'planted' in the 'pagan lands'. And the people there were also to be helped by being introduced to the real or imagined 'benefits' of Western-isation. The frontiers at that time were seen in geographical terms, and the missionaries were seen as heroic people who left their homelands to work in alien lands. They were specialists who prided themselves on their toughness and audacity. They were trained to be independent, to take initiatives, to endure long journeys through tropical rain forests or into the remotest deserts.

The renewal of theology, which in the Catholic Church was associated with Vatican II, called us to move on from the milit-ant theology of church on which this model of mission was based. Deprived of its foundation, it has been dying a painful death over the past generation. But it still lingers on in two ways. First, it endures in the mentality and attitudes of some of the 'old time' missionaries formed according to the old model. Secondly, this crusading conception of mission still lingers on in the minds and hearts of some of those who provide the support of interest, prayer and finance on which most missionary instit-utes depend.

An Alternative Model
Though we must leave behind the 'crusader model' of mission, we can retain the best elements of it – the commitment and zeal, the endurance, the audacity to take on great challenges. However, these must be embodied in a new way by today's mis-sionaries. The world as Christians see it today is:
– a world where we look for and find the Spirit at work outside the present boundaries of the church,
– a world where there is a genuine pluralism and where we appreciate, respect and learn from the religious beliefs of others;
– a world where Western civilisation is no longer identified with the Christian message and where we see many ways in which non-Christian cultures may be far closer than we are to the Christian vision and values;
– a world where we have an *integral* concept of human liberation and development, replacing the sharp dualisms of body and spirit, of this life and the next life, of church and world, of nature and grace.

– a world where patriarchal values and models of thought and action are being questioned and where we are called to give the feminine its full value;
– a world where the missionary can no longer be 'a lone ranger' but must be a team and community person.

Some key aspects spring to mind as characteristic of the new missionary approach and style. First of all, missionaries of today and tomorrow no longer wish to be described in militaristic words such as 'crusaders' or 'commandos'. We may perhaps see ourselves instead as explorers, people whose special vocation and mission is to go beyond the existing frontiers, to discover some of the myriad ways in which God's Spirit is already at work there – and also to learn the ways in which sin has distorted these different worlds.

Furthermore, we have learned to be wary of our urge to change people, of our need to be always in the position of the ones who give. Our aim is to be in genuine solidarity with those who are beyond the frontiers or on the margins, receiving and giving in a spirit of dialogue and sharing. We take as our model Jesus, who 'emptied himself' (Phil 2: 7) to take on our humanity and be in solidarity with humankind.

Another phrase from St Paul offers more light about an appropriate approach to dialogue with those on the margins or beyond the frontiers. He speaks of being 'ambassadors for Christ' (2 Cor 5: 20; cf. Phil 1: 9). Those missionaries who think of an ambassador in terms of banquets and flowery speeches may be reluctant to identify with such a role. But in our world today, more than ever before, there is a new breed of diplomat or ambassador: men and women who see themselves as peacemakers and who devote endless hours to the search for mutual understanding and reconciliation. Similar qualities of diplomatic sensitivity are called for in anybody who engages in the delicate task of inter-religious dialogue, or the even more delicate work of promoting reconciliation in deeply troubled parts of the world. Christ may be served better today by missionaries who see themselves not as crusaders but as patient diplomats, peacemakers in the service of the Prince of Peace.

The 'Sending Out Image' of Mission

Having looked at different *models* of mission I want now to look at different images which influence the way in which we think about mission. The image which the older generation of Christians grew up with and took for granted may be called 'the sending out image'. It has a very solid scriptural basis. It begins from the sending of Jesus into the world by the Father (e.g. Jn 5: 23, 30, 36-7; 12: 49) and then focuses on the sending by Jesus of the apostles to the nations (e.g. Mt 28: 19; Jn 20: 21). In the past, these biblical texts tended to conjure up an image of a pyramid, which could also be pictured as a kind of fortress. At the apex was God the Father, *sending* Jesus into the world. A step lower down was Jesus *sending out* his apostles to convert the world. At the next level one imagined the apostles appointing and *sending out* their successors the bishops. These in turn sent out priests as their collaborators. Bishops and priests could partly share their mission with catechists. Members of religious congregations fitted in to the pyramid somewhere lower than priests and higher up than 'ordinary' lay people.

Lay people were at the bottom of the pyramid. They were told that their daily lives were missionary in some manner that was not specified very clearly; but it involved sharing in the mission of the church above all by prayer, by 'offering up' their sufferings, and by supporting the church financially. Their task was also to reach out beyond the boundaries of the fortress to the outside world. This involved giving good example to people, influencing them and, where appropriate, actively inviting them to join the church. It also meant working to change the structures and laws of the world so as to make it conform as closely as possible to the ideal expressed in church teaching. In this way the mission of the church was to transform the secular world into a Christian world.

This image of mission is so closely linked to a purely institutional and hierarchical model of church that it does not fit in easily with an understanding of the church as a communion, as the People of God, or as a prophetic servant of the world. It tends to reduce lay people to being agents or instruments of the clergy in the task of mission. And it suggests that mission is a one-way activity, taking little or no account of the prior presence and activity of God in the world – in the great world religions, in the primal religions, and in the secular world.

The pyramid/fortress image of mission needs to be replaced. But we should not throw out the baby with the bathwater. It is still crucial to the notion of mission to see Jesus as being sent into

the world. And there is a real sense in which Christians are
called and sent forth by God, and led by the Spirit, to share in the
mission of Jesus. There is a solid basis for this not only in scripture but also in our own religious experience.

The 'Gathering In' Image

The notion of mission as a 'gathering in' has been put forward
by the Nigerian scripture scholar Sister Teresa Okure SHCJ, as a
direct challenge to the notion of mission as 'sending out'.[1] She
insists that, in the New Testament perspective, the mission of
the disciples/church is essentially a gathering rather than a
going forth. She argues that 'the Greek name for the church itself
(ekklésia) is derived from the Hebrew qahal (synagogé) meaning a
gathering or assembly.' For her the church is mission because it
is itself a gathering, one which has the duty to bring into communion fellowship all God's scattered children. She maintains
that, in the New Testament, the purpose of the proclamation of
the disciples was to draw others to join their fellowship with
God and with Jesus Christ.

The notion of mission as a 'gathering in' finds further support in the fine book by David Bosch, entitled *Transforming
Mission*. Bosch maintains that in early Christian times many people found the life and worship of the Christian community very
attractive.[2] So the mission of the church was exercised not so
much by going out as by drawing people in.

This 'gathering in' image is very powerful; but taken on its
own it would be inadequate. However, it has a solid biblical
foundation and it rings true to the experience of many missionaries. So it is a very helpful supplement and corrective to models
of mission which focus mainly on the sending out of missionaries to bring the good news to others.

Solidarity Image

Nowadays we need to supplement the other two images by pict-
uring Jesus *in the midst of* his people. If we adopt this as the central image, we can then take the word 'solidarity' as a key to the
understanding of the mission of Jesus. Using the image conjured
up by the word 'solidarity', we focus on the coming of Jesus to
share the life of ordinary people, to experience their daily struggle for survival, to share their pain and their celebrations, to be
in touch with their experience of God and of their own history as

NEW MODELS, NEW IMAGES, NEW ATTITUDES   191

a people loved and saved by God. We then appreciate that it was out of his experience of solidarity with the common people, his own people, that Jesus came to have a sense of direction, of mission. This becomes an invitation to build our understanding of the mission of the church and of every Christian around the idea that it is a call to follow Jesus in being in solidarity with people all over the world and in every human situation.

The solidarity image is not in conflict with the 'sending out' image or the 'gathering in' image. In fact it can go some way towards integrating what is best in them. This is very clear in the approach of Teresa Okure, the champion of the 'gathering in' image. She goes so far as to suggest that those who go forth without solidarity with those to whom they come, are not genuine missionaries but exploiters and colonisers. Those who are not in solidarity with people are all too likely to deprive them of their self-esteem and despoil them of their cultural heritage. The sense of solidarity with people ensures that one can declare God's year of favour to them and bring them true liberation from God.

The word 'solidarity' can take us deeper and give us an indication of what lies at the very heart of mission. We see this by looking closely at the mission of Jesus. He did not come with a 'message of revelation' in the sense of some abstract 'truth'. God gave Jesus the mission not just of being with us and telling us things about God, but of living a fully human life. His mission was not some task which he took on over and above becoming human. Rather, we can say that the sharing of our life was his mission – provided we draw out the full meaning of that phrase.[3] Jesus explored the heights and plumbed the depths of what it really means to be human. He emphasised this by choosing for himself the title 'the Human One'. (As I said in the chapter on evangelization, that is the best translation of the Greek words which are usually translated as 'the Son of Man'.)

Since solidarity was at the heart of the mission of Jesus it must also be central to the mission of the church and of any Christian who engages in missionary work of any kind. Like Jesus, we are called to share the life of the people among whom we feel called – and have chosen – to work. For each of us, mission cannot really begin until we are able, with some authenticity, to experience the people we live and work with as 'my people'. For us, as for Jesus, sharing in the life of a community is not just a preliminary to mission but is the very core of mission. For it is our solidarity with others which is the basis both for our openness to *receive* what they have to offer and for our willingness and eagerness to *share* with them the gift of faith in Jesus and the other gifts we have been given.

This sense of solidarity with others normally finds its focus in a particular community of people. But it is not limited to them. We become aware that the local group is part of a wider national or regional community and that its welfare is bound up with that of the wider society. John Wesley was a man who had a vivid sense of this broader human community, a man who felt a truly missionary call. He summed up that call when he coined the phrase 'the wide world my parish'. This could become the motto of all who feel called to reach out to the frontiers and beyond.

Nowadays, we are more conscious than ever that we live in a global society. This means that solidarity with the people of any one grouping can be fully authentic only when it extends out to include the whole human race. And it does not end there. People are beginning to appreciate that the human community is itself part of the wider community of nature and the cosmos. So we are called to take our share of responsibility not only for our immediate neighbours, not only for the welfare of the human race as a whole, but also for the earth which nourishes and sustains us. Implicit in the experience of solidarity is the call to mission to the whole wide world. And a sense of mission rooted in the experience of solidarity is far less likely to become distorted by arrogance or feelings of superiority.

QUESTIONS FOR REFLECTION

1. Is it really possible to combine the call to work 'on the frontiers' with the call to work as part of a team? What kind of formation is required to help people be pioneers while at the same time being community-builders who are able to work easily with others?

2. Do you see the traditional missionary attitude and style as being 'masculine'? If so, what would a truly 'feminine' missionary style look like?

CHAPTER 12

The Purpose of Mission

Having looked at different models and images of mission, I want now to explore the purposes and aims of those who engage in various kinds of missionary work. For almost a hundred years, up to quite recently, missiologists insisted that the primary purpose of mission was to 'plant' or establish the church. Within the past generation, however, theologians have come to distinguish more clearly than in the past between the church and the reign (or kingdom) of God. Quite recently this distinction began to be applied to the theology of mission. So (as I pointed out in Chapter 5) some theologians began to shift the emphasis of mission on to promoting the reign of God, rather than just founding the church.

For several years I resisted this idea, feeling that it did not do justice to the reality of mission as I experienced it in the work overseas of my colleagues and myself. For the reality was that those of us engaged in parish ministry spent almost all of our time building up Christian communities and training catechists or other Christians to minister in various ways to these communities. A small number of my colleagues worked in seminaries. They, too, were obviously engaged in building up and serving the local church.

Very recently, however, I have come to believe that in approaching this issue I had been unduly influenced by the fact that I am a *priest*. I realised that I had been giving too much weight to that clerical experience of mission. It can hardly be denied that the primary concern of most missionary priests and ministers, and of those who work closely with them, is the establishment and nurturing of Christian communities. But their work should not be taken as the only paradigm or pattern of what mission is all about. There are many fine missionaries whose immediate concerns are by no means the same as those of the typical missionary priest or minister.

Two Categories of Missionary

I now find it helpful to make a distinction between two different categories of missionary:

– Those who focus primarily on the building up of the church both as a community and in its institutional aspects; and

– Those who are primarily concerned not about the church but about certain key Christian values – living these values, giving witness to them, and promoting them in society. They may, for instance, be devoting their time and energy to building up a primary health care system, or to literacy work, or to the promotion of human rights, or to working for liberation, or reconciliation.

I want to insist that there is no question of giving a higher status to one of these categories over the other. And of course there is a considerable over-lap between the two.[1] But it is helpful to distinguish between them because the two categories of missionary may at times have quite different priorities.

In the past, this distinction was not really made, even though there was an obvious practical basis for it. A generation ago, the first category (building up the church), if it had been recognised, would have been made up almost entirely of priests or ministers. The second category (witnessing to key values), if it had been recognised as separate, would have been made up mainly of the thousands of missionaries who devoted their lives to setting up and staffing schools and medical centres. In the Catholic Church, most of these were religious Sisters and Brothers. In this category, too, were a relatively small but committed number of lay missionaries, as well as some priests who devoted themselves to teaching, or managing schools or, occasionally, to some other profession. In most of the Protestant Churches there was a similar differentiation between clerical and lay roles, though the number of lay missionaries was greater.

Up to fairly recently there was no particular reason to make the distinction I am now making between two categories of missionary. This was because theologians and church people had failed to make any clear distinction between the church and the kingdom or reign of God. So the focus remained very much on the church, even when missionaries were engaged in what we would now name as various kinds of development work. In those times it was generally taken for granted that the establishment of educational and medical services was somehow part of the establishment of the church. The schools and hospitals were 'used' to some extent to give the church credibility, even though they were valued for their own sake as well. So people did not think of making the kind of distinction I am now making between missionaries whose priorities are to set up the church and missionaries whose priorities are to witness to Christian values.

Now, however, we make a clear distinction between the church and the kingdom or the reign of God. This provides a solid *theological* basis for the distinction between missionaries who focus on building up the church and those who give priority to witnessing to reign of God values. But, of course, it is important not to split off one from the other entirely.

There is nowadays a much less rigid boundary between the work of the clergy and the work of other missionaries. Consequently, the first category of missionary (those whose focus is on the church) is no longer the preserve of ordained ministers. Quite a lot of lay people (and, in the Catholic Church, very many missionary Sisters and Brothers) have become catechists or taken on ministries such as forming and nourishing basic Christian communities or training leaders for church activities. All of these fit into the first category of missionaries – those whose priority is building up the church community and the institutional church.

The other category of missionary includes all those who are not directly involved in setting up or staffing the structures of the church. They are the people involved in the provision of health services, education, social services, community development, ecology work, empowerment of women and of the poor or marginalised groups, and those involved in education for human rights, democracy and civic responsibility. So this second category includes most lay missionaries and Sisters and Brothers, as well as a number of clergy who have gone into various specialised ministries not immediately related to building up the church.

The Christian values to which this second category of missionaries give witness are, for the most part, moral and political values; this is evident from the list I have just given of the various activities involved. Nowadays there is a far stronger and more conscious focus on these values than in the past. The theological basis for this lies in the awareness that the church is called to be at the service of the world. This change of focus began to come to the fore in the Protestant Churches in the

1950s. In the Catholic Church it came into favour during the second half of Vatican II; and it found expression in the 'Pastoral Constitution on The Church in the Modern World' *(Gaudium et Spes)*. In my book *Spirituality and Justice*, I noted a further development of this idea, namely, the realisation that it is not enough to think of the church serving the world; one must ask, 'which world?'. Is the church serving – and colluding with – the world of the rich and powerful, or is it serving – and empowering – the poor and exploited who make up the great majority of the world's population?[2] It is at this point that we move from what may be called 'secular liberal' values to the values of liberation and option for the poor.

Religious Values too
Most missionaries of the second category devote themselves to the kind of moral and political values I have just listed. But it is important to note that in some cases missionaries of the second category may be committed to promoting values which are specifically *religious*. A small but growing number of missionaries are now focusing on expressly spiritual or religious values such as mysticism, the spiritual journey, and dialogue with people who are on a spiritual search for meaning.

It would be easy to assume that those who concentrate on such religious values and activities should be included in the first category of missionaries, namely, those concerned with building up the church. But our Western church is in such an activist mode that these deeply mystical, contemplative and dialogue values may at times be in danger of being undervalued and neglected. Some missionaries have noticed this gap and have set out to devote themselves specifically to these profoundly spiritual activities. In some cases they have been able to do so in a way which keeps their specialised ministry at the very heart of the local official church life. When that happens it is a great benefit to the church, because this special emphasis on contemplation, prayer, and dialogue with 'searchers' demonstrates in a very practical way that the church is there not just to organise people, to train leaders, or to provide sacramental services; it is there to pray and to help its members (and others) find God and live in the presence of God.

There are, however, times and places where the relationship with the institutional church is not so easy for those who feel a special call to the mystical life or to engage in dialogue with religious searchers. They may find that their priorities can at times be quite different from those of missionaries engaged in other church ministries. They may have the sense that the institutional church is, like Martha in the gospels, busy and concerned about many things while undervaluing 'the one thing necessary'. So they may feel obliged to opt out of the usual round of meetings, training programmes, and involvement in church building projects. They do this in order to focus on meditation, or simply on 'being with' people who are looking for meaning and purpose in their lives. Consequently, they may be seen as shirking the normal responsibilities of church workers; so they may find themselves distanced to some extent from the local institutional church. For this reason I would place them in the second category of missionaries – those whose priority is to give witness to fundamental Christian values.

The point I am making is that the basis for the distinction between the two categories of missionary is *not* that the first group deals with spiritual matters and the second group focuses on secular or developmental matters. It is rather that the first group make the building up of the church their first priority – whether that involves celebrating liturgies or digging the foundations of a church building. Those in the second category, on the other hand, give priority to 'reign of God values', whether these be obviously spiritual like contemplation, or overtly political like struggling for the fundamental rights of prisoners.

Why make this Distinction?
Why bother distinguishing between two categories of missionary – those whose focus is on establishing and building up the church and those who concentrate more on giving witness to Christian or reign of God values? After all, when I make this distinction I have to admit at once that missionaries in the two different categories generally work hand in hand together. Not only that, but there may be a considerable overlap between them, in the sense that some missionaries engage in both kinds of work. Nevertheless, I think it can be very liberating for many missionaries to make this distinction.

Christian values such as justice, reconciliation, and contemplation are worthwhile in themselves, even apart from any direct connection they may have with the church. The distinction I am proposing between two categories of missionary ensures that these values are given full weight in the missionary enterprise. If we fail to recognise the two categories, there is a real danger that all missionary work will be valued only in terms of its contribution to the building up of the institutional church. This would mean the adoption of a utilitarian attitude which defines success in terms of numbers of converts or visibility of church projects. But it is contrary to the authentic Christian spirit to judge the success of missionary activity mainly in terms of the extent to which it contributes to increasing the numbers of Christians, or even in terms of the extent to which it contributes to the image or credibility of the church.

The distinction between the two categories can be particularly helpful for Sisters, Brothers and lay missionaries. For these are the people who are less likely to be directly involved in building up the institutional church. In the rather clericalised church in which we live there is a constant danger that 'priestly' work will be given priority or seen as the norm against which other kinds of missionary work are judged.

Sometimes the more church-oriented missionaries are inclined to believe that what they are doing is the *real* missionary work. They imagine that missionaries who devote themselves to, say, the promotion of human rights are *only* doing development work, as though this were, at best, a second-class type of missionary work. In this situation, the insistence that there are two categories of missionary provides a safeguard for those missionaries who devote themselves to development work of some kind. It is important to insist that promoting and witnessing to the values of the reign of God may not be treated as though it were merely a means to achieve the end of building up the church; this work can be just as authentically missionary as building a church or preparing people for the sacraments.

Both kinds of work have their place on the wide spectrum of missionary activity. Each contributes to the other. The institutional church is not an end in itself. Its whole purpose is to help people live out and share their Christian values. On the other hand, the promotion of these values ensures that the church does not degenerate into an empty shell – an institution which has forgotten its deepest meaning. I shall take up a different aspect of the question of witnessing to Christian values in Chapter 14 on 'Missionaries and Development Workers'.

A Fuzzy Boundary

I sometimes meet members of an older generation of missionaries who are inclined to think (or, perhaps, to *feel*) that promoting and witnessing to values of justice or ecology, however good it may be, is not quite what mission is all about. I myself am a missionary who went through my missionary formation at a time when the taken-for-granted belief was that the purpose of mission is to establish communities of believers who live the Christian way of life. So I have a lot of sympathy for those old-style missionaries. They are so convinced of the centrality of the church that they can hardly help feeling that all this emphasis on values is either a distraction from the main task, or just a matter of preparing the ground, or some kind of second-best missionary activity. The following comments are an attempt to address the concerns of such people. Starting from the viewpoint that the building up of the church is central to mission, I want to suggest that this perspective can be expanded to encompass witness to 'reign of God values' even where there is little or no formal emphasis on church.

It sometimes happens that missionaries find themselves in situations where it is impossible or unrealistic in practice to gather people into Christian communities or found a 'young church'. They may, for instance, be working in the kind of situation which exists in Iran at present, where there is a total ban on anything that could be perceived as Christian 'proselytising'. Again, they may be allowed into a country such as China only on the clear understanding that they avoid 'missionary' work in the usual sense of the word. In other situations there may be no official ban on missionary activity but the prevailing non-Christian culture may be so strong that there are very, very few converts to the church. (This is the case in North Africa and in many other predominantly Muslim countries; and it may also arise among Muslim minorities in Western countries.)

Recent mission theology can bring great consolation to missionaries who find themselves in such situations. We now recognise that the Christian way of life is not an all-or-nothing package. The clear-cut boundaries of the institutional church are a very poor guide to determining who is living the Christian way of life and to what extent they are doing so. It is easy to count the numbers who are registered church members. But it is far more difficult to measure the numbers of people who, though they are not registered as members of the Church, live their lives partly or wholly on the basis of the Christian vision.

There are many people who are, formally, non-Christians but who accept the truth of the Christian story (at least to some extent) and who find spiritual nourishment in Christian rituals and symbols. There are many more who have been deeply influenced by the Christian value-system and have largely adopted it, even though they do not call themselves Christians. I am thinking of the thousands of people who went through the Christian school system in, say, Japan or India or Malaysia. There are clear indications that many of them were profoundly affected by their contact with Christian missionaries in these schools and colleges. Furthermore, the Christian values adopted by such people have not remained in the private and family sphere. Frequently, they have been inserted into public and political life.

A further point is that when it comes to the insertion of Christian values into public life we are no longer confined to individual countries but have to look at the wider global context. An obvious example is the fact that there are non-Christian lawyers and journalists and Buddhist monks in various countries in Asia who have made a truly authentic option for the poor. I am not, of course, claiming that this makes them unconscious Christians, or even that the witness of Christians in their own area led them to make such an option. But, on the other hand, we have to acknowledge that the courageous option for the poor made by many Latin American church people has had an impact far beyond their own church and their own continent and has played some part in inspiring non-Christians in Asia and elsewhere to make a similar option.

All this has practical implications for missionaries who find themselves unable to establish or extend the church in the conventional sense and who focus instead on promoting or witnessing to 'reign of God values'. They do not have to feel that what they are doing is some kind of second-best activity, justified only on the ground that it prepares the way for 'real' evangelization. In so far as their work promotes understanding or acceptance of Christian truths, values, or symbols it is authentic evangelization. Another way of expressing this point is to say that the work of missionaries – or of anybody who engages in the task of evangelization – is not merely to found the church but also to promote the Reign of God.

The success of missionary work cannot be measured in terms of the extent to which the official church is established. We may think of a wide penumbra around the church, a zone where Christian values, truths, rituals, and symbols have an impact on the lives of people who are not church members. A very important part of the evangelization work of missionaries is to widen and deepen this sphere of influence since it is a key element in the incarnation of the faith in the local culture and society.[3] The ideal, of course, is that the founding of the institutional church should go hand in hand with this broader and more intangible work of enabling the faith to permeate the society, and that each of these two aspects of missionary work should support the other.

QUESTIONS FOR REFLECTION

1. Are there practices in the church which give a counter-witness to the values which the church proclaims? If so, can you name some and suggest ways of ensuring greater coherence between Christian values and the actual practice of the church?
2. Do you feel drawn to give particular emphasis to any important Christian value? Do you find support in your local church for doing so?

CHAPTER 13

New Frontiers of 'Mission to the Nations'

Some months ago I was working with a group of priests from my own missionary society on the outskirts of São Paulo, Brazil. Some of the issues they were dealing with were more or less the same issues as missionaries are facing in the more 'developed' areas of other countries, such as Korea, the Philippines, Kenya, or Malaysia – and many other countries where Western missionaries have been working for the past couple of generations. Our members have been working in this area for over thirty years. They played a big part in establishing a network of about sixty parishes across the whole western side of that enormous city and, over that period, they have handed more than fifty of these parishes back to the local church. As the people from the northeast of Brazil kept pouring in to the city, and its periphery kept expanding outwards, they continued to move further out to the poor and undeveloped areas on the new periphery. By now these areas are separate dioceses, with their own local personnel.

The church in that area has now become well organised. The missionaries find that the bishop is asking them to come to meetings and to submit plans and do all the kind of things that frontier missionaries were able to avoid. They regret that they no longer have the same missionary freedom as they had in the past. They see themselves being sucked into a more traditional bureaucratic church.

In this situation there were three different responses by the missionaries. Several of the older ones were convinced that they should continue working in the same general area where they had been for the past twenty or thirty years. They justified this by pointing to the urgent need for missionaries in view of the continuing shortage of fulltime church ministers in the São Paulo area.

A second group, mainly younger or more active missionaries, said: 'Our work here is done. São Paul is no longer frontier

territory; it is time for us to move elsewhere.' They discerned together for a year, then decided to move to a very remote area a
thousand miles in to the interior – an area where the institutional
church scarcely exists. The first four members of this group are
just settling down there at present.

The third group came up with a very different response.
They saw the present situation as a challenge to redefine their
missionary role, not in terms of moving *geographically* but in
terms of staying in the same geographical location but specialis-
ing in new *frontier ministries* there. They had in mind ministry to
prisoners, to the unemployed and exploited workers, to people
suffering from Aids, and other specialised ministries.

The responses of the second and third groups of these
missionaries helped me to clarify what it means to work on a
missionary frontier and how it differs from other aspects of the
overall mission of the church. At this time of ageing and dimin-
ishing numbers it is difficult for missionaries to have to recognise that what was authentic missionary work twenty or even
ten years ago may no longer be frontier mission today. It is very
hard for them to face the challenge of uprooting themselves
physically, psychologically and spiritually. But on the other
hand, many missionaries find that, if they linger on past their
missionary 'sell-by' date, they become uneasy or disillusioned.
So a transition of one kind or another seems to be the only fruitful way forward, at least for those who are still in good health
and still have energy for mission.

Changing Frontiers
The exciting thing about the present time from a missionary
point of if view is that it is now becoming much clearer what
'mission to the nations' *(ad gentes)* is really about. Basically, it is
about working on the frontiers. And we cannot any longer be
satisfied with easy answers which define the frontiers entirely in
terms of geography. Of course the geography is still important.
As Pope John Paul pointed out in his mission encyclical,
Redemptoris Missio, there are still areas of the world where the
gospel has not really been heard and where the institutional
church scarcely exists (RM 37). But nowadays there are places in
almost all of what we used to call 'missionary countries' where
Christianity is no longer in a frontier situation and where the
church is well established. Some of the pastoral and educational

work being done within the so-called 'young churches' can no longer be called 'mission to the nations'. It is rather part of the general pastoral work of the church, quite similar to what goes on in 'the home churches'. Many 'foreign missionaries' sense this and become uneasy, feeling that while they remain *foreign* they may no longer be *missionary* in the strict sense.

This means that the mere fact that I am working in Korea or Kenya or Brazil is no guarantee that I am on a missionary frontier. The issue today is *in what part* of these countries am I working and *what kind of ministry* am I engaged in there? The point is that there are different kinds of frontier situations. *Some* of them can be defined geographically, while *others* cannot. For instance, work with non-Christian ethnic minorities is truly frontier work – even when such minorities are defined not in terms of geography but by employing cultural, religious, or political terms. Similarly, we have to use social or economic terms to define victims of famine, and political or economioc categories to define refugees.

Historical Background
It may be helpful at this point to look back at how the notion of 'mission to the nations' was defined in the past. We can begin by noting two extreme approaches to the issue. At one end of the spectrum is what may be called the medieval Catholic notion of mission. This presupposes that there is a clearly defined geographical reality called Christendom, surrounded by 'the heathen world'. Mission is then a one-way going out from Christian lands to 'save souls' and to extend the boundaries of Christendom.

A less extreme version of this outlook was common during the heyday of Catholic mission from 1860 to 1960. During that period, 'the West' was still thought of as 'Christendom', which implies that it was seen as already evangelized (more or less). Most other parts of the world were seen as 'missionary territory'. This means that at that time Catholics still defined mission almost exclusively in geographical terms. It was during this period that most Catholic missionary congregations and societies were founded. Their task was at first seen as 'saving the souls' of 'pagan' people. From early in the twentieth century the priority began to be changed to 'planting the church'. But the location was still 'foreign lands'. So it is not surprising that the idea of mission as expressed in the constitutions of these organisations was mainly geographical.[1]

At the other end of the spectrum is the extreme evangelical view which sees the church as composed of a relatively small group of 'the converted' and which thinks almost entirely in terms of these individuals reaching out to other individuals on a one-to-one basis, calling them to accept Christ as their personal Saviour and thus to join the ranks of 'the saved'. In this view there is need for such a mission in the USA or in Ireland just as there is in China or Pakistan.

The way most missionaries today define mission is some-where in between these extremes. By and large, Protestants tend to be somewhat nearer to the evangelical view. However, main-line Protestant Churches do not reduce mission to promoting a 'one by one' conversion as the extreme evangelicals do. Nevertheless, they often speak of 'mission in six continents', a phrase which implies that mission is everywhere.

Transculturality
In recent times, Catholic missionary agencies have either abandoned or carefully nuanced the geographical definition of 'mission to the nations'. In general they have moved cautiously from geography to *ethnicity* or *culture* as the main criterion for defining their specific role.[2] Many of the revised constitutions of missionary congregations speak of working on an inter-cultural basis.

All this seems fairly acceptable so long as we stay within the rather narrow world of the missionaries – a world which is now shrinking quite rapidly. Outside this world, among thinking members of the wider Christian community, there is very little interest in these distinctions. I have hardly ever met anybody outside the missionary community who is impressed by the dis-tinctions we 'professional missionaries' make. Most committed Christians (apart from ourselves) tend to have a broad concept-ion of mission. When foreign missionaries try to make a careful distinction between mission *ad gentes* ('to the nations') and other forms of mission many home church personnel are quite resent-ful. They feel that it is an attempt to claim a monopoly of the term 'mission' or to present work on the foreign missions as in some way superior. Indeed overseas mission has lost some of its romantic appeal. Those who define themselves as foreign mis-sionaries today find themselves on the defensive. Yet they are the ones who are asking some of the most difficult and challenging questions about the nature and validity of mission *ad gentes*. The missionary movement is suffering from a crisis of confidence.

John Paul's Mission Encyclical
Against this background we can look at the contribution of Pope John Paul II in his mission encyclical, *Redemptoris Missio*, issued in late 1990. It set out to restore missionary morale, by making a clear distinction between mission *ad gentes* and other aspects of mission by defining the boundaries of mission *ad gentes*.

In this encyclical (RM 33 and 65-6) John Paul maintains that, while there is one universal mission of the church, this mission is carried out in three different situations (even though the boundaries between the three 'are not clearly definable').

The first of these three situations is 'mission to the nations' *(ad gentes)* in the strict sense. It is the situation of 'peoples, groups and socio-cultural contexts in which Christ and his gospel are not known, or which lack Christian communities sufficiently mature to be able to incarnate the faith in their own environment and proclaim it to other groups'. The second situation is in sharp contrast with the first. It is a 'pastoral' situation where 'there are Christian communities with adequate and solid ecclesial structures'. The third situation is distinct from the two others. It is an 'intermediate situation, where entire groups of the baptised have lost a living sense of the faith, or even no longer consider themselves members of the church, and live a life far removed from Christ and his gospel'. 'In this case', says the Pope, 'what is needed is a "new evangelization" or a "re-evangelization"', rather than 'mission to the nations' in the strict sense (RM 33).

When it comes to clarifying the boundaries of what constitutes mission *ad gentes*, it is clear that the encyclical moves further away from the geographical approach than most Catholic missionary congregations and societies have done. John Paul suggests that there are a whole series of different 'worlds' which together form 'the nations' *(gentes)*; these are the special concern of the missionary. These include the 'worlds' based on ethnicity and culture (e.g. 'the Chinese', 'the Japanese' etc.). But they extend also to 'the world of the media', 'the world of youth', 'the world of women and children', 'the world of the poor', 'the world of the mega-cities', 'the world of justice, peace and ecology', 'the world of art, culture and the sciences' and 'the world of those who search for a deeper meaning in life'.

Extending the Frontiers

I think the Pope's way of identifying mission *ad gentes* is very helpful. It continues to pay particular attention to culture but does not claim that culture is the only objective basis for defining mission *ad gentes*. I believe we can develop this approach of John Paul and throw further light on the specifically missionary vocation *ad gentes* by seeing it as *work on the frontiers of the church*.[3]

I want first to mention three very obvious ways in which the frontiers of mission 'to the nations' *(ad gentes)* can be expanded. The first is the *ecological* question and I illustrate it by taking as an example the Columban missionary and writer Seán McDonagh.[4] He now has an international reputation as a spokesperson on issues relating to justice, ecology and religion on a world scale. His missionary work in the Philippines provided him with a solid experiential basis for his activity on these issues. But his present commitment is not confined to 'the South' (or what used to be called 'the Third World'); for he sees that the issues are *global;* and in fact he now lives mainly in 'the North'. His work is fully missionary, according to the criteria of the encyclical; for in it the Pope speaks of 'safeguarding the created world' as one of the 'new sectors in which the gospel must be proclaimed' (RM 37).

The issue of *international debt* – particularly the debt of the countries of 'the South' – has become a very urgent one in recent years. Missionaries have first-hand experience of the devastating effects which this debt has on millions of the poorest people on earth. So when missionary institutes bring home some of their most active and committed members to be spokespersons and activists on such issues, this is not a loss to 'the missions' but simply a transfer from one sphere of missionary activity to another.[5] The encyclical makes it clear that the same must be said of other global justice and peace issues such as racism, cultural oppression, the development and liberation of peoples, the protection of human rights and the advancement of women (RM 37).

The work of *dialogue* between the different religions of the world has come to be of particular importance in recent times. Missionaries who have worked on the ground in the East or 'the South' bring to this work a wealth of practical experience which is at least as valuable as academic study of the religions. It is a matter of secondary importance whether this inter-faith dialogue takes place in, say, India (where there are many centres devoted to it) or in Chicago. What makes the work authentically missionary is not its geographical location but the fact that it is truly on the frontiers of the church.

One way of summarising the above points is to say that mission *ad gentes* should now be seen as embracing not just *foreign* mission but also *global* mission. In using the term 'global mission' I am referring to major issues – such as ecology, international debt, and dialogue with other religions – which are truly global in scope and importance; they affect the world as a whole and the role of the church in the world.

Examples of Other 'Worlds'
The way in which the encyclical opens up new frontiers for missionaries is by speaking of the different 'worlds' into which the missionary is called to enter (cf. the 'worlds' I mentioned above). To fill out what is meant by a 'world' I shall now give several examples of other 'worlds'. They provide particularly vivid instances of zones which are beyond the usual frontiers of the church. The first example is the 'world' which Edwina Gately entered some years ago when she began to work among the prostitutes of Chicago. Edwina had been a lay missionary in Uganda and she had already shown herself to be a pioneer by founding The Volunteer Missionary Movement (VMM). She did not see herself as *ceasing* to be a missionary in taking up her new frontier ministry. I do not think that missionaries would be entitled to say that it is not 'real' mission *ad gentes* to do what this prophetic woman has done, namely, to attempt to cross the frontiers from our familiar world into the very different 'world' inhabited by prostitutes.

A second example is the 'world' of handicapped people which Jean Vanier entered many years ago when he set up the movement known as 'l'Arche', and which he has done so much to reveal to others over the past thirty years. A colleague of mine who worked for many years in Africa now shares the life of the people in 'l'Arche'. I see this change, not as an abandonment of mission *ad gentes*, but as a switch to a different aspect of it.

Another example comes from my own experience. Nearly twenty years ago I was one of a group of missionaries who founded a movement called 'Partners in Mission'. It promotes the empowerment of deprived groups and individuals. It does this mainly by providing them with training in leadership skills, social analysis and community organising. The focus of the movement is on what is called 'capacity building'. This means that the training programme is designed not so much for experienced community leaders but more particularly for groups or individuals who are poor and who feel they can do little to change their situation. There is a culture (or sub-culture) of poverty and powerlessness. The founders of the programme and most of the present facilitators inhabit a very different 'world', one that is more typical of middle-class people. So a serious social frontier has to be crossed when the 'Partners' training programme is introduced into a deprived area.

Over the years many of the key leaders in this movement have been people who worked as foreign missionaries for several years. They have been able to bring into the Irish situation the experience and skills they picked up when working as missionaries in Africa, Asia or Latin America. Some of them may be content to call themselves *former* missionaries while others may insist that their present work for marginalised groups in Ireland is missionary in the full sense. Whether or not they themselves name their present work as 'missionary', I am convinced that their empowerment of the poor and of laity is truly frontier work and that it fits within the definition of 'mission to the nations' as outlined in John Paul's encyclical.

A further example relates to the women's movement. In recent years the 'Sophia' movement has played a significant role in the promotion of Christian feminism in Ireland. A key person in this movement is Sister Claire Murphy SHCJ who worked as a missionary in Nigeria for twenty-five years. She is now working in her home church. But if we accept the approach adopted by Pope John Paul we should say that she is still a missionary in the *ad gentes* sense. For his mission encyclical mentions working 'for the advancement of women' as an instance of mission *ad gentes* (RM 37). But how can one claim that work for the promotion of Christian feminism is frontier work? Does such a claim imply that the gospel has not permeated the world of women? Not at all. But there is certainly a wide gap between 'the world of women' and the patriarchal world inhabited by most of the leaders of the Catholic Church. Claire Murphy has chosen to work on the boundary or frontier between these two worlds and that is why her work can be seen as an instance of mission *ad gentes*.

Another example of crossing a frontier into an different 'world' is provided by a colleague of mine. Having worked for half a life-time in Africa, he has now taken on the very difficult task of trying to enter in some degree into the 'world' of paedophiles, in order to work as a therapist with them. I imagine that his previous experience of adapting to a foreign culture is of some help to him in his effort to understand and empathise with those who occupy this very different 'world'. I consider that this work fits into the category of 'mission *ad gentes*'.

My final instance of a sphere which poses a frontier challenge in our time is the 'world' of what may be called the 'searchers'. These are the people who are looking for a deeper meaning in life than mainstream Western culture offers at present. Pope John Paul points out that in the midst of consumerism and materialism 'we are witnessing a desperate search for meaning, the need for an inner life, and a desire to learn new forms and methods of meditation and prayer' (RM 38). He goes on to identify this as a sphere which is to be evangelized. Sharing the gospel with what we may call this 'world of the searchers' is therefore one aspect of the church's 'mission to the nations'.

There is no doubt that most of those who inhabit this 'world of the searchers' are quite untouched by the regular pastoral work of the church. To reach out effectively to them is a truly missionary task, requiring a change of mentality and strategy. My colleague and friend, Fr Michael Rodgers, worked for many years in Africa and from there he was elected to serve as a member of the General Council of our missionary society. Having completed his term of office in 1990 he did not return to Africa. Instead, he went to live in Glendalough, which is one of Ireland's holiest places. There he is developing a Celtic and ecological spirituality and has a ministry to many 'searchers' who have little contact with the regular home church. His previous experience of working in an African culture, and of trying to develop there a holistic vision of human growth and healing, has helped him in his present ministry of being available to those who inhabit the 'world of the searchers' and of coming into solidarity and dialogue with them.

I venture to add a word about my own work in recent years – as a kind of postscript to what I have just been saying. Having worked in non-Western cultures for several years, and having been a consultant to missionary groups for over thirty years, I now spend much of my time running specialised workshops and retreats. In them I facilitate 'searchers' in exploring the twilight zone between psychology and spirituality, between psyche and soul. I find it demanding and exciting and I believe that it, too, is a kind of frontier work.

Too Broad?

How will Catholic missionary congregations and societies respond to the insistence of the Pope that there are many new frontiers for 'mission to the nations' today? There is a danger that they may acknowledge the existence of the new frontiers in principle, but limit themselves in practice to working in the traditional 'missionary world', arguing that this is their particular charism. To do so would be to reduce *charism* to *tradition* and in this way to block or inhibit creative change. The charism of a group is not past tradition alone; it is a living, growing, self-correcting tradition which springs from the interaction of *past* tradition with the call of the Holy Spirit to meet *new* challenges in the future.

My experience over the past twenty-five years has been that both the general membership and the elected leadership teams of Catholic missionary congregations and societies are quite reluctant to broaden their definition of mission *ad gentes* along the lines proposed in John Paul's mission encyclical. They seem to be afraid that if the traditional boundaries of 'mission to the nations' are eroded, then missionaries will be left floundering without any clear sense of their identity or of their specific role in the church. They fear that if all the different areas mentioned in the encyclical are included under the heading 'mission to the nations', then the definition becomes so broad that nothing is left out. They feel that if the definition includes *everything* then it has *nothing distinctive*. More specifically, they fear that if they were to broaden their scope as widely as the encyclical indicates, they would lose the overseas thrust which is so much part of their own tradition. They may even be afraid that they would have to cope with a large influx of missionaries returning from overseas in the hope of finding some 'easier' kind of missionary work in their own home areas.

My aim here is to show that *re-defining* the frontiers of missionary activity is by no means equivalent to *abandoning* the whole notion of a distinctive missionary activity. There is no adequate basis for the fear that there will be a loss of identity by missionaries and missionary institutes if they acknowledge in practice that 'mission to the nations' can be exercised on frontiers other than the geographical one. In fact this approach offers exciting challenges and the possibility of a new lease of life for institutes and individuals committed to mission *ad gentes*. It opens up new frontiers while still being in organic continuity with the past. I have been trying to illustrate this by pointing out some of the new and inspiring frontier activities in which missionary institutes or individual missionaries are actually engaged at present. But it would be a serious mistake to imagine that a broader definition of mission *ad gentes* provides an easy option for missionaries to return home. Quite the contrary; it requires a high degree of creativity, energy, and dedication to work on any of the frontiers of the church, whether they be situated at home or abroad.

Furthermore, a heavy price may be paid by those who refuse to take seriously the broader definition of 'mission to the nations' proposed in the encyclical. By clinging to an unduly narrow definition of 'the nations' they run the risk of provoking the very crisis they wish to avoid. For the Pope is not being *arbitrary* when he proposes a broader definition of mission *ad gentes*. Rather he is articulating and making explicit what the Spirit is already saying to Christians through what theologians call 'the sense of the faithful' *(sensus fidelium)*. An exclusively geographical definition of mission is increasingly felt to be inadequate by most reflective Christians.

There is a real danger that those of us who belong to specifically 'missionary' congregations or societies may be so focused on overseas mission, that we blind ourselves to the changes taking place around us and even to the new directions outlined by Pope John Paul. I think of the mediaeval military religious orders like the Knights Templars who were so specialised that when the situation changed they could not adapt. The same fate could befall the missionary institutes which have developed highly specialised structures on the basis of the older model of mission *ad gentes*. If they are unwilling to change with the times, they might linger on like the Knights as quaint ghosts from the glorious past, imagining that they are still on the cutting edge of the church. But they might no longer be effectively present on the frontiers where the church really intersects with the world of today and tomorrow.

Two urgent challenges face missionaries today. Firstly, we must be open to the Spirit in working out a model of mission appropriate to our time and our world; this new model must be based on a new vision and embodied in new structures and traditions. Secondly, we must find ways to ease the transition for people who have been brought up on the old 'commando model' of mission.

If those in leadership roles in the missionary institutes read 'the signs of the times' correctly they will be able to help their members in the field to reach a broader understanding of 'mission to the nations' along the carefully nuanced lines proposed in Pope John Paul's mission encyclical. But if the leaders dig themselves deeper into old trenches then many of the more reflective missionaries in the field (and many of those who find themselves under pressure or struggling with disillusionment) may well *abandon* the traditional conception entirely rather than *replacing* it with the Pope's broader definition. This is a situation where the most effective way to survive is to adapt and grow, by exploring new frontiers.

The Way Forward
The call of the Spirit is most likely to be heard first 'on the prophetic edge' of any given group; the task of those at the centre (in general assemblies or in central leadership) is to be open to such a call coming from the margins, to encourage those who feel called, and eventually to facilitate a general discernment about whether this may be a call directed to the group as a whole.

When those in leadership roles in a missionary institute are faced with a call among their own members to such a new ministry it is not enough for them to judge it in terms of whether or not it fits in neatly with what the group has traditionally been doing. If they wish to be true to the church, they should ask rather whether it is truly a frontier ministry, along the lines spelled out in John Paul's mission encyclical.

It is clear that a missionary group cannot take on corporate responsibility for every new missionary call experienced by one of its members. There is, however, the possibility of approving such commitments on an *experimental* basis. This would mean that an individual or small group are given the support of those in authority – but without any commitment that the congregation or society will continue their work. We could expect that some 'experiments' of this kind would come to an end after some years, when those engaged in it die, or retire, or move on to other work. But other 'experiments' would flourish, would attract more members, and would eventually be taken on formally by the missionary institute as a whole. This would be a very practical way to ease the transition into new kinds of frontier ministry.

To adopt a new model of mission is to undergo a quite radical transformation. The change that is required is not only in the consciousness of individual missionaries but also in the traditions and structures of missionary institutions. Individual missionaries may feel called to pioneer work on the new frontiers. But they need the moral and material support of their sisters and brothers in their own congregations or societies and in the wider missionary movement; this calls for a change in the corporate mentality of whole groups of missionaries. The pioneers must also be encouraged and helped to develop new agencies and organisational structures if their vision of frontier mission is to become operative on the ground.

It will not be easy to ensure a smooth transition from the older vision, model, and structures to the new vision, the new model, and the new structures to which we are called today. A special responsibility in this regard falls on two groups. The first of these are the leadership teams of missionary congregations or societies. The second group are the people who have energy to explore these issues and dialogue with others about them.

We have to respect each other in the exploration process. If changes come too suddenly many missionaries will be left floundering like stranded whales, unable to move on the shore on to which they have been pushed and at the same time unable to get back into the familiar ocean. On the other hand, if no bold initiatives are taken, many missionaries could end up like ageing commandos, living on the glories of the past but feeling unable to cope with the new situation. Those who cling to an outdated model of mission are losing touch with the Spirit who is leading the church into the future. No wonder, then, that they feel lost and defensive. So long as they fail to flow with the Spirit they cannot expect many young people to join them and bring them new life. Missionary life, like all other forms of life, can survive only by facing change. We must trust the Spirit, the one who brings new life out of chaos (cf. Gen 1:2).

An Alternative View

The wider definition of missionary activity found in the encyclical was welcomed by some missionaries because the broader
definition of missionary work which it offers still allowed them
to make a fairly clear distinction between 'mission *ad gentes'* and
other aspects of the work of evangelization. But I do not think
the encyclical succeeded very well in its main purpose which
was, I think, to boost the morale of missionaries. A major reason
is that many theologians and other reflective Christians saw the
encyclical as an attempt to shore up an outdated concept of
mission *ad gentes.*

In this regard, the missionary anthropologist and theologian,
Aylward Shorter, gives clear expression to the more implicit and
inchoate opinions of many missionary theorists and practitioners.
So it is not unreasonable to take him as representative of those
who disagree with the approach of the encyclical on theological
grounds. Shorter disagrees with Pope John Paul on two significant points in his mission encyclical. These differences are not
matters of purely academic interest. They have important practical
implications for missionary societies, congregations and institutes.
The two major differences between Shorter and the Pope are as
follows:

– First, Shorter does not believe there are adequate grounds for
the distinction made by the Pope between 'mission *ad gentes'*
and the kind of 'new evangelization' which the Pope holds to be
necessary in so-called 'post-Christian' countries.

– Second, he does not agree with the Pope on how to define
mission *ad gentes.*

Three Categories or only Two?

I want to look briefly at the first of these objections before moving on to spend more time on the second. John Paul's encyclical
distinguishes clearly between 'mission *ad gentes'* and the kind of
'new evangelization' which is required in the more secularised
parts of the Western world. For the Pope this distinction is based
on the fact that even very secularised Westerners live in countries where Christian principles remain embodied in the culture
and affect people's lives.

Shorter does not accept the validity of this distinction. He asks,
what difference does it make if a country had a Christian past?
He insists that culture 'does not have some kind of impersonal

existence of its own'. He goes on to argue that, far from being enriched by their former Christian culture, those who live in a post-Christian society 'have suffered a far-reaching cultural impoverishment'.[6]

Shorter's position offers a major challenge to those whose task it is to establish the policies and direction of missionary institutes. Should they take on 'missionary work' in secularised Western countries? If they accept Shorter's view, there is a strong case for doing so; and this would be a significant change of direction.

My own view on this issue is rather closer to that of the Pope than to Shorter. I agree with Shorter in stressing the loss by Western countries of much of their Christian heritage. Nevertheless, I think the Pope is correct in maintaining that the residual Christian elements in a secularised culture may influence people's attitudes. Take, for instance, the principle of the fundamental dignity and equality of all people. I think this is a value which has its roots in the Judeo-Christian tradition and which has had an enduring effect on all 'Western' people – even those who now live in a so-called post-Christian society. For this reason I am inclined to accept the validity of the Pope's distinction between 'mission *ad gentes*' and 're-evangelization'.

Situational or Personal Definition of Mission

I move on now to Shorter's second objection to John Paul's approach; it concerns the basis used to define mission *ad gentes*. The difference can be summed up briefly by saying that John Paul uses a *situational* criterion, while Shorter uses a *personal* one. The Pope holds that there are certain geographical, sociological and cultural 'worlds' which are not yet evangelized; and for him the task of the missionary *ad gentes* is to insert Christianity into these 'worlds'. Shorter rejects this view as linked to an 'obsolete paradigm' of mission.[7] For Shorter it is not that some situations are objectively missionary while others are not. What makes the difference is the person engaged in the evangelizing activity. 'Missionary evangelization occurs when the evangelizer crosses a human frontier to build the kingdom in another culture, another language, another nation or local church.'[8] So, according to Shorter's view, a Korean who preaches the gospel in the USA or Ireland would be just as much a missionary as an American or an Irish person preaching the gospel in Korea.[9]

While I recognise the arguments for adopting Shorter's approach, I must say that I am not fully convinced by it. I think that despite Shorter's great emphasis on inculturation, his definition of mission *ad gentes* does not take sufficiently seriously the Christian call to truly *embody* the faith in every human culture. It seems to me that it is more or less inevitable that there are degrees of success in this undertaking – in other words that there are some cultures and situations (or 'worlds') in which the faith has been embodied fairly effectively while in others the task has scarcely begun. This difference provides an *objective situational* criterion for determining the boundaries for mission *ad gentes*. If we accept that there are some cultures in which the Christian faith has as yet been scarcely incarnated (for instance, the Tibetan and perhaps the Japanese and Chinese cultures), then John Paul is quite right to insist that the geographical frontier remains a significant one.

It is easy to opt for the *personal* definition of mission *ad gentes* if one contrasts it only with a crude and old-fashioned conception of the situational definition which limits it to a purely geographical notion of mission. But before dismissing the traditional situational approach I think it is important to explore the possibility of updating and enlarging it. That is what Pope John Paul did in his mission encyclical; and earlier in this chapter I developed this a little and added some further nuances.

A Practical Proposal

To draw this chapter to a conclusion I now propose my own tentative answer to the issue of whether missionary societies, congregations, and institutes ought to adopt a situational definition of mission *ad gentes* (as outlined in John Paul's mission encyclical) or replace it with Shorter's *personal* definition. My response is that the best practical approach for us at present is to use *both definitions together*. But precisely because we use both, we can afford to be somewhat flexible in applying one where the other is already fulfilled.

This means, on the one hand, that we recognise that the mere fact that one is working in Japan, China, Tibet, Pakistan or Morocco in a maintenance or chaplaincy capacity is not a proof that one is engaged in mission *ad gentes*. If the work there is to qualify as truly mission *ad gentes* then it must involve a serious effort to embody the faith in the local culture and to engage in serious dialogue with those who do not share the Christian faith. But, on the other hand, I think we do not have to demand an immediate withdrawal from an area such as Iran when there are no obvious openings for inserting the gospel into the culture. Furthermore, we can allow for some flexibility in allowing – or even encouraging – some older missionaries to stay on in parts of Africa, or Latin America, or Korea even after the gospel has already been fairly well inserted into the local culture.

The other side of the coin is that missionary institutes should not lightly give up their commitment to working overseas. For the geographical frontier remains a significant one. Apart from the great challenge of embodying the faith in these cultures there is also the fact that the great majority of the world's population lives in the non-Western continents. There is also a further reason why mission in 'the South and the East' remains important for those who are from the West: to live for some years in these very different cultures poses a powerful challenge to the Eurocentric or Western worldview which is so dominant in this part of the world.

This challenge arises not just from 'book knowledge' but from lived experience. Those of us who have worked as missionaries in radically different cultures and in the midst of peoples with a very different religious outlook found ourselves challenged to develop a pioneering mentality and approach. We often found ourselves almost compelled to adopt a new *attitude* to the people among whom we worked, a new *strategy* of evangelization, and even a new *vision* of the church. This experience of changing our mindset is a great advantage when later we find ourselves on new frontiers which may no longer be geographical. So our missionary work overseas is an invaluable learning experience. Furthermore, our efforts to enter a foreign land with a radically different culture becomes a powerful symbol of the challenge of entering other 'worlds' which cannot be defined in neat geographical terms.

For these reasons it seems reasonable to me that, for the foreseeable future, specifically missionary groups should continue to put some emphasis on geographical and cultural frontiers. In practice, this would mean that they would normally expect *all* of their members to devote some years to overseas mission. They would do so even in cases where some members feel a particular call to work in their own home country in a different frontier ministry. After some time working abroad, these members, if they still felt called to this other mission frontier, could be allowed and encouraged to follow the call of the Spirit, even if it meant returning to their home countries to do so.

In proposing this kind of policy, I am well aware that it is already beginning to happen. Missionary institutions are adopting a more flexible approach in regard to allowing their members to become involved in a much wider variety of frontier ministries than in the past. This is happening mainly because the leadership teams of missionary institutions are no longer able to exercise strict control on the activities of their members. So what I am offering here is not really an invitation to adopt a radically new policy. It is more a question of providing a solid theological basis for a gradual shift in policy which is already taking place. If policy is clearly grounded in a coherent theology there is a better chance of ensuring that the distinctive *ad gentes* charism of these institutions will be preserved. Then the changes which take place are more likely to come, not on the basis of who pushes the hardest, but as a response to genuine inspirations of the Spirit.

QUESTIONS FOR REFLECTION

1. Do you personally feel drawn to any specific frontier ministry? How have you responded? What supports have you found?
2. Do you see similarities between foreign mission and mission to various marginalised groups? What attitudes and specialised skills are required for such work?

PART FOUR

Foreign Missionaries

CHAPTER 14

Missionary Strategy:
Vehicles of Evangelization

There are four chapters in this fourth and final part of the book. In these chapters I shall examine certain very practical issues which arise for those who work 'on the frontiers'. I shall focus mainly on these questions as they arise for those who work as *foreign* missionaries, mainly in the so-called 'developing world', because it is in these situations that they arise most acutely. But the points and proposals that I am making are generally applicable, with a little adaptation, to people engaged in frontier ministries in their own home countries. I begin with an important question of missionary strategy.

During the heyday of the modern missionary movement (from about 1860 to 1960) the Christian churches expanded very rapidly in most of sub-Saharan Africa, in the Pacific and in several Asian countries. Despite the great differences between these areas there was a remarkable similarity in the methods of evangelization used by the pioneer missionaries in the various countries. In almost all cases the missionaries spent a great deal of time and energy in establishing a system of Western education and developing Western-style hospitals and health services. In many respects this missionary strategy was not particularly original – it was very similar to the approach used one or two generations earlier in Ireland, Britain, North America and Australia.

Nowadays we look back with some misgivings at the enthusiasm with which these Western systems were introduced into non-Western countries; and later in this chapter I shall point out the reasons for these misgivings. But first of all it is useful to look at the advantages of this missionary approach. The peoples in these countries wanted very much to have schools and hospitals. So when the missionaries set about building schools and establishing health centres they were responding to the expressed needs of the local people. They were not seen simply as outsiders whose only interest was in the introduction of new religious beliefs and practices. If the missionaries had not become involved in the provision of Western education and medicine, they might well have been seen by the local people as evangelists of a rather odd sect – in much the same way as we now see the Mormons or the followers of Hare Krishna. But because of their involvement in the schools and the health services there was no likelihood that the missionaries would remain on the margins of the life of the people. They had found an entry-point into the everyday 'worldly' concerns of the people.

The missionaries were not using education and health services simply as a kind of bribe to induce people to become converts – or at least that is not how they wanted it to be. Rather they took it for granted that Western medicine and schooling were fundamental to the welfare of the people among whom they were working – and this was a view shared by the great majority of their people. The missionaries saw an intimate connection between the good news of Jesus Christ on the one hand and the schools and hospitals on the other. They were not interested in spending time in working out a profound theology to express this connection. In fact the theology of the time was quite inadequate for this purpose – it was too sharply dualistic, setting 'spiritual' affairs in sharp contrast to 'temporal' matters, and over-stressing the next life in comparison to the present life.

Though hampered by this weakness in the formal theology of the time, the missionaries developed an unexpressed theology of their own – a practical spirituality which was richer and more genuinely Christian than anything they had studied in the theology textbooks. This spirituality led them to be concerned not just with the 'spiritual' needs of their adopted people but with their overall human welfare. (Nowadays we would say that the missionaries were concerned about the 'integral human development' of their people – but it is only within the past generation that this term became a normal part of missionary vocabulary.)

There were, of course, some untypical situations in which the word of God had to be preached without any significant involvement by the missionaries in the provision of Western schools and medicine. For instance, those missionaries who worked in certain strongly Islamic countries had little or no opportunity to become involved in health care or education. So, in principle, there was a clear distinction between preaching the fundamental message of the gospel and the promotion of Western education and health care – even though in practice they were very closely intertwined in the work of so many missionaries. Missionaries of that time did not work out any exact language to express the close link between the two and the distinction between them. So I want to propose a phrase that can help us to articulate the connection. I would say that Western education and health care were 'vehicles of evangelization'.

By a vehicle of evangelization I mean something that can 'carry' many of the basic values of the Christian faith. A good example is a healthcare system that is accessible to all, that respects the dignity of everybody and that shows special concern for individuals or groups who are disadvantaged in society. Such a system is a practical embodiment of Christian faith. When missionaries or other church people are involved in establishing and staffing such a system they witness to non-Christians what Christianity is about. Similarly, if missionaries devote their lives to setting up and developing a system of education which embodies these values, they are very effectively proclaiming in practice the Christian good news. Another way of putting it is that these missionaries belong to the second of the two categories of missionaries which I referred to in Chapter 5: their primary concern is not the building up of the institutions of the church but rather the promotion of Christian or 'reign of God' values.

There are many such 'vehicles of evangelization' which have been used at various times by missionaries – for instance, redemption of slaves, engagement in science, and the establishment and running of 'lazar' houses for the care of lepers. It is not possible for all missionaries to be involved in all of them at the same time. Therefore, a key element in good missionary strategy is the wise choice of the 'vehicle of evangelization' which is most appropriate for the particular time, place and situation. One reason for the success of Christian missionaries in many areas in the first half of the twentieth century was their choice of education and healthcare as their two major 'vehicles of evangelization'.

Advantages

One of the most notable advantages of this choice was that it provided the missionaries with a most effective contact-point with the local community. Working to establish schools and health clinics, they came into daily contact with community authorities and leaders of all kind. The missionaries came to be respected by local chiefs or leaders for their ability to bring services which were keenly wanted by most of the local people. The missionaries also found themselves playing a significant role in the national development policies of the countries where they were working.

A second great advantage of becoming involved in the provision of educational and health services was that it offered the missionaries plenty of opportunities for rallying the local Christian community around worthwhile activities. At the very least, this meant that the missionaries had something to talk about with the Christians. They might not be very fluent at the language and might therefore have difficulty in having a dialogue about the beliefs and values of the people. But many missionaries developed close friendships with local leaders as they decided together where best to build a school and how to raise the money and get volunteers involved in the building.

This led on to a further advantage of this line of approach. It meant that the Christians were not concerned merely with 'churchy' matters or in promoting just the interests of their own church. Rather they saw themselves as serving the community as a whole. In other words they were not just building up the church but promoting the reign of God – even though at the time they might not have used these words to describe what they were doing. This gave them a better understanding of the real purpose of the church – which is meant to look outward to the wider society. Furthermore, the Christian community was clearly seen by others to be concerned about such broader issues – and this made it more attractive.

A Changed Situation

In recent times the missionary situation has changed very considerably. The building and running of schools and hospitals has largely been taken over by governments. Even in countries where the church still plays a role in this kind of work, its contribution is relatively small. For this reason alone, commitment by the church to establishing or running schools or hospitals is no longer such a striking means of witnessing to the basic values of Christianity. In the new situation, the hospital and the school may no longer be the most appropriate 'vehicles of evangelization'.

But there are also other good reasons for questioning the appropriateness of commitment to schools and hospitals as the best missionary strategy for today. The church cannot easily compete with the state in providing education and healthcare for the masses, since it does not have access to funds from taxes and other large sources of revenue. Therefore church-owned institutions have to make a difficult choice. On the one hand, they may choose to rely heavily on funding from abroad – and this dependency undermines the self-sufficiency which is a mark of authentic development in a country. The alternative choice is for the healthcare and educational institutions owned by the church to become fee-paying. In this latter case the result, in practice, is that church schools and hospitals are no longer catering for the needs of the very poorest of the local people.

There are deeper objections to the choice of schools and hospitals as the prime 'vehicles of evangelization'. Many people now believe that Western schooling and Western medicine have played a major role in undermining local culture in the so-called developing countries. This view is put forward in a very radical form by those who believe that Europe and America have imposed a cultural imperialism through Western schools and Western health systems (as well as through the church itself).[1]

A less radical view is that the problem is not so much the schools and hospitals in themselves but the fact that they have not been properly integrated into the local way of life. For instance, the educational curriculum has not taken sufficient account of the local culture and does not prepare people to meet their real needs. It is clear that in many of the 'developing countries' the hospitals have been unable to meet the health needs of the people. Furthermore, the Western-style education and health systems have given rise to social injustice – largely because they are not well integrated into the fabric of the society and the local culture. They tend to widen the gap between the rich and the poor; and for the privileged people who work within them they often provide opportunities for corruption.

Loss of Traditional 'Vehicles'
Partly because of increased involvement by governments in education and healthcare, and partly as a result of the kind of questioning outlined above, missionaries today rely far less on these two traditional 'vehicles of evangelization'. In fact it often

happens that foreign missionaries are more disenchanted with schools and hospitals than are the local church leaders. So, over a period of years the missionaries have gradually phased themselves out of these institutions, in much the same way as religious Sisters have largely phased themselves out of schools and hospitals in Western countries. But in many places they have not found other 'vehicles' which can carry the values of the Christian faith in today's world as effectively as the schools and hospitals did in the past.

If missionaries or other church leaders fail to commit themselves to some major vehicles of evangelization this has a number of negative effects. First of all, the church tends to turn in on itself – which means that its missionary thrust becomes much weaker. It becomes rather marginal in society because it is no longer addressing the questions that are of pressing interest to most of the local people. Church leaders in this situation exercise their ministry mainly *within* the Christian community rather than *vis-à-vis* the wider society as missionaries did when they were the main providers of schools and healthcare. The consequence of this is that the Christian community as a whole begins to take on a complexion that is closer to that of a sect than was the case in the past.

A second result is that there is a great fall-off in the number of mature *men* who take an active part in church life. The men who remain on in the church are mainly those who are attracted to various 'churchy' activities such as being choir-master, church warden, catechist, or chairman of a church committee. The church tends to become mainly a community of women, children, and old or disabled people. Of course it is very good that the church should appeal to women and to such marginal people as those who are disabled, old, or widowed – and even that it should give them a privileged place. But there is something lacking in a church whose adult practising membership is drawn very largely from these groups, with only a small proportion of able-bodied adult men.

It would appear that men feel attracted to institutions where they can exercise some kind of leadership role. A small number of men meet that need by becoming involved in the 'churchy' activities listed above (e.g. teaching catechism or playing a leading role in the parish council). But only a minority of men are attracted to this particular kind of involvement – and indeed there is room for only a relatively small number. So long as the church was turned outward, seeking to respond to pressing 'worldly' needs of society (such as the provision of education and health-care) there was an opportunity and an incentive for many men to be involved actively and to exercise their leadership potential to the full. But the number of committed men begins to drop off when the church ceases to be a key actor in shaping society, as it was in the past through its involvement in schooling and health-care.

It could be argued that the drop in the number of men who are active in church life shows that most of the men were not interested in the 'real' work of the church. The claim would be that the men's concern was only in having schools and hospitals, which are not of the essence of the Christian faith. But this is an unfair way of describing the situation; for, forty years ago, the schools and hospitals were genuine 'vehicles of evangelization', carriers of Christian values and beliefs. Those who devoted time and energy to promoting education and health were fulfilling their proper Christian calling as lay people. They were trans-forming their society in the light of Christian values. Indeed it could be argued that they were doing so at least as authentically as the people who got involved in more 'churchy' work such as leading the choir. It does not seem right, then, to blame the men for their lack of active involvement in the life of the church in more recent years. The problem lies rather with the church lead-ers themselves. They have failed to find alternative 'vehicles of evangelization' to replace the former ones of schools and hospi-tals. The result is that the church is left on the sidelines of society far more than it was in the past.

Alternatives
Missionaries and church leaders might like to 'get off the hook' by saying that this kind of 'sidelining' of the church is inevitable – an intrinsic part of the increasing secularisation of modern life. But that is not true. In fact there have been some missionary situ-ations in recent years where the church has begun to play a far more active role in shaping society than it had in the past. An outstanding example is the role played by the Brazilian church in the defence of human rights in the late 1960s and the 1970s. During those difficult years the church provided the only 'space' (literally and metaphorically) where people could meet to discuss

the gross abuses of the military regime. It was largely under the aegis of church organisations that an effective resistance to oppression emerged.

In the 1980s this work was taken up in what is called 'the cone' of South America (i.e. the southern tip of the continent). At that time both Chile and Argentina were governed by extremely repressive regimes. The security forces were guilty of gross offences against human rights; and people were 'disappearing' daily. Church leaders in these countries, actively supported by Brazilian church leaders, set up offices for the defence of human rights and campaigned with great courage and persistence against these abuses.

The result was twofold. Firstly, the church helped to bring about a situation where, despite the efforts of the tyrannical regimes to cling on to power, people were eventually able to install governments that were somewhat more democratic. Secondly, the church came to be seen as a champion of the oppressed and the victimised. Consequently, it attracted other such champions – notably the corps of dedicated lawyers and journalists who devoted their energy and risked their lives in a non-violent struggle against oppression. In the past, many of these people would have been alienated from the church or actively hostile to it. But, because of this new line of action, these champions of justice often became actively involved in church life; and the Christian faith became for them a source of life and energy, a beacon of hope in a oppressive society. This is a good example of the church discovering a new and powerful 'vehicle of evangelization'.

Something similar, but on a less dramatic scale, is happening in many parts of Africa and Asia and also in the less privileged parts of Dublin, London, New York, Sydney and other cities of the industrialised world – and, to a lesser extent, in towns and rural areas as well. Committed church people have become very involved in working with marginalised groups such as prisoners, and working for human development of all kinds with people in poor or deprived areas. Many members of religious communities and committed lay people have moved out of teaching and the administration of schools and into various kinds of informal education. For instance, they have become involved in initiating or running programmes with groups of women to help them have a better self-image and to facilitate them in meeting some of their urgent needs such as a crèche or recreational facilities. Similarly, many of those who had previously been involved in staffing and running excellent hospitals have now chosen to move out into the community and have become involved in health education or primary healthcare programmes.

Option for the Poor
Why this major change of direction? Undoubtedly a most important inspiration has been the notion of an option for the poor which originated in Latin America around the time of the Medellín Conference in 1968. This concept has by now percolated into many other parts of the world – especially places where there is a lot of poverty and deprivation. Inspired by this ideal, committed Christians have begun to look closely at the role they have been playing in society. Many committed Christians are moving out of hospital work and into primary healthcare. They do so because they believe that the present hospital system is not an adequate response to the health needs of the great majority who are poor and underprivileged.

Similarly, many of those who had devoted their lives to providing high-quality education for young people have come to believe that by doing so they have not been contributing to the building of a more just society. In fact they now believe that such high-class education played a part in widening the gap between the privileged classes and those who are poor and underprivileged. When I was working, in the 1970s, in a slum area on the fringes of Lagos, one of my colleagues there was a missionary Sister who had devoted twenty-five years to educational work. She had been a dearly loved headmistress of excellent second-level girls' schools both in Nigeria and in Ghana. In her fifties she left this work, trained as a community organiser, and moved into this very deprived area where a million people lived a life of grinding poverty and marginalisation. She kept in contact with many of her past pupils who by then were in key roles in society – as business people, in high positions in the civil service, and even, in one case, as the chief of police. They simply could not understand why she had chosen to live with the poor in a part of the city which was so dangerous and 'wild' that they called it 'the jungle'. They made vague promises to visit her there and help with her work – but none of them ever came. For her, this reaction of theirs was a vindication of the rightness of her choice.

I noted earlier that many foreign missionaries are troubled by doubts and questions about the effects of Western schools and hospitals on the culture and society in non-Western countries. These doubts become much more serious when they are situated within the context of the recent emphasis in most missionary organisations and communities on making an option for the poor. Many missionaries feel that the arguments in favour of moving out of schools and hospitals into other ministries are even more compelling in 'the South' (i.e. the so-called Third World) than in the industrialised countries.

The Latin American churches (or, more accurately, certain key sectors of these churches) have led the way in this regard. Their analysis of their own situation led them to refocus the church's commitment in society. Their resources of personnel, time and money are now devoted far less to schools and hospitals and far more to work for the promotion of justice and human rights.

Inspired by this Latin American change of direction, many foreign missionaries in other parts of the world have been looking for appropriate ways to make an option for the poor in their own situations. They want to find more effective ways of inserting Christian values into society and the local culture. So they are seeking new ministries to replace, or supplement, the apostolate of the school and the hospital. In other words, they are looking for 'vehicles of evangelization' which are more relevant in their world today. Some indigenous church leaders have engaged in the same kind of discernment – and indeed the initiative has sometimes come from them. But, sadly, the proportion of local church leaders who take this line is often quite small; and at times they resist the new approach of the foreign missionaries, and even feel let down or betrayed when foreign missionaries decide to let go ownership or control of some famous school or hospital.

It is in the context of this search for more appropriate 'vehicles of evangelization' that we can make sense of the notable shift towards work for 'human development' in the missionary enterprise within the past generation. Of course, the provision of schools and hospitals can also be classed as 'human development'. So it would be more accurate to see what is taking place as a re-orientation within development work. It involves a shift away from large institutions staffed by professional people towards small, more informal activities. These are much more participatory in their management style and they provide openings for harnessing the leadership gifts of people who may have little or no formal qualifications.

A Vehicle for Today?

Among those who find themselves in leadership roles 'on the frontiers' there is a good deal of experimentation in the search for effective forms of human development and liberation. This is true not just in 'the foreign missions' but also (and perhaps even more so) on the other missionary frontiers which I referred to earlier (e.g. inner city areas, or work with refugees or immigrants). Some 'missionaries' are convinced that the church needs to get involved in agricultural development; for others the way forward lies in credit unions; and there are some who think that involvement in literacy work will provide the church with the ideal vehicle of evangelization. (I am putting the word 'missionary' in inverted commas to remind the reader that what I am saying applies not just to *foreign* missionaries but to anybody trying to insert Christian faith into any 'frontier situation'.)

In practice, it often depends on the whim of the 'missionary' or other church leader which one of the many possible 'vehicles' is chosen; there may be little or no consultation with the local people about what *they* want. Is it any wonder, then, that many of these programmes never 'get off the ground' and that when one does get started it often grinds to a halt again when the founding figure, whose brainchild it was, goes off to work somewhere else?

In the past, the pastoral strategy of the church in a particular area was often determined by the inspired guesses of one or two gifted or strong-headed missionaries. But it is likely that for every right guess there were many wrong ones, pointing the church in mistaken directions. Indeed we may assume that, where truly suitable vehicles of evangelization were chosen, this took place because some gifted pioneers were able to 'hear' their people – to pick up and articulate the deep desires of those among whom they had come to live and work. But, whatever about the past, the determination of church policy and strategy should not nowadays be left to guesswork and arbitrary experimentation. For it is the very antithesis of real human development and liberation to leave people at the mercy of the whims or special interests of a 'missionary' or other church leader.

However, it is not easy for missionaries to avoid this trap, since people in the areas where missionaries work are often apathetic – partly because of their poverty and partly, perhaps, because they have seen many so-called development projects fail in the past. So they often leave it to the missionary to take the initiative. What is required, then, is some way in which those who have a leadership role can evoke real involvement by local people, but without imposing any ready-made agenda on them. There is need for some way in which 'the ordinary people' (or at least those of them who are willing to work for improvement in the community) can be inspired to come together and decide how they want to work for the development of their community; and they need some process which will help them reach consensus on their priorities.

It is important, too, that when people do come together they make their decisions on the basis of a realistic assessment of their needs. So they need a methodology which will enable them to engage in a careful study of their situation, in order to identify the fundamental problems which they are facing – and then go on to uncover the root causes of these problems. Furthermore, there is need for some process which will allow real consensus to emerge on important issues. Finally, it is very important that the process used be one which recognises and nurtures the leadership talents that are already present within the local community.

The Psycho-Social Method
What all this amounts to is that the most important question is not *which* of the different kinds of human development work people become involved in. The really important thing is *how that choice is made.* Is it something imposed on the community – either by an outside person, or by one or two of their own people who think they know what is best for all? Or, on the other hand, is it a choice based on a careful study and assessment by the whole group, leading to a real consensus? There is one insight which is essential for anybody who wishes to promote the human development of a community. It is that development is not something which begins *after* a decision is reached about what kind of development is needed. The making of that decision is *itself* a key step in the development of the community; and how that initial decision is made will determine the whole pattern of future activity in an area.

Perhaps the most significant contribution anybody can make towards the human development of a community is to help them in using a process that really *empowers* people. The method of decision-making must not leave them dependent on leaders from outside. Rather it must enable all the members of the group to play an active role in decision-making. It must also encourage those who have a special talent for leadership to use that gift for the welfare of the community. Frequently this means enabling people to see that real leadership is not a matter of dominating or controlling others but rather of encouraging them to work for consensus and inspiring them to carry out the commitments which are taken on by the whole group.

Obviously, such an approach to human development and liberation requires a wide range of skills. Fortunately, there is available a training programme which can help people to develop these very skills. Inspired by the insights and approach of the great Brazilian educator, Paulo Freire, Anne Hope and Sally Timmel developed a practical method for working with grass-roots people and local leaders. They used it mainly in Kenya at first but before long it began to be used widely in at least twenty African countries as well as Ireland.[2] By now this training programme has become known in every continent of the world, so those who use it can draw on a great wealth of experience. The programme uses what is called 'the psycho-social method'. It goes under a wide variety of names in different parts of the world e.g. 'Training for Transformation' 'Community Action Teams', 'Christian Development Education', 'DELTA' (Development Education and Leadership Teams in Action), 'Action-Reflection', 'DELES' (Development Education and Leadership Services), 'Partners in Mission', 'Ecumenical Development Education Programme', and 'PSM' (Psycho-Social Method).

There are variations from place to place in the way the training programme is carried out. But the essential elements remain the same. Fundamentally, the psycho-social method enables those who use it to engage in a type of human development and liberation which is very *participatory*. It is one which truly respects the 'ordinary' people, by giving them a sense of their own dignity. It empowers people to take responsibility for their own lives, for the welfare of their community, for promoting justice and human rights in the wider society, and for the preservation of earth.

Because it embodies these fundamental values I would say that the psycho-social method is a very important 'carrier' of the Christian value-system. It is one of the most effective vehicles of evangelization which can be used by missionaries, one that can play the same vital role today as was played by schools and hospitals in Western countries in the second half of the nineteenth century and in so many 'missionary countries' in the first half of the twentieth century.

At first it may be difficult to realise that something as intangible as a method of working with people and helping them make decisions can itself be a vehicle of evangelization. This difficulty arises especially if we are accustomed to using schools or hospitals as carriers of the Christian value-system. But those who use this 'psycho-social' approach for some time come to appreciate the deeply Christian values which it embodies and promotes. They realise that in the past it was their own anxiety to achieve something, to produce visible 'results', which led them to take the short-cut of imposing their own ideas and plans on others. Missionaries and other church leaders who use the psycho-social method find that it leads to their own evangelization as well as to that of the people for whom they are working! They learn to be patient with people – and this puts them in a frame of mind where they can respect and appreciate the values and gifts that are already present in the community. They see that the Spirit has been at work there, long before they themselves arrived.

Those who *begin* their involvement in human development work by using the psycho-social method will find it fairly easy to ensure that this approach pervades the various development programmes which are started as a result of the initial community reflection and commitment. So it frequently happens that there emerges in a given area a whole variety of projects, all using this method. These may range from primary healthcare to youth work, from women's awareness groups to human rights groups, and from literacy programmes to income-generating projects such as agriculture or craftwork. Each of these programmes or projects can then become a very powerful *specialised* vehicle of evangelization which carries fundamental Christian values into a particular sphere of human living.

Take, for instance, a situation where the psycho-social method has been used seriously by the women of a community in planning and setting up, say, a lace-making project. This method will help them face up to such difficult issues as price-cutting by some members of the group who are tempted to sell more of their goods at the expense of the rest of the group; for already the members of the group will be used to co-operating together and ensuring that the competitive instinct does not get out of control.

The psycho-social method can also help a development group not to base their action solely on the narrow self-interest of their own particular group, but to take account of wider development issues of the whole community. Suppose the farmers in an area decide to co-operate in an agricultural project. If their pro- gramme has emerged as a result of their use of the psycho-social method then they are far more likely to appreciate how wrong it would be for them to hire farm-labourers from outside at ex- ploitative rates. A further example: a youth project arising from use of the psycho-social method is far more likely to avoid the dangers of domination by one or two strong members. In all these ways, fundamental Christian values such as respect for others and care for the whole community become embodied in the everyday life of society. It is in such practical ways that 'missionaries' can work to help bring about the reign of God.

The Church as Vehicle

It seems obvious that the institutional church itself should be a powerful vehicle of evangelization. It should give witness in its own structures and procedures to the Christian values of soli- darity, justice, accountability, participation, respect for the views of all, and particular concern to make those who are 'on the margins' feel valued. But we are all aware of many situations where this is not the case. Quite often, people are hurt, angry, shocked or alienated because they find that their views are not really listened to by policy-makers in the church. They see that decisions are made arbitrarily, and that there are few structures which encourage active participation by lay people.

What is the root cause of this failure by the church to witness in its own life to the values it preaches? It is the tradition of cleri- calism which gives bishops and priests a great deal of power with very little accountability to the Christian community. One of the most effective ways of changing this situation is by a widespread use of the psycho-social method in the church itself.

In saying this I am basing myself on practical experience. I know of two dioceses in Kenya, one Anglican and one Catholic, where the church became involved first in using the psycho-social method to promote the more *secular* aspects of human development such as agricultural projects or primary health care. But gradually the laity, the priests and the bishop became aware that this participatory method could be of great value for parish councils and other groups concerned with the *pastoral* and *religious* aspects of church life. So it came to be used in all the organisational aspects of individual parishes and of the whole diocese. Diocesan synods could then be organised from the ground up rather than from the top down. There was widespread consultation of people even in remote rural areas. The views of 'grassroots' people were fed 'up the line' by locally chosen representatives and in this way diocesan policies came to be based on an assessment of their situation by the whole community.

The use of the psycho-social method leads in this way to an important change in the structures of decision-making in the church. Lay people are given real responsibility and challenged to use it. Clergy are expected to be accountable for their actions and to make use of procedures in which the voice of the community is given its full weight e.g. planning sessions, workshops, exercises of working for a common vision, evaluation processes, etc. The use of good participatory processes (e.g. breaking occasionally into small interest groups) helps to keep in check the neurotic need to dominate others which many people experience in varying degrees. It is no longer presumed that the bishop or the priest has to be 'in the chair' at every meeting in which he takes part. This means that the clergy are free to play their proper role, to inspire and persuade others on important *religious* issues rather than getting involved in the struggles about authority which are often the lot of the chairperson.

Parallel to these structural changes – and equally important – are changes in attitude which can be brought about by widespread use of the psycho-social method. Clergy find that it is relatively easy to let go of the undue power which they had in the past. They no longer feel so threatened by fear of what might go wrong if they were to relinquish the right to have the first and last word on every issue. They are no longer so reluctant to attend meetings, for they know by experience that planning sessions can be fruitful and even enjoyable. Lay people, having had the experience of being asked for their views and really being listened to, find that they can let go of the hurt and anger evoked by bad episodes in the past. The good atmosphere in meetings leads to a lessening of the aggressive or passive-aggressive behaviour which often mars meetings. There is a growth of trust all round and church meetings of all kinds, instead of being a burden, often become an occasion where those involved share their faith with each other at a deep level.

Many Christians today experience themselves as trapped in very clericalised parishes; and they are crying out for change. They believe that the solution has to begin with a major reform at the highest level of the church. But the danger is that while pining for such major changes they may neglect the opportunities they have at present to foster a truly respectful and participatory approach in the parishes and local projects where they are working. If, on the other hand, they succeed in turning these agencies at the grassroots level into truly effective vehicles of evangelization, then there is some hope that this may lead on to the changes at the 'higher' level which are also required.

The great pioneer church people and missionaries of the past used schools and hospitals to carry the Christian value-system into the fabric of daily life. Those who today wish to follow in their footsteps have available to them a vehicle of evangelization which can be just as effective. The psycho-social method can bring basic Christian values into all aspects of human development work and can transform the institutional church itself so that it gives more effective witness to the good news of Jesus Christ.

QUESTIONS FOR REFLECTION

1. What, in your experience, has been the most effective 'carrier' of Christian values in society?
2. Do you see a need for the church in your area to put emphasis on different 'vehicles' now than in the past? If so, where should the new focus be?

CHAPTER 15

Missionaries and Development Workers

Most missionaries are aware that if they are looking for help from support agencies they need to make it clear whether their project is to be presented as one of 'evangelization' or one of 'development'. For there are different sources of funding for these different kinds of projects. 'Evangelization projects' are supported by specialised agencies such as the 'Pontifical Works' based in the Vatican and the well-known German agency *Missio*. 'Development projects' are supported by a very wide range of agencies. Many of these are church agencies, such as Christian Aid, CRS, Cafod, SCIAF, *Trócaire*, Australian Catholic Relief, and *Misereor*. Yet they, like their secular counterparts (such as Oxfam and Concern), make strenuous efforts to ensure that projects they support are not 'pastoral' activities (such as building a church or training catechists) of their own church or any other church.

Nevertheless, the distinction between the two kinds of project is not at all as clear as it seems at first sight. Some years ago I was a member of the Projects Committee of a well-known development agency. Our task was to look at the various project proposals which came in from 'developing countries' and decide whether they fitted into the category of 'good development' as specified in the agency's guidelines. These guidelines made it very clear that 'pastoral projects' could not be considered. One project that came before our committee was from Brazil. It was a proposal to design a set of Stations of the Cross (scenes from the passion and death of Jesus). One might have thought that this would be seen as 'evangelization' rather than 'development'. But in fact the projects staff and the members of the committee were quite enthused about it and were very willing to support it. This was because they knew from the project description, and from personal knowledge of the priest who sent it in, that it would promote the liberation of the local people. It would link the passion of Jesus with the sufferings of the poor in that slum parish in Brazil and would help to animate the people to struggle against poverty and injustice. So it was seen as authentic human development.

A few years earlier I was on the staff of an educational institute in Africa which focused on the moral development of teachers. The participants included Muslims as well as Christians of many different denominations. Clearly, this was a development project. Yet it was partially supported by one of the Roman agencies concerned with evangelization.

These two examples indicate that there can be a considerable overlap between 'development projects' and 'evangelization projects'. The meaning of both of these words is rather fluid. If 'evangelization' is taken in the broadest sense it includes human development of all kinds. On the other hand, if 'development' is taken in a wide sense it can include liberation projects centred on the gospel.

Questioning Development

There is a very inadequate concept of development which is commonly adopted by Western governments and intergovernmental agencies like the International Monetary Fund. They are inclined to limit development to purely *economic* development, and effectively reduce that in turn to economic *growth;* and they would assume that evangelization means simply proselytisation.

I have written quite extensively about the notion of development in four books which are still in print so I will be quite brief in what I say here about this topic.[1] Firstly, the whole notion of 'development' is a relatively new idea. It came to the fore with the dramatic success of the Marshall Plan after World War II, when the USA put up large amounts of money in grants and in investment to help the war-devastated countries of Europe get back on their feet again. This was taken as a model for how the so-called underdeveloped countries could overcome poverty. Before long the churches came to adopt the concept of development. They recognised that charity is not enough, that there has to be real human development. A theology of development began to emerge. It is against this background that the major church development agencies came into existence.

A crucial point that was learned early on by most people associated with church-sponsored development agencies is that genuine development programmes are about *people* rather than about *projects*. The results which a development agency should look for are not big buildings but people who have learned to believe in themselves and have gained the skills of planning and working together to overcome poverty and injustice. Sadly, the international development agencies such as the World Bank have been much slower in learning this lesson.

A further point that the more progressive church-sponsored development agencies now take for granted is that poverty is not just an *absence*, a state of not having yet learned how to be efficient and successful. It is *created*, caused by the way the wealthy and powerful have used their power to take advantage of the weak. So almost invariably there has to be a component or dimension of *liberation* built into any authentic development programme. In Latin America the more progressive social scientists became extremely sceptical of the whole idea of 'development'. They saw that what was being presented as development was a form of neo-colonialism. The progressive theologians accepted this view and came to believe that what was required was not a theology of development but a theology of liberation. On the other hand, in most African countries (apart from South Africa) church people looked much more favourably on the theology of development and my impression is that they are still rather scared of the word 'liberation'.

The truth is that quite a lot of what goes on under the name of 'development' is in fact exploitation of people or of the earth. For instance, many so-called 'development projects' in poor countries have involved transnational corporations taking over enormous tracts of the best land from the local peasants – land which the peasants needed for subsistence farming. The displaced farmers and their families are forced to move to the cities or to work on the estates as seasonal labourers at exploitative wages. For the poor in these countries the quality of life has become immeasurably worse than it was in the past.

Furthermore, workers are frequently replaced by high-tech machines, in the name of 'development'. It is then left to the wider community to bear the cost of the resulting unemployment. Again, a lot of Western-sponsored 'development' in poor countries involves digging up unduly large quantities of irreplaceable raw materials such as copper or oil. This over-production leads to competition between the poor countries and a drastic fall in the price of these valuable materials.

The language of 'development' can also be deceptive. By speaking of the *production* of oil or copper, the development lobby disguises the fact that the oil and mining corporations are not really *producing* these products but are actually *consuming* them – and in doing so could be said to be stealing resources from future generations. Indeed, a lot of so-called 'development' is leaving to future generations a legacy of nuclear waste and depleted resources.

All this indicates that we need to take a very critical look at what is presented as 'development'. Part of the task of the church – and of other 'prophetic' agencies – is to challenge 'development workers' to look again at the work they are doing, to decide whether it truly merits the title 'development'. Against the gross over-simplification which reduces development to economic growth it is important to insist that human development properly understood must take account of social, political and cultural development. This means that authentic development includes spiritual values of all kinds.

A Useful Distinction

Some people would argue that the distinction between 'evangelization' and 'development' is a Western notion which has little relevance in other cultures. This claim contains some truth but I do not fully accept it. My belief is that despite the frequent distortions and misunderstandings (or because of them) it is still useful to make a distinction between evangelization and development – but more from the point of view of the funding agencies than from that of the recipients. When Christians are asked to donate money for worthy causes, it is important that they recognise the difference between, on the one hand, evangelization projects such as support for 'young churches' or for promoting the Christian vision and, on the other hand, development projects such as helping those who are struggling to defend human rights or helping the poor to help themselves.

If we fail to distinguish between evangelization projects and development projects there is a danger that we may use the wrong criteria in choosing which to respond favourably to. But why should there be different criteria for the two kinds of project? The easiest way to answer this question is to take two simple examples. Suppose there are thousands of starving refugees who have been displaced by a war or an earthquake. It would be wrong to support a project designed to feed only the Catholic refugees (or only the Protestants) – or designed to help them feed themselves; that would be a misguided approach to *development*. But, on the other hand, suppose there are Muslims and Christians in a given area; there is nothing invidious about supporting an *evangelization* project designed to provide Bibles for the Christians.

Development Workers and Missionaries

Within the past generation, many committed lay Christians – medical people, teachers and other professionals – have gone to work in the so-called 'Third World'. The majority of these good people see themselves as 'development workers'. They do not think of themselves as doing missionary work – and they generally feel uncomfortable or even angry if they are named as missionaries. Yet they may well be doing work which is more or less identical to what some missionaries are doing – especially the second category of missionary to which I referred in Chapter 5 above, namely, those whose focus is not so much on building up the church as on promoting fundamental 'reign of God values' such as justice, empowerment, and ecological sensitivity.

In order to clarify the relationship between missionaries and development workers I want to locate both groups within the context of an overall framework of the different categories of people who go to work in 'the developing world' (as it is euphemistically called). As I see it, such people can be located somewhere on the following spectrum:

Commercial people	InterGov Dev e.g World Bank	Secular NGO Dev & relief Oxfam, Goal, Concern	Christian-inspired Devel & relief Trócaire, CRS, Christian Aid	Christian witness e.g. literacy, AIDS	Official Church e.g. catechists

The three categories at the left end of this spectrum are secular. The two categories at the right end of the spectrum should be counted as Christian missionaries. Those who come third from the right are not to be seen as missionaries, even though they are working for development agencies which are inspired by Christian motivation. This is not to cast any aspersions on the work of the many deeply committed Christians who operate under the auspices of Christian development agencies. It is simply a matter of respecting their particular motivation and the way they see themselves and their work.

Those who work for secular agencies such as Oxfam may or may not be motivated to do so by Christian faith; but their personal motivation is not of any direct concern to the agency under whose auspices they are working. On the other hand, those who work for Christian-inspired development agencies, such as CRS, *Trócaire*, Cafod, SCIAF, or ACR, have to acknowledge that their agency is part of the church's outreach; and their own work is part of that. They are to be seen as 'development workers' whose work is not strictly missionary but is part of the church's commitment to the relief of suffering, the promotion of human development, and the safeguarding of human rights in the world.

Christian 'development workers' know that there are times when their credibility would be compromised if they were identified as missionaries. Suppose, for instance, the Irish church agency *Trócaire*, or Australian Catholic Relief, undertake development work in Pakistan, or China, or Iran. Those who come may be involved in a humanitarian project such as helping refugees, or a development project such as literacy, or a justice project such as defending the fundamental human rights of prisoners. If they identify themselves as missionaries, the government or the local people may no longer trust them. There may be a suspicion that they have an ulterior motive in the work they are doing – that their ultimate purpose is to make converts. Furthermore, by refusing to think of themselves as missionaries they themselves become more clear about their own motives; and this may help them to be more respectful of the beliefs and values of the people among whom they are working.

Does this imply that those who *do* identify themselves a missionaries have an ulterior motive? Does it suggest that they are using their development work to 'soften people up' so that some may eventually become 'converts'? Not at all – or at least not if they really understand what missionary work is about. For a crucial part of missionary work is a genuine and sensitive dialogue with the beliefs of the local people; and this rules out such a disrespectful attitude. But, having said that, I must add at once that these missionaries may see the development work they are doing as a 'vehicle of evangelization', as described in the previous chapter.

Overlapping

Now that I have tried to clarify the difference between Christian-inspired development workers and missionaries, I have to acknowledge that the boundary can at times be somewhat fuzzy. Development workers may in practice be doing work that is a more or less identical to the work of quite a lot of those who call themselves missionaries. At times the only obvious difference may be whether or not the people involved are willing to call themselves missionaries. But behind that there is often a subtle but important difference in *motivation* and *purpose*.

Christian development workers are likely to be inspired or motivated by Christian compassion or the Christian emphasis on justice; and the purpose of their work is to bring that justice and compassion into the situation where they are working. The missionary may be inspired in just the same way. The Christian development worker and the Christian missionary both see their work in the context of a broader perspective. At the front or back of the Christian's mind lies an image of an ideal world – the world as God wants it to be. All of the work of the missionary and of the Christian development worker fits into that pattern. But at this point we can locate the difference between the two.

The explicit, overt purpose of the missionary is to promote the reign of God and to give witness to fundamental Christian values. The development worker may have the same Christian vision; but this ideal vision is not brought explicitly into the public arena. The agency which employs the development workers – and the development workers themselves – freely acknowledge that they are acting on the basis of the Christian commitment to justice and concern for the poor. They even invite others to share their commitment to these values. But they do not invite the *beneficiaries* of their development work to share the good news and the vision which for the Christian is the ultimate basis for these values.

There is a further complication which has to be taken into account. It frequently happens that those missionaries whose focus is on 'reign of God' values receive funding as development workers! Their decision to apply for such funding is a purely pragmatic one. Governments are willing to fund development workers but they would not be willing to fund people who said their work was evangelization. Therefore many lay missionaries, who would otherwise find it almost impossible to get funding, apply for support for the development work they are doing. There is nothing dishonest or underhand about the decision of these missionaries to present themselves to governmental funding agencies as development workers. For what they are engaged in is genuine and respectful development work. The funding agencies are not concerned that these people *also* see themselves as missionaries – provided they are not using their development work to put pressure on people to become Christians.

Focus on Values
Those who are engaged in development work generally wish to adopt a pluralist approach. They want their agricultural programmes, their literacy work, their advocacy of human rights, etc, to be of benefit not just to the local Christian community but also to people of other faiths or none. At this point it may be helpful to recall the distinction I made on page 86 above between four major aspects of evangelization, four categories in which the Christian way of life is embodied and passed on – story/truths, values, rituals, and institutions. It could be said that those who engage in an integral evangelization will necessarily be concerned with all four of these aspects of the faith. On the other hand, those who focus their attention on the human development of the community are concerned mainly with the area of *values*. For instance, they may wish to ensure that all members of the community (not just the Christians) have the right to political freedom, access to meaningful work, etc. Such values are compatible with a wide variety of different systems of belief and ritual (Muslim, Catholic, Protestant, etc).

Genuine human development presupposes a set of values (such as the dignity of the human person and the importance of participation) that lie at the heart of Christianity. However, these values are not exclusive to the Christian faith since they are shared by people of other beliefs. Neither are they an exhaustive or comprehensive expression of Christianity; there are fundamental Christian beliefs (e.g. the centrality of Jesus and his teaching on forgiveness) which cannot be brought explicitly into development work in a pluralist context. These are aspects of integral *evangelization* which are not included in the usual understanding of integral human *development*.

This means that, from the point of view of a missionary,

commitment to human development in a pluralist society is just one aspect of integral evangelization. It still leaves room for pastoral activity which links concern for fundamental ethical values with commitment to Christian truths, rituals and institutions. Acceptance of this distinction provides a basis for mutual respect and co-operation between those engaged in pastoral activity and those whose main focus is development work.

Restricted Concept of Evangelization
I referred above to simplistic notions of development and evangelization held by many policy-makers and planners in Western governments and inter-governmental agencies. I must now add that there are equally simplistic concepts of evangelization and development put forward by some senior church people. They speak as though evangelization were concerned with purely spiritual matters while development concerns temporal or material or earthly affairs. This involves ignoring or playing down the 'worldly' aspects of evangelization and the more spiritual aspects of human development. To make things worse, it often leads on to a very distorted and damaging understanding of evangelization, namely, a restriction of this term, in practice, to clerically controlled pastoral projects such as the building of churches or the training of priests and catechists.

At this point we touch on painful misunderstandings and tensions which sometimes arise between missionaries and development workers. I would say that a more careful analysis would show that the tension is not really between missionaries as such and development workers. It is between, on one side, a particular category of missionary – namely, those whose primary focus is on establishing the institutions of the church – and, on the other side, development workers and those missionaries who are more directly concerned with promoting 'reign of God values'. In fact the tension revolves around the issue of the relative importance of 'pastoral work'.

Many missionary priests and a growing number of Sisters, Brothers and full-time lay church workers concentrate their attention on pastoral activities such as building up and servicing a Christian community, through the provision of prayers services, celebration of sacraments, training of catechists, building churches etc. They, rightly, see this work as 'evangelization'. But, in my experience, some of them go further by *restricting* the use of the word 'evangelization' to such pastoral activities. They do not recognise the other category of missionary activity (promoting 'reign of God values') as 'evangelization'; they see it rather as 'development work'. From their point of view, 'development work', while good in itself, is of secondary importance; and this applies whether such development work is being carried out by people who call themselves 'development workers' or by people who call themselves 'missionaries'.

Funding
A good deal of the tension springs from a resentment felt by some missionaries engaged in pastoral work. They see lots of money coming from abroad to support 'development projects'. But they often find it difficult to get support for the more traditional church activities in which they are engaged. They cannot understand why they should be excluded from access to such funds for their own work which they consider to be perhaps more important and urgent – and more central to Christianity. So they wonder if there is a prejudice against 'evangelization'.

There is no easy way out of this quagmire of misunderstanding. All I can offer here are a few considerations that may carry some weight if people can be persuaded to broaden their understanding of both 'evangelization' and 'development'. A first point is that those who are unable to get access to outside funding may find some consolation in the thought that dependence on such help can be counter-productive in the long run. Of course it is convenient not to have to rely on the slow and difficult work of raising money locally. But most missionaries know from their own experience that heavy reliance on outside help makes it almost impossible to achieve effective local commitment. Dependence of this kind is the greatest single obstacle to genuine human development as well as to really effective evangelization. For this reason the slow building up of a local self-reliant Christian community, and the gradual formation of local leaders to full participation in decision-making in the life of the church, may be a more authentic contribution to both evangelization and development than high-profile 'development projects', or grandiose church buildings, which remain dependent on outside resources. It is no coincidence that the Swahili word for 'useless' is *'bure'*, a word which literally means 'for nothing'; anything got for nothing is assumed to be of no value.

Furthermore, it should be acknowledged that one of the reasons why money is brought in from outside to support specific 'development projects' is because most of the available local sources of church funding are already tied up in supporting *pastoral* projects such as building churches and support of the local clergy. This is not a healthy situation for a young church to be in. One way to rectify the balance would be for the clergy to allow wider participation in the control and use of local finances. Over a period of time this could lead to more support at local level for both pastoral and developmental programmes.

Links between Evangelization and Development
There is a close link between evangelization and human development, at the level of method and approach. Those who are engaged in genuine development have worked out a wide range of techniques, e.g. ways of enabling a group to agree on a common vision, ways of helping them to sort out their priorities and reach consensus about their goals and plans, ways of doing a social analysis, and methods of evaluating their work. As I pointed out in the previous chapter on 'Missionary Strategy', these techniques are very useful, even necessary, for those who are engaged in pastoral activity or religious education.

This means that there is a very considerable degree of overlap between pastoral and developmental work; and each can benefit greatly from the other. In fact the use of human development techniques has proved enormously helpful to those whose aim is to build up basic Christian communities, or to foster the emergence of deeply committed parish councils and committees. Without the use of such methods there is a very real danger that clergy or other leaders will take on too much and will not allow themselves to be challenged to share power with others.

Even today, quite a lot of missionaries do not have much familiarity with these empowerment skills. One aspect of the renewal work which they undertake should be to provide them with a repertoire of techniques to promote collaboration and participation both in the church and in the local community. Renewal programmes should also provide a more theoretical and theological component to help missionaries have a clearer understanding of the different aspects of evangelization and of what genuine development involves. This may help to overcome some of the misunderstandings of the past. It should also provide a basis for mutual appreciation by missionaries and development workers of each other's aims and purposes and should help both groups to find more fruitful ways of moving forward together.

QUESTIONS FOR REFLECTION

1. How would you explain to young people in your home country the difference between missionary work and development work?
2. Where does liberation come in? Do you see it as an aspect of evangelization, or of development, or of both?

CHAPTER 16

Moving On or Staying On

Introduction

Missionary activity is not primarily a matter of getting more and more people into the church. As I explained in chapter 12 on 'The Purpose of Mission', it has two aspects: it aims to witness to fundamental Christian values in a milieu where the Christian faith is not yet inserted; and it is concerned with establishing a self-reliant young church. By its nature, then, missionary activity is time-conditioned; in normal circumstances it should not continue indefinitely. Since its purpose is to push back the frontier, there should come a time when this has been achieved. At that point the missionaries would expect to hand over to others, while they themselves move on to new frontiers.

This means that those who engage in work that is on a missionary frontier generally have to face up at some point to the question whether their work in this particular area or sphere of activity has been in some sense 'completed'. Is it time for them to move on? This issue of 'moving on' versus 'staying on' lies at the heart of the missionary vocation. In this chapter I shall deal with the question as it arises for *foreign* missionaries. But the same issue arises in relation to any project that can be called missionary, whether it be the work of a foreign missionary working far from home or whether the frontier is defined, not geographically, but in social or religious terms; so what I am saying requires very little adaptation to make it apply to other missionary frontiers.

The question of moving on has to be addressed from two distinct points of view – that of the local church and that of the missionary. I shall consider each of these in turn.

SECTION I: FROM THE POINT OF VIEW OF THE LOCAL CHURCH

The Acts of the Apostles suggests that, in the very early church, missionaries like St Paul did not feel it necessary to stay a long time in any one area; they moved on quite quickly to new frontiers. In recent centuries, however, it became common for missionaries to commit themselves for life to a particular region. They generally chose some central town as a base and moved out from there in an ever-widening circle. Only rarely did they think of up-rooting themselves completely to move to an entirely different mission area. This made sense in a period when travel was far more difficult than it is today. But perhaps a more fundamental reason why they could not follow the example is St Paul is that the church today is far more institutionalised than it was in time of the first Christians; so it takes much longer to initiate people into it. Without making any judgement on the past, I want to suggest that the model used a hundred years ago is not the best model for today. It is better that, in coming to any given area, or to any 'frontier' project, missionaries should presume that their commitment there will be for a *significant* but *limited* duration.

Missionaries are not living up to their vocation if they do not settle and become rooted in the area or sphere of activity in which they have chosen to work. If their time-commitment is only a couple of years, there will be little incentive for them to devote an adequate period of time to learning the local language, to becoming really familiar with the culture, and to developing close friendships with the local people. On the other hand, if their time-commitment is open-ended, the missionaries are in danger of building up a church which is unduly dependent on them and which is very slow in becoming self-reliant. So the attitude of mind and heart with which the missionary becomes rooted is very different to that of an emigrant. In coming to live and work on a 'frontier', missionaries should have at the back of their minds the assumption that their call to settle there will at some stage give way to a call to move on, leaving behind a community which no longer needs them.

Missionaries who do not keep this in mind are in danger of seriously undermining the value of their own work, by failing to foster a healthy self-reliance in the local Christian community. I think that some Catholic missionary societies and congregations of priests have, in the past, failed to distinguish clearly between a life-long commitment to mission and a life-long commitment to a *particular* mission. This also happened, but to a lesser extent, among missionary Sisters and Brothers and among Protestant missionaries. As a result, many missionary priests tended to act as though they were settled diocesan priests in the area to which they came; and quite a number of life-long missionary Sisters and Brothers never thought seriously of moving to a different frontier area. In this way they may have lost some of their missionary edge. So it is particularly important that all of these professional missionaries be invited to keep on their agenda the issue of whether they are still working on a truly missionary frontier.

Viability

When missionaries begin to reflect on whether it is time for them to move on, there is a danger that they will see the question mainly in terms of the gaps they would leave behind. How many mission stations would have to be closed down or amalgamated with others? In the mission school or hospital how would the local staff cope without the presence of experienced missionaries? Of course these are important questions; but if we do not set them in the context of more fundamental issues it is unlikely that we will ever find a time that is right for the foreign missionaries to move on.

The growth of a local church cannot be seen simply in terms of linear expansion – greater numbers of Christians, more outstations, and expanding schools, healthcentres, and development programmes. The church is a living entity which comes to birth in a particular area. We must take seriously this metaphor of birth. So the crucial issue is whether or not the local church is *viable*. Is the Christian community in this area both able and willing to function independently without relying on outside help?

There are missionary churches which seem to be flourishing: they have lots of committed expatriate and local personnel who are engaged in all kinds of valuable work. But there comes a disruption – perhaps as a result of a political upheaval – which forces the missionaries to leave; and within a short time the church runs down. This shows that it was not really viable – it was unduly dependent on the foreign missionaries to keep it alive. On the other hand, there have been many situations where war or a political crisis forced the foreign missionaries to depart hastily and long before they or the local church leaders would have thought they should go. Yet, despite the crisis – and perhaps even because of it – the local church grew from strength to strength. (Obvious examples which spring to mind are the flourishing of the church in India after new foreign missionaries were barred, and the remarkable expansion of the church in the Igbo-speaking parts of Nigeria after most of their expatriate missionaries had to leave.)

This helps us to realise that, in the founding of a young church, at some stage there has to be the risk of birth. The infant has to emerge into a harsh world which is quite life-threatening and which involves an interruption of the progress which has been taking place up to that time. We cannot expect a totally smooth transition of a young church from being in a state of dependence on foreign missionaries to independence and self-reliance. It is not enough for the missionaries to ensure that a local bishop is installed and to hand over responsibility for some other key ecclesiastical positions. That does not yet constitute the birth of a self-reliant young church. The turning point is rather when the local community and its leadership spontaneously feel that the church is theirs, that they are responsible for the direction it takes, and that they are not going to 'pass the buck' to foreign missionaries.

Letting Go

The right time for the missionary to move on has to be judged not so much in terms of statistics as in terms of the psychological state of the young church. It is partly a question of whether foreign missionaries are holding on to leadership roles which could be filled by locals – in parishes, schools, hospitals or other projects. But even more important is the *manner* or *style* of their presence. Do local church leaders perceive them as still 'breathing down their necks', watching their every move in a judgmental way, or even watching over them in a motherly way, fearful lest they fail? The missionaries have to learn to let go ultimate responsibility quite some time before they actually leave the young church.

This lesson is likely to be painful. How painful it will be depends on the temperament and sensitivity of the missionaries and of those who are taking over responsibility. Some time ago I

devoted several years to setting up a leadership training programme in West Africa. In this task I was part of a team made up
of some foreign missionaries and some local church people.
About three years after the programme began, we were engaged
one day in one of our regular planning sessions. An African
woman challenged me quite strongly in regard to what had
seemed to me to be a rather minor proposal I was making. I was
very hurt that she seemed to misunderstand me. But, fortunately,
the depth of feeling in her voice gave me a clue that there was
more at stake than the particular topic under discussion.

I realised that the fundamental question was: whose voice
should carry the most weight, whose ideas should be most
favoured. I was being challenged to let go of the privileged
weight which had been accorded to my views. For me it was a
moment of truth, a moment of great pain but of great grace. An
unusual and almost instantaneous change took place within me:
my sense of hurt was transformed into a very deep joy – though
the joy still contained a good deal of pain. I was joyful that the
woman who was challenging me had come into her strength,
that she felt able to claim the major responsibility in our programme for herself and the other local people involved. My joy
was deepened by the fact that she had chosen her time well and
had issued her challenge respectfully and with dignity. I was
truly happy to yield.

There is no doubt in my mind that this was a turning-point in
the development of the programme – the moment when effective
leadership changed hands, even though we continued as before
to make decisions in a collegial way. It was two or three years
later before I actually left the area; but from that moment I felt
free to go when the time was right. I knew I was still wanted and
appreciated. I would be missed when I left, and I would leave a
gap that might not be filled for some time. But the local leaders'
sense of dependence had been broken, at least in principle. For
my part, I had to relinquish whatever unconscious or half-conscious sense of 'ownership' of the programme I had felt up to
that point.

Hand-over Difficulties
Reflection on this experience makes me very aware of two
problems which generally arise in relation to the handing over
of responsibility by foreign missionaries to local leaders – the

problem of *ownership* of projects by one person and the problem
of the *qualifications* of those who are available to take over. The
programme which I have just referred to was untypical in relation to both of these issues. Firstly, the responsibility had been
shared from the very beginning; and our decisions had always
been taken jointly. In this it was quite different from very many
church projects which are initiated by one person and effectively
'owned' by this founding person. Once a project is started in this
way it is exceptionally difficult for the founder to hand over
responsibility. Even if the founding person manages to avoid
the temptation to cling on to control, it is still very hard to get
somebody else to take on responsibility for the project. So the
founder is quite likely to feel obliged to stay in charge longer
than he or she would have wished – and then eventually to hand
over to an unsuitable person.

The only way I know to avoid this difficulty is to ensure from
the outset that the project is an embodiment of the vision of *several* people; in this way the responsibility will be shared from the
start. In this situation the founding group can arrange that they
be replaced one by one over a period of time. This works well,
provided that at regular intervals the leaders and other 'stake-
holders' re-define the vision or purpose of the project. In this
're-visioning' process the newcomers who replace those who
have left will have an opportunity to share their ideals for the
project and their views about how to carry it through. This allows
them to 'buy into' the psychological ownership of the project.

Our programme was also unusual in church circles in relation to the question of qualifications. It was not controlled by
clergy. Some members of the leadership group were priests but
these did not seek – and were not given – any special authority
in comparison with the other men and women who founded the
programme. It was accepted from the beginning that when any
of the leaders was relinquishing a position of responsibility this
could be given to any other suitable person. This policy was in
sharp contrast to what generally happens when foreign missionaries set out to hand over responsibility of a project to local people. Quite commonly, the most important issue is the *official
qualifications* of those who are taking over rather than their *real
leadership potential*. The new matron, the new school principal,
the new accountant – all must have paper qualifications; and –
perhaps most starkly – ordained ministers can only be replaced

by other ordained ministers. This commitment ties the young church into a very elaborate system, designed according to Western standards, a system which leaves the local church in a state of dependence for years and years.

It may be argued that this long state of dependence on outside leadership is necessary to ensure that a well-educated and responsible leadership takes over. But the question is, what constitutes an appropriate education? Most of the professions – and the clerical profession perhaps most of all – tend to treat candidates as though their previous experiences were more or less irrelevant. In sharp contrast to this, in our leadership training programme we found that many participants already had a gift for leadership and a variety of experiences in exercising responsibility. So the amount of *specific* training they required was relatively small; it could be covered in a series of workshops spread over two or three years. In other words, the secret of success was to recognise the gifts which people had before ever they entered into this particular training programme.

St Paul was able to recognise the leadership potential of many of his converts. In preparing them to take over leadership in the Christian community he could build on all the knowledge and experience they already had. But the churches today are much more rigidly structured, especially in regard to the conditions that are set for those who are called to be its official leaders. So long as they remain trapped within a rigid clericalist system there is no easy solution to the problem of the handing over of leadership by missionaries to local counterparts.

The difficulties can, however, be greatly lessened if the missionaries establish a pattern of shared leadership from the very beginning – and especially if responsibility is shared with local leaders whose authority comes from their acceptance by the local community rather than from any professional qualification. Then, when the time comes for the expatriates who have held professional positions to be replaced by local professionals, a considerable degree of authority can still remain in the hands of the non-professional leaders of the local community. A really effective sharing of leadership with local non-professional people does not happen spontaneously. There is need for a fairly elaborate set of techniques to ensure that it works smoothly. The 'psycho-social method' to which I referred in Chapter 14 provides training in such methods. In my book, *Integral Spirituality*,

I have spelled out some techniques that can be used to build a common vision and bring about effective joint planning.[1]

Discerning the Right Time
It is only natural that missionary institutes and individual missionaries should look for some general guidelines to help them decide when they ought to move on. But no guidelines can relieve them of the responsibility of making a careful discernment in each particular situation. The best they can hope for is to have some criteria on which they can base their judgement. Missionary institutes sometimes assume that they should apply the criteria which they used for judging whether or not they ought to work in a particular area in the first place. For instance, they may conclude that it is time for them to move on if they find that the area in which they are working is no longer one of those 'situations where the need is most urgent' or 'where there are no others to announce the gospel'.[2]

This is helpful, but I think it does not take sufficient account of the difference between a missionary agency deciding whether or not to come to an area in the first place and the same agency deciding many years later whether the time has come for them to move on from an area to which some of their members may have devoted half a lifetime. In this latter situation there is need to take far more account of the psychological factors referred to above. Suppose it happens that the local church is well-developed in terms of personnel and institutions but there remains serious doubt about its capacity or willingness to be self-reliant in relation to management and resources of personnel and finance; in that situation it would be irresponsible of the missionaries to pull out immediately. The challenge faced by that church's leadership – and especially by expatriate missionaries – is that of taking radical action to break down as quickly as possible the relationship of dependence on outside help that has developed in it. This may involve scaling down or even abandoning various projects which expand the numbers and influence of the church in the area but which foster continued dependence on foreign missionaries.

One of the strongest arguments in favour of missionaries moving on is the fact that, so long as they remain, the local church leaders will find it almost impossible to rid themselves of a certain crippling ambivalence in their attitudes towards them.

On the one hand, they will appreciate the good work done by the foreign missionaries and will feel indebted to them. However, the local church leaders may at the same time have a certain sense of being watched and judged by the missionaries. Naturally, this gives rise to some degree of resentment.

Ambivalence of this kind often arises between people of two different races or cultures – above all when there is a legacy of past racism which led those who belonged to one of the groups to imagine that they were superior to the others. Warm friendships may develop between foreign missionaries and local church leaders, but the equality of friendship is constantly threatened by the legacy of the former unequal relationship. It often happens that local church leaders feel they can really be themselves only when the missionaries have moved on.

However, it occasionally happens that, some years after this decisive break, it is possible for a small number of missionaries to return – not, of course, in a rescuing role but in a much more limited capacity. At that point they are far less likely to be perceived as a threat by local leaders. When foreign missionaries come back in a certain 'guest' capacity there is less chance that they will be an inhibiting factor in the development of the self-confidence and self-reliance of the local church.

A Missionary Thrust

At this point we need to distinguish between an authentic self-reliance and an entirely wrong kind of self-sufficiency which can be found in many sects. The members of a sect are often content to be a small minority within society, provided they have the resources to service their own members and to look for new converts who will join the sect one by one. This attitude contrasts sharply with the missionary sense of a Christian community which experiences itself as *church* rather than as a *sect*. In a church community the numbers may still be relatively small but there is a real commitment to *transform society* as a whole, to help bring about the reign of God. For such a church to be self-reliant in the authentic sense is to be able, from its own resources, to maintain this thrust outward to the wider society, this insertion in the real world, rather than existing in its own narrow ghetto.

One aspect of the outward thrust is a commitment to geographical and numerical expansion. A living church will be characterised by a psychology of growth. This will normally find expression in the opening of new mission out-stations and the founding of new basic communities. If this expansion comes to a halt there is a real danger that the church in that area will begin to die. The first symptom of that slow death is the loss of a missionary spirit. There are many formerly 'missionary' areas where all of the mainline churches have tacitly settled for their present limited 'slice of the cake'. They provide services for their members but they are not fired by any strong sense of mission towards the un-evangelized villages all around them – or, in urban areas, towards the sprawling slums that have sprung up around the fringes of the cities. In these situations a vital element is missing from the life of the church. There is need for some local or expatriate people who, fired by missionary zeal, enable this church to move out again to the frontiers.

Outreach to the remote villages or to needy urban settlements in the area is only one aspect of the vibrant missionary drive which should mark a church which has become truly viable. Such a Church must also have a wider missionary thrust. This in turn takes two forms – *foreign* mission and *global* mission.

Foreign mission, as the name implies, means accepting some responsibility for the evangelization of peoples in distant lands. Such a commitment cannot wait until the task of evangelization is more or less complete on the 'home' scene. For no matter how needy the particular church may be, it is very likely that there is some other area in still greater need. Perhaps an even more important consideration is that any community which is to be truly Christian, truly church, must have a universal vision and concern; and it must make this concrete through an outreach 'to the nations' *(ad gentes)*, which will lead on to links with Christian communities in other parts of the world.

One of the most effective ways for a young church to grow in self-confidence is to take on a foreign missionary commitment. The Christian community will be invigorated by its sense of pride in the courage of the men and women who volunteer to go abroad. Their zeal and enthusiasm is catching; it brings new life to the Christian communities from which they have come. The sense of being responsible for evangelizing people in far away places helps the local church to become truly self-reliant.

Missionaries from the West are aware that many of the countries where they have been working are facing a growing impoverishment. This leads them to wonder whether it will ever

be possible to break the sense of dependence on help from overseas which has developed in the churches there. But it is well to
remember that the great surge of missionary enthusiasm which
arose in countries like Ireland early in this century came at a
time when most of the people there were very poor. When they
sent out missionaries to every corner of the globe it was not out
of any sense that they had already solved their own economic
and political difficulties. On the contrary, the departure of the
missionaries played an important role in the development of a
sense of self-confidence not only in the church but even in the
nation. There are indications that something similar is happening
in the young churches of Asia, Africa, Latin America and the
Pacific.

Global Mission
I have suggested that if a young church is to avoid becoming a
mere sect it needs to develop a commitment to foreign mission
and to global mission. The former term is well-known but the
term 'global mission' is less familiar. I have already employed
this term in Chapter 13 on 'New Frontiers' (page 208 above). I
use it to mean a commitment to certain fundamental values
which are vital to the wellbeing of society and of the earth as a
whole. The followers of Jesus are called to share his interests and
his work – the bringing of life and good news to all the peoples
of the earth. In our world today this implies commitment to
human rights on a global scale, as well as engagement in the
development of an equitable political-economic world order
and the protection of the patterns of the natural world and the
integrity of creation.

   If church people neglect these values and focus their concern
mainly on 'churchy' matters like religious services and the gain-
ing of new converts, then they have missed the main point of
what it means to be Christian. In recent times the churches have
become less significant actors in the provision of educational
and health services in many countries. This gives rise to the danger that churches would turn in on themselves. The leaders
could become more concerned about their own power and status
than about what is taking place in society and in the world; and
the interest of the membership might become rather narrow and
'churchy'.

   In the young churches of 'the South' the diminishment of the

influence of the church in society has happened to coincide with
the departure of many of the missionaries. The missionaries
who remain have a particular obligation to do what they can to
ensure that the church remains outward-looking and that it
develops new ways of being an effective presence within society.
They ought to relinquish the roles of maintenance of church
structures which are often thrust upon them. They should instead
look for ways of moving the local church out to the frontiers. For
example some of them might devote themselves to promoting
ecumenism and dialogue between the religions. Others might
give the bulk of their time and energy to programmes concerned
with the care of the earth, or the protection of human rights, or
the empowerment of women, or the development of the local
culture of the area.

By devoting their final years in the young church to projects
which promote global values, the missionaries will be doing
what they can to ensure that what they leave behind is not a sect
but the church of Jesus Christ. However, in taking on any initiatives of this kind, missionaries must make a special effort to
ensure that the vision of the enterprise is not theirs alone. From
the outset, local people must be given a key role in articulating
the idea and in planning its implementation. Otherwise it will be
just another foreign imposition which will probably languish
and die soon after the missionaries depart.

SECTION II: FROM THE POINT OF VIEW OF THE MISSIONARIES AND MISSIONARY INSTITUTES

Clearly it is part of the missionary vocation to experience a certain tension between the call to stay with the people to whom
the missionary has been sent and the openness to a call to move
on. (I am not dealing here with the question of missionaries
leaving an area in order to retire but rather of moving to a new
area or sphere of mission.) In the previous section I have been
exploring aspects of this tension from the perspective of the
young church. In this section I want to look at it more from the
point of view of its effect on the missionaries themselves.

It is essential for missionaries in any particular area to keep a
balance. Undue emphasis on the call to move on would inhibit
them in making a generous and unrestricted commitment to the
people and the local church where they are working at present.

This could lead to an undermining of the morale of those missionaries who choose to stay on in the area. On the other hand, to give excessive weight to the need to stay on is to run the risk that the missionaries will become too rigid – unwilling to move on when the good of the church requires such a move, and perhaps even psychologically and spiritually *unable* to do so. The leaders of the young church could then be left in a state of frustration and/or of continual dependency.

It is obvious that many of the older generation of missionaries showed remarkable commitment in dedicating almost their whole lives to founding and serving a local church – and they should be warmly commended for this. However, missionaries today find themselves facing a much more fluid situation. Recent experience suggests that in the future many more missionaries will be called to uproot themselves from one missionary situation in order to immerse themselves in a new one.

The manner in which such a change takes place should allow for a three-way consultation between the missionaries on the ground, the leadership team of their missionary institute, and the leaders and members of the local Christian community. The ideal is that there be adequate time to reach full consensus about the proposed move. There should also be opportunity for the departing missionary and the local Christian community to show their appreciation of each other. This can be expressed in a ritual or liturgy of closure.

In practice, however, the withdrawal of missionaries has at times to take place in much less auspicious circumstances. Political upheaval or ecclesiastical dissension may lead to a hasty and undignified departure. Ill-health or some personal crisis may bring about a withdrawal which is inopportune and unwanted and may well be beset with dissatisfaction, hurt or a sense of failure. So it may happen that even those who are most determined to stay with their adopted people to the end may find that they are compelled to withdraw and go elsewhere: 'When you were young you put on your own belt and went where you wanted to go; but when you grow old you will stretch out your hands and somebody else will put a belt around you and take you where you would rather not go.' (Jn 21:18)

The experience of a wide variety of missionary groups has been that, in whatever form it comes, the call to move on to another missionary situation is often extremely demanding and painful. The disruption and pain are particularly serious if the transition takes place suddenly or in adverse circumstances – and especially if the missionary has not previously faced up to the reality or possibility of change.

The leaders or co-ordinators of the group of missionaries have the task of ensuring that the process of withdrawal and re-assignment is carried out in a respectful and sensitive manner. But the task cannot be left entirely in the hands of the authorities. The difficult transition can be greatly eased if the departing missionary receives full support and sympathy from companions and co-workers.

Transition Time

Having departed from the place where he or she has been working, the missionary needs to spend time in personal and pastoral renewal before moving on to a new appointment. Some time ago I facilitated a 'Think-In' on this topic by a group of the leaders of about twenty missionary institutions, under the auspices of the Irish Missionary Union. Those who took part were very insistent that uprooted missionaries should take time – and must be given time – to reflect on their experience before moving on. They need to integrate their experience by acknowledging what they have done and what has happened to them. It is important that they affirm their successes and grieve over the things that went wrong. They need especially to let in the pain of leaving their mission. The person who does not take time to experience the pain will be unable to let it go, and will find it almost impossible to settle down anywhere else.

The period after withdrawal from an area or sphere of mission is a time when many missionaries can benefit from counselling or therapy. This is especially true if the departure has been sudden or traumatic. Even where the move has been well planned and everything has gone according to plan, it may still be useful – or even necessary – for the missionary to get some counselling help. One reason is that this transition often co-incides with, or precipitates, a move by the missionary into the second major phase of adult life. There is a turning inward, a search for the deeper meaning of life and for a richer, more experiential spirituality. This is a time when women and men begin to explore the hitherto latent side of their personalities. It may well be a time when the missionary moves from an emphasis

on inspiring or empowering others to a new emphasis on what I
have called (in chapter 10 above) 'fulcrum power' or 'flowing
power' or even 'yielding power'. Such a change is very enriching but it can also be quite upsetting since it calls the missionary
to discover a new mode of being.

New Challenges

As the time set aside for reflection and integration draws to a
close, the missionary will move into a process of discernment
about the future. This may not be easy, even when the withdrawal from the previous mission was relatively painless. In
cases where the withdrawal was traumatic or difficult, those
responsible for the welfare of the missionary have a particularly
delicate task to perform. They must help this uprooted person to
see that a new apostolic opportunity is implicit in the present
painful circumstances. The disruption of the work in one area
can be understood as an invitation to face the challenge of
engaging in a fruitful ministry elsewhere. If this challenge is presented too quickly, the uprooted missionary is deprived of the
opportunity to grieve for the loss of a major part of his or her life.
On the other hand, too long a delay can be equally disastrous: a
sense of aimlessness can develop, sapping the life-energy and
leaving the displaced missionary open to serious depression.

At times, the call to move on is so painful that to answer it the
missionary may require a generosity that is more than could be
expected of a normal human person. Yet, by the power of God, a
lot of missionaries have been able to answer this call. Many of
those who have done so acknowledge that they have grown as a
result. Despite the pain of being uprooted, despite the sense of
helplessness they experienced in facing a new situation and having to learn a new language, they have found new life and energy
for themselves in the change. And they have brought this gift of
new life to the group with whom they work and to the new missionary situation which they have entered. It is clear that the
weakness and vulnerability which they have experienced have
become for them a source of grace and have given them a deeper
understanding of their missionary vocation.

On the other hand the disruption and pain of withdrawal –
especially forced withdrawal – can be so great that the person
may find it almost impossible to settle successfully into a new
missionary situation; this may be because of age or health or

temperament. Those who are in a position of leadership must do their best to help such people not to feel that they have failed or have been reduced to a marginal position in the whole missionary enterprise. Sometimes the best that can be done is to find such people congenial work in their own home area, while enabling them to keep in touch with their colleagues overseas.

The new theology of mission should reassure those who find themselves in this situation: they are still able to have a missionary mentality and approach even if they are no longer working in any of the traditional geographical areas of mission. For instance, they can still work to promote the 'global values' which are especially important to one who feels called to be missionary 'to the nations' in the sense outlined in this book. (I shall return to this question in the next chapter.) Unfortunately, however, it often happens that the very people who are most in need of this kind of theology are the ones who are not aware of it or not open to it. This goes to show how important it is that all missionaries be encouraged to take time for updating and renewal.

The demands of mission in the future will make it necessary that missionaries everywhere hold themselves open to the possibility of a change to a new mission. However, the possibility of movement in the future must not be used as an escape from the demanding task of insertion into the present missionary situation. A missionary's decision to move on should not be based on an unwillingness to stay with a young church which is going through the difficult period prior to self-sufficiency. The missionary should rather be motivated partly by a desire to ensure that the young church move beyond a state of dependency and partly by an awareness of the urgent need for a missionary presence in other areas or spheres of activity.

The experience of various groups of missionaries is that those of their members who were able to make a successful change to a new missionary situation have gained in openness and adaptability. This constitutes a strong argument for a greater degree of mobility and flexibility in missionary commitments. There is a lot to be said for the adoption of a policy where full-time missionaries would no longer assume that their assignment to a particular area is for life. Perhaps the assignment should be for a period of ten years at the most. After that time the missionary would be expected to spend about a year in renewal programmes of various kinds. This period would conclude with a time of discernment about a missionary appointment for the next ten years. Such an approach would allow the missionary ample time for full insertion in a given missionary area. But it would also ensure that he or she would be aware that the good of the church and the good of the missionary might well call for uprooting and reinsertion elsewhere. This whole process of taking time out for renewal and discernment could be repeated at ten-year intervals.

The Remnant

There are times when the redeployment of missionaries is partial. By this I mean that, while the majority of the missionaries move elsewhere, a small number of the group ask, or are asked, to continue working in an area where the church is now judged to be viable. The morale of those who find themselves in such a 'remnant' situation may suffer, and their missionary energy may be sapped unless there is a careful re-definition of the role they are to play in the young church.

It is usually better that the length of stay of this 'remnant' of missionaries should not be left open-ended. There is need for a clear understanding, both by themselves and by the local church authorities, that they are staying for a specific time-period. The fact that they look forward to a definite time of departure may give a new focus to their work and can be a source of new missionary energy for themselves.

As the number of foreign missionaries in an area begins to dwindle, those who remain can react in a variety of different ways. Sometimes they attempt to continue on as before; this often results in them taking on a greater workload to cover the gaps left by those who have departed. This leads to an even more rapid reduction in numbers, as the extra work takes a heavy toll on the physical health of those who have stayed behind and puts extra psychological pressure on them. On the other hand, those who remain may retreat to a marginal position in the local church; those who choose this option often find it hard to avoid making harsh or cynical judgements about the 'young' local personnel who have replaced them.

A third possible option for the remaining missionaries is to take on specialised positions for which they are qualified by virtue of their long experience. This may at times be a good approach. But it gives rise to difficulties if it puts the foreign missionaries in positions of authority or financial control. If at all possible they should avoid taking on roles which are likely to bring them into conflict with up-coming local church ministers; they should not allow themselves to be seen as fighting a rear-guard action against the directions favoured by the new generation.

Missionaries need to be particularly careful that they do not allow themselves to be 'used' by local bishops or other authority figures as a way of avoiding facing up to the difficult issue of giving local ministers and leaders a real share in the running of the church. One of the main advantages of missionary redeployment is that it enables the local church leadership to take on primary responsibility for the life of the Christian community in the area. This distinct shift of responsibility will be less evident if a few experienced missionaries are perceived as 'hanging on' to monitor the process and to 'pick up the pieces' when anything goes wrong. So it is generally better that the missionaries who stay should have limited and somewhat specialised roles. Ideally, these roles should not be ones which give them high status. In fact they might well stay on in positions which offer them an opportunity to make a clear option for the poorest and most marginalised people in the area. Other suitable roles are ones in which they devote themselves to ecumenical work, to 'global values' such as justice or ecology, or to building up the missionary dimension of the young church.

QUESTIONS FOR REFLECTION

1. How would you try to help a colleague whom you believe is making himself or herself indispensable for the continued existence of a project? Do you think any of the advice you would give to your colleague might be applicable in your own case?
2. What elements would you put into a renewal programme for a displaced missionary?

CHAPTER 17

Bringing it Back Home

Missionaries for Life

There is a very interesting passage near the end of Pope John Paul's mission encyclical. The Pope says:

The special vocation of missionaries *'for life'* retains all its validity; it is the model of the church's missionary commitment, which always stands in need of radical and total self-giving, of new and bold endeavours. (RM 66; cf. RM 84)

One can interpret this passage to mean that people who volunteer to work in foreign missionary situations for only two or three years are somehow second-class missionaries, because their missionary call was not life-long. But I prefer to think that what the Pope has in mind is quite the opposite, namely, that those who go abroad for a couple of years can remain life-long missionaries when they return home – provided they continue to have a frontier mentality and seek out frontier situations in their home church situations. This interpretation fits in well with the encyclical's insistence that one can answer the call to mission *ad gentes* (to the nations) not only in distant lands but also in social or cultural 'zones' or 'worlds' near home – situations where Christ is not really known and the church is not truly present.

This means that there are three different models of the missionary vocation. The first is what I may call the classical image of the missionary: the women and men who leave their homes to devote their whole lives to working in geographically remote mission situations. The second is represented by the pioneering Christians who, staying in their home area, move on to a frontier that is not geographical but social or cultural, e.g. dedicated work among refugees or prostitutes. The third is one which has become much more common within the past couple of generations: committed Christians who spend some significant period of time working in foreign mission situations and then return home, bringing with them a missionary vision, energy, and attitude. In this final chapter I want to explore the contribution that this third group can make to their home churches.

The reason why this type of missionary has become more common in recent years is that air travel and easy electronic communication between distant parts of the globe have brought about a fundamental change in foreign missionary activity. In the past there was something almost irrevocable about setting off to work as a missionary in another continent. But the effect of modern communications is that it is far easier to travel to remote areas – and relatively easy to retain one's links with home. Furthermore, the fact that English or Spanish have now come to be used so widely throughout the world means that in many situations it is no longer essential for all missionaries to spend years in mastering a local language; so it is now possible to do significant missionary work within a few years. The churches have responded to this situation by encouraging committed Christians to take on relatively short-term missionary assignments. For instance, Pope John Paul's mission encyclical has high praise for diocesan priests who go on temporary mission abroad (RM. 68). Short-term missionaries, whether clerical or lay, are living witnesses to the *solidarity* that can exist between the different churches and the exchange of gifts between them.

Because of the way the Catholic missionary movement is organised, it is usual for lay missionaries to spend only two to four years working in the traditional 'missionary countries'. But when they return home very many of these lay people still see themselves as missionaries. In fact the lay missionary groups have been to the forefront in challenging the rigidly geographical conception of mission which prevailed in the past. The Irish lay missionary group called *Viatores Christi* were always quite unwilling to accept the older division of the world into 'missionary' and 'non-missionary' areas; their approach had more in common with the 'Protestant' notion of 'mission in six continents'. John Paul's encyclical partly vindicates them in this – at least to the extent that it recognises that there are other missionary frontiers besides those of geography.

'Reverse Mission'

'Reverse mission' is a phrase which became popular in missionary circles about twenty years ago. It refers to the activity of missionaries who have returned from overseas and have tried to apply in their own home church some of the insights and strategies which proved effective in the young churches. There is a certain amount of resistance to the use of the phrase 'reverse mission' – mainly because some returned missionaries have at times been insensitive, giving the impression that they have solutions to problems which have baffled the church leaders and ministers of their own home churches. Despite such occasional brashness, returned missionaries have contributed quite a lot to the renewal of the churches from which they have sprung, particularly in the areas of human liberation, working with the poor, and community-building. By and large, local church leaders and ministers have welcomed their contribution and have been willing to try out approaches borrowed and adapted from the young churches.

The first example that comes to my mind springs from an initiative taken nearly twenty years ago by the Columban Sister Maura Dillon. At that time she was a member of the team of the Mission Centre which had recently been established by the Irish Missionary Union. Maura's work in the Philippines had led her to appreciate the contribution made in that country by religious Sisters committed to the struggle for human liberation. So she founded 'Sisters for Justice' as a kind of 'ginger group' to work on justice issues and on behalf of the poor and deprived in Ireland. This group quickly became an important agent of change in the Irish church and in Irish society. Her initiative is a good example of 'reverse mission'.

Maura also had the idea of promoting partnership and mutual sharing between missionaries working overseas and committed church workers in Ireland. She proposed that the Irish Missionary Union should sponsor a three-week workshop entitled 'Partners in Mission' as a way of bringing this about. She invited me to help in planning and running this workshop; and she accepted my suggestion that we invite Anne Hope to play a central role in the team facilitating it. Over the previous decade, Anne had worked in South Africa and Kenya and, together with Sally Timmel, had worked out a very effective model of education for justice and leadership training, inspired by the well-known Brazilian educator, Paulo Freire. They developed the 'Training for Transformation' programme to which I referred in Chapter 14 on 'Missionary Strategy'.

The first of the 'Partners in Mission' workshops took place in 1981. It was an enormously exciting and empowering experience for those who took part in it. Many of them look back on it as a turning-point in their lives. In the following years, other workshops were run, using the same approach and techniques. On every occasion, most of the participants found that for them the workshop was both a kind of 'conversion experience' and a training in useful strategies for working with deprived people.

Within a few years, 'Partners in Mission' had established itself as a movement; and before long it had expanded to a point where it required some fulltime staff and a corps of 'contract facilitators' to run its workshops. It has continued to provide training programmes in community leadership for committed people in many of the more deprived areas of the cities and also in rural parts of the country. In the first few years of the programme the participants in these training workshops were committed Christians. In more recent years, however, the Irish church has lost much of its credibility and the proportion of practising Christians has dropped dramatically. So at this stage many, if not most, of the participants have little or no church affiliation. However, all are interested in working for social change in their own areas; and they share the vision of the founders of 'Partners' – a vision of a more just and participatory society. Many of them have gone on to become very effective social activists. In Chapter 13 above, I referred to the 'Partners in Mission' programme as an illustration of one of the 'new frontiers' of mission. Here I can add that it is also a good example of reverse mission.

A third example of 'bringing it home' also began about twenty years ago, at a time of great difficulty in Ireland. The struggle in Northern Ireland was at its height. The British government led by Margaret Thatcher had refused to allow IRA prisoners to wear civilian clothing in jail. In response, they made a series of protests, culminating in a hunger-strike; and prisoners began to die one by one. Tensions mounted and ecumenical relationships came under increasing strain as Catholics sympathised with the prisoners and Protestants with the government authorities.

In this stressful situation, returned missionaries, Catholic and Protestant, felt a particularly urgent need to promote dialogue. They had had experience of working for reconciliation as part of their foreign missionary commitment. They had learned how easily 'tribal' loyalties can stir up very strong feelings which may make people deaf to the Christian call to break down barriers between peoples. As a result of their overseas experience, the missionaries could stand back a little and then try to reach out to cross the divide that had opened up between the Protestant and Catholic communities on this painful issue of the hunger-strike. They formed a Mission Dialogue Group where they came together to explore topics of common missionary interest. This initiative may have contributed in some small but significant way to the promotion of reconciliation. The Mission Dialogue Group has continued to meet every month; and over the years it has helped to foster the present warm and friendly relationships which exist between mission-minded members of the different churches in Ireland.

An outstanding example of 'reverse mission' is the Justice Desk of CORI (the Conference of Religious of Ireland). Seán Healy SMA and Brigid Reynolds SM were missionaries who worked in a justice ministry in Nigeria. Returning to Ireland they became involved in similar work at home. Since the early 1980s they have turned the Justice Desk of CORI into the most effective voice for justice and alternative development in Ireland. Underpinned by highly professional social and economic analysis, their advocacy work on behalf of the poor and the marginalised has had a major impact on government policy. It is a prime example of how a church agency can play a very effective prophetic role in society and of how foreign missionaries can apply in their home situation the skills and commitment they developed abroad.

What 'Missionary' Contribution can they make?
Those who go to work in a completely foreign situation are bound to suffer a certain degree of 'culture shock'. If they survive this, they often begin to look at the world through new eyes. When they return home again with this fresh vision, they are likely to see frontier situations which they had overlooked in the past. They see people who are sorely in need of hearing good news; and they may become aware of whole spheres of life which are in need of such evangelization. Furthermore, their experience of working in another culture makes them more keenly aware of the need for the gospel to be truly inserted into the everyday life and culture of the people who live in these un-

evangelized 'zones'. Putting that in more technical language we can say that they see the need for the inculturation of the gospel not just in foreign countries but in key parts of their own home areas. They may also become convinced of the need for their home church to engage more actively in the struggle for liberation and to make a more effective option for the poor; and perhaps also for the church to play a more active role in working for reconciliation and the healing of ancient struggles and grievances in their home countries.

Readers may recall that in Part Two of this book I devoted a chapter to each of these five topics – evangelization, inculturation, struggle for liberation, option for the poor, and reconciliation. What I am now saying is that all of these topics are very relevant for those who return from missionary work abroad and feel called to apply the same missionary attitude in their home situation. I have just given two examples of returned missionaries pioneering new ways of working for liberation and of making an option for justice and for the poor; I also gave an example of missionaries drawing on their foreign experience to promote reconciliation in their home situation. In the following pages I hope to spell out some other ways in which they can make an important 'missionary' contribution to their home churches.[1]

Everything depends on their continuing to have a missionary attitude or approach – being willing to take up a prophetic stance in relation to their home 'world' and home church. (It would be invidious to suggest that they are more prophetic than those who have never left home; suffice it to say that their experience abroad gives them a grace-filled opportunity to contemplate their home situation through fresh prophetic eyes.)

Evangelization and Inculturation
I have said that missionaries who return from abroad often have a sense that people in their home areas need to hear good news, which means, of course that they need to be evangelized in some respects. One starting point for such an evangelization is not to think in terms of bringing them good news from outside but of helping them come to a clearer awareness of the many ways in which God is already touching their lives.

For instance, many people find themselves occasionally suffused with gratitude for something that has happened to them, or in a more general way, for the gift of their lives. Such moments may be undervalued simply because they are not named.

It is a real evangelization to help people to recognise such events as moments of deep meaning, as gifts of real prayer, as oases in the midst of desert days, providing nourishment on the journey through life.

Again, for many women today the most privileged experiences come in their personal and interpersonal exploration and celebration of what it means to be a women and in their cultural and political struggle to have that recognised by others. Furthermore, for a growing number of people today the really special way to religious experience comes from a renewed relationship with the earth itself. They allow themselves to be nourished and uplifted by contemplating the beauty of nature, or the power of the ocean; and they go on to commit themselves to protect the earth from destruction and exploitation.

All of these peak experiences are situations where we feel ourselves more fully human – and that is precisely why we can find God in them. For that is the core of the good news of Jesus: that God is not somewhere 'up there' or 'out there' but is at the heart of our lives, most fully present to us when we are most fully human. This is the message that missionaries have been communicating abroad. When they come home they often become very aware that there are many in their own home area who have not yet heard this message.

Another aspect of evangelization concerns freedom of spirit. In his own time Jesus invited the ordinary people to get out from under the religious tyranny of scribes and Pharisees who claimed that God imposes on people a burdensome legalism and an elaborate ritualism. Many missionaries spend their time abroad communicating the same message to their adopted people. Then they return home and find vast numbers of people who are weighed down by a legalistic, moralistic, clericalist and almost superstitious conception of Christianity. So they feel an urgent call to facilitate people in working towards true freedom of spirit; and to give affirmation and encouragement to those who have the courage to practise this freedom. They are aware that this will help not only those Christians who are trapped in legalism but also many non-Christians or non-practising Christians – people who have rejected a version of Christian faith and practice which they experience as legalistic or superstitious.

When foreign missionaries return home and are still in the process of seeking a congenial place to put down their roots, they often come in touch with people who have set out on a personal spiritual search for meaning and hope in their lives. The missionaries may be surprised to find that many such 'searchers' scarcely think of looking to the church for inspiration. A glance at the selection of religious books in our bookshops shows that the 'searchers' generally look for enlightenment to the religions of the East or the pre-Christian religion of the past. The rich heritage of Christian faith and spirituality seems to be just 'dead wood' for most of them. In fact, a large part of their spiritual journey seems to be the dismantling of the burdensome legacy which they received from the church of the previous generation – a legacy of unwarranted certainties in doctrinal matters and guilt in moral matters. Returned missionaries who share some aspects of their search – and who have had a far more positive experience of church – are in a position to dialogue with these 'searchers' and perhaps to share sensitively with them some aspects of their own personal experience of the good news.

These are instances of what may be called personal evangelization. But they are, at the same time, examples of inculturation, insofar as they are attempts to insert the gospel into the everyday life experiences of Western or Westernised people. It is important to free ourselves of the assumption that inculturation is concerned mainly with incorporating local music or dances in the liturgy. It is primarily about enabling the good news to find a point of insertion in people's lives.

An Option for Women

The above examples might give the impression that the missionary call in the home church involves mainly a ministry to individuals. But it also involves a call to a ministry that concerns society as a whole and even the earth itself. It is an invitation to offer prophetic comfort and challenge to all the strata of society, since the good news is addressed to all. I think that in the Western world, at the present time, this can be expressed as a call to make three major options: an option for women, an option for the earth, and an option for the poor.

Missionaries working overseas often become painfully aware of how women are oppressed or treated as second-class citizens in very many non-Western cultures. A good deal of the missionaries' time and energy may be devoted to allowing the gospel to challenge this injustice; this is done by animating women to take leadership roles in civil society. Furthermore, while working abroad, missionaries often have the joy of empowering women to play leading roles in the local church – holding leadership roles in Christian communities, leading prayer services, and sometimes being the main minister of a Holy Communion service which may well be experienced by the community as more-or-less the same as a eucharist.

Returning to their home areas, many women missionaries, and some men, are struck by the extent to which women in the West are still disadvantaged in a myriad of ways. Despite the relative success of the women's movement over the past generation, women still own or control only a small fraction of the *economic* resources. They are *politically* under-represented at all levels of government. And from a *social and cultural* point of view they still suffer in many ways from the assumptions of the past that they are second-class citizens and are expected to carry the main burden in looking after children, homes, husbands and old people.

When these missionaries return to their home church they find that many women feel that they are treated as second-class citizens even in the church – or perhaps *especially* in the church. It is not uncommon for women missionaries to react to this with anger and outrage while their male counterparts may feel burdened by guilt and a sense of complicity in the marginalisation of women in the church. Both men and women are struck by the fact that in many non-Western cultures the church is an agency of liberation for women, while in the Western world today many women perceive the church not as a solution to their disadvantaged state but as a major part of the problem.

There are many women, including religious Sisters, who are quite scandalised when they become aware that over many centuries the traditional spirituality in the church was marked by a deep-seated fear of women. They are shocked at the degree of prejudice against women that characterised much of Christian theology. They are angry that the official church is so slow in allowing itself to be converted from the sin of sexism and the legacy of centuries of patriarchy.

In these circumstances, returned missionaries are called to make a serious option for women. What that will mean in practice will vary from one area to another. But it is clear that it must always have two aspects to it. On the one hand, it will involve efforts to support women in their struggle for justice in the economic and political spheres. On the other hand, it must also involve a determined effort to restore credibility to the church in its claim to be a defender of the rights and dignity of women. This means ensuring that women are more actively involved in church life – not merely in roles of service but more particularly in leadership and ministry roles of all kinds. It also involves making a clear commitment to undoing the many ways in which women have been disadvantaged in church life and in Christian spirituality and theology. Furthermore, it calls for finding ways to compensate for past wrongs – for instance, by instituting a temporary period of positive discrimination in favour of appointing women to leadership roles.

An Option for the Earth

While working abroad many missionaries become keenly aware of ways in which the Western model of development leads to an exploitation of the earth. They are privileged to experience the close partnership with nature presupposed and generated by the traditional pattern of life. And they often experience the sharp contrast between that and the ecological damage caused by efforts to introduce modern Western-style development. This frequently leads to ecological concern becoming a significant element in their work of evangelization.

Coming home from this kind of foreign ministry, it is not surprising that missionaries become concerned about environmental issues in their home country. They often find themselves appalled by the sheer waste of precious resources which they see going on all around them. Some of them left their home countries at a time when people's lifestyle was still quite modest. Returning home, they are shocked at how rapidly the mentality of 'the consumer society' has become the norm in their home countries. I know returned missionaries who find themselves almost compulsively turning off hot-water taps – or even cold-water taps; or who are quite unable to discard 'old' or out-of-fashion clothes; or who baulk at buying Sunday newspapers because of the huge amount of paper they consume.

Such reactions could be dismissed as quaint if there were unlimited resources of water, energy, and trees. But any serious analysis of the state of the earth will show that these and other precious resources are limited – and that they are being shamefully squandered in the wealthy countries. So 'an option for the earth' becomes a matter of concern for all Christians and of particular concern for missionaries. In Chapter 13 above on 'New Frontiers', I cited the Columban missionary Seán McDonagh as an example of a missionary who has focused attention on this urgent 'global issue'. What I am now saying is that other returned missionaries could very usefully follow his lead. They can make their personal and corporate contribution to the campaign to 'save the earth' by protecting its resources and rich diversity. By doing so they serve not only their home church and the wider Christian community, but also the whole human race and the earth community.[2]

An Option for the Outcasts
I want now to suggest some ways in which the gospel can be brought to two distinct strata or categories of the poor, namely, the outcasts and what I may call the 'ordinary' poor. Firstly, the church must be seen to follow its master, Jesus, in being unequivocally in solidarity with those who are most 'outcast' in society. But who are the most outcast in the West today? I think they include three groups:
– those who have contracted Aids; these are often treated today as the lepers were in the time of Jesus;
– prostitutes, who today are just as exploited and rejected as they were when Jesus was alive;
– and dislocated and uprooted groups such as refugees, migrants, gypsies and 'Travelling People'.
    Missionaries often have a good deal of experience in responding to the special needs of these three categories of 'outcast' people. It is a body of experience which may well be welcomed by the home church, which may have its attention and resources so focused on the regular 'maintenance' of mainline Christians that it hardly knows how to respond to these marginal groups. But whether this experience is welcomed or not, returned missionaries have a serious obligation to put it to use and to take a stand on behalf of the 'outcasts'. Of course, it is not a question of every individual returned missionary having to give primacy to this call; but missionary organisations should certainly take the obligation seriously and should support those of their members who feel a particular call to this specialised ministry.

Solidarity with the Poor

I am now moving on from the 'outcasts' to what we may call the 'ordinary' poor. In seeking to be in effective solidarity with the poor we can learn an important lesson from the Latin American church. When they made their famous 'option for the poor', church leaders there set out to disengage the church from its former alliance with the rich and the powerful. In the West, too, the church must distance itself from 'the establishment' – the groups and sectors of society who profit unfairly from the present model of development which is creating so many human and social problems and is putting the earth itself at risk. At present, the weaker and more vulnerable groups in society tend to perceive the church as part of the powerful 'establishment'. So they feel that it is colluding in the injustices which they suffer. The result is that, by and large, the church is not in a position to be, for them, an effective prophetic witness to good news.

Many of those who have returned from foreign mission have had practical experience of what is involved in making an option for the poor. In the situations where they worked the choices were very stark. Some church people were perceived to be colluding with oppressive governments and to be providing ideological-theological support for injustice. Others opted to be in solidarity with those who were politically and economically oppressed – and they were made aware every day of the price that had to be paid for making this option.

In the Western world, the choices are generally much less stark and clear-cut. For one thing, 'the poor' are more likely to constitute perhaps 25% of the population rather than 90%. Furthermore, the exploitation which benefits the better off is less likely to be an obvious and direct exploitation of the local poor people. Instead, it is generally a less obvious exploitation of workers in the 'Third World' from where cheap clothing, footwear, fruit, minerals, and oil are imported. It is also an exploitation of the earth itself, justified under the name of 'development'. In this situation, returned missionaries can play an important role in nudging the church towards making a more credible and effective option for the poor. They do so by giving first-hand accounts of the ways in which they have witnessed exploitation taking place and by linking it to the consumerist life style of the Western world; and, perhaps more effectively, by giving witness to their convictions though the lifestyle they adopt.

From Services to Social Activism
In the past, the church played an effective prophetic role in society by providing a variety of services for the poor – education, health services, shelters, and soup-kitchens. More recently, many church people have become involved in community development, so that the poor may regain responsibility for their own lives. This is already an important step and earlier in this chapter I indicated how returned missionaries played a key role in the development of one such initiative – the 'Partners in Mission' programme.

In several parts of Latin America, and also in parts of the USA, prophetic church people have gone one stage further: they have moved on from the ministry of human development to a more overt ministry of social justice. There is need, and there are opportunities, for the church in all the Western countries to adopt a similar approach. We might begin by providing a 'Social Justice Advisory Service' for deprived groups. This would lead on to helping the victims of social injustice to find redress through the courts. (In Ireland, some important steps in this direction have been taken by a movement for the empowerment of the 'Travelling People' – a movement in which a key role was played by John O'Connell, who had worked as a missionary in the Philippines and had learned there the meaning of an option for the poor.)

Where this kind of work is continued over a period of time, the result is the building up of a legal framework for the protection of the weaker sections of the community. This could be supplemented by various other kinds of quasi-political involvement in the shaping of society – all with a view to making it more just and humane. Publicly recognised 'church people' can offer a great deal of help to groups organising and campaigning for social justice (e.g. trade unions, tenants' associations, organisations for the unemployed, and action groups in support of refugees.)

In this kind of work returned missionaries have a particular contribution to make. This is because they find themselves in a home church where overt political involvement is frowned upon in favour of discrete behind the scenes 'dialogue-lobbying' between senior politicians and senior church leaders. The missionaries have learned how, at its worst, this can lead to 'cosy' understandings and unacceptable collusion between church and state. In reaction to this, many of the missionaries while abroad have already taken the first difficult steps of moving into the sphere of overtly political action. This experience can be put to good use in the home church – provided it is done sensitively and without undue brashness. Returned missionaries are also in a good position to bring out the links between working for justice at the local level and commitment to social justice at a global level.

Solidarity with the 'Troubled Middle Classes'
It is vitally important that returned missionaries take account of one of the most notable differences between their home church situation and the so-called 'Third World' situations in which most of them worked. The difference is that when they worked abroad the vast majority of the people were desperately poor, whereas in the home church the poor are a minority. In my opinion the brashness of some missionaries in trying to introduce liberation theology in the Western world springs from a failure to take full account of this difference. From a strategic point of view, it means that the task of working for social change in the West is even more difficult than in poor countries. In 'Third World' situations those who work for radical change know that they are working for the liberation of the majority of the people. In the West, by contrast, anybody who works for social change and is also committed to democracy has to find ways of developing some kind of 'rainbow alliance' which can engage the allegiance of a majority of the people.

I believe that returned missionaries can make a significant contribution to the development of such a 'rainbow alliance'. It would be composed of three elements – women, the poor, and what I call 'the troubled middle class'. It should be clear, from what I have already said, that it is in the interests of women and of the poor to work for a major transformation of Western society. I am not, of course, assuming that all women or all poor people will be convinced of the need for change or be willing to devote themselves to bringing it about. But I dare to hope that, with appropriate education and stimulation, a sufficient number would make an option for a new world order. The changes required are not just in the socio-economic structures but also in the prevailing cultural ethos. I am thinking, for instance, of the common assumption of the business world that typically feminine qualities and values are not economically useful or relevant. I have in mind also the half-conscious assumption of many 'comfortable' people that the poor remain poor largely because of their lack of initiative or intelligence. I do not propose to elaborate any further on these points. But I need to explain what I mean by 'the troubled middle class' and why I think they could become part of an alliance for change.

The people I have in mind know they are privileged *vis-à-vis* the poor all around them. They feel uneasy, rootless or alienated because they sense that they are locked into a system that is immoral. But they have no clear idea how that situation can be changed or what part they might play in bringing about the radical change they know is required. It is easy for returned missionaries to feel in solidarity with such people, because many of them are themselves part of this 'troubled middle class'. But how can they be faithful to the radical prophetic message of Jesus? It is not enough to wallow in guilt or slip into paralysis. Genuine solidarity with these troubled people means seeking with them a way out of the morass. One of the most effective ways is by being actively involved with them in exploring and promoting alternatives to the present economic order which is grossly unjust and environmentally unsustainable.

People in this situation are often lacking in knowledge about possible alternatives. But the core of their difficulty is not so much a lack of theoretical knowledge as the shortage of practical models of what a just alternative might look like in practice. This is a glorious opportunity for committed church people – and particularly for returned missionaries who have personal experience of the viability of other patterns of living besides the present dominant Western model. They can help in the project of working out the alternative models of human living of which people are so much in need. In doing so they will be putting into practice their option for women, for the poor and for the earth. They will be witnessing to the values of the reign of God and giving people hope by showing them a foretaste of the future to which God is calling humanity and our world.

'The Impossible Dream'
The task is no easy one, because the church does not have a ready-made divinely revealed solution to offer. But we do have important resources:

– Firstly, we have the assurance that the Spirit of God will be with us in our search, in solidarity with other committed people, for a model of life that respects people (especially women and the poor) and shows care for the earth.

– Secondly, we have a legacy of fundamental values which make up the social teaching of the church.

– Thirdly, we in the church have available to us the resources of hope, inspiration, wisdom, energy, spirituality and theology of a significant number of people who are dedicated, committed and prepared to devote their lives to what may seem to be an impossible dream.

Most returned missionaries will find themselves in one of two groups. On the one hand, there are those who concentrate their energy on working out ways to transform the present system from within, in a piecemeal and gradual way. On the other hand, there are those who opt out of the present system and seek to build an alternative 'from the ground up'. Both groups need wholehearted support from the leadership of the church and from the Christian community as a whole. For the prophetic challenge they have taken on is so daunting that it is almost impossible for individuals or small groups to sustain it without support within the wider church.

Any proposed alternative model of human development must be ecologically sustainable, so that it respects the rights of future generations to a fair share of the resources of the earth. This means partnership with nature rather than exploitation. It must also seek to eliminate the drudgery and alienation which arises when workers have no personal involvement in the product they produce and no say in determining the conditions of their work. So there should be incentives to encourage workers to play an active part in planning their work, and to develop a friendly and supportive environment in the workplace; and this should facilitate solidarity and participatory decision-making in other spheres of life, even outside the workplace. Furthermore, those who seek an alternative model of economic and social development should not make the mistake of identifying 'work' with 'employment'. For it seems likely that any successful future model of human development will involve having less people who are working as employees for others; instead there will be many more workers' co-operatives as well as more self-employed people.

Those who dedicate themselves to the task of forming alternative communities are giving prophetic witness to the future which God has promised. In doing so they are undertaking the modern equivalent of the founding of a religious order. In such new prophetic initiatives the vows of poverty might be replaced (or supplemented) by a commitment to ecological sensitivity. Corresponding to the vow of chastity taken in religious orders there could be a commitment of fidelity to the network of alternative communities. And corresponding to the vow of obedience there is need for a commitment to decision-making and action based on the participation of all. If we choose to belong to or support such committed communities, each of us can find new hope in our lives – and we will be engaged in a truly missionary work, bringing the prophetic good news of Christ more effectively into our churches and into our world.

QUESTIONS FOR REFLECTION

1. Can you name two or three prophetic initiatives which you know of that were taken by returned missionaries? What difficulties did they face? What supports did they find?
2. What elements would you put into a programme intended to help returned missionaries to re-insert in their own culture while retaining their missionary vision and energy?

Notes

*(See the bibliography for full titles and bibliographical information
on books and articles referred to in the notes.)*

NOTES TO INTRODUCTION (pp 7-13)

1. Donal Dorr, *Divine Energy*.
2. In this book I am not examining the important issues of dialogue *within* individual churches or ecumenical dialogue *between* the Christian churches, because my focus is on looking outward to other religions and ideologies and to the secular world.

NOTES TO CHAPTER 1 (pp 16-25)

1. Cf. *Redemptoris Missio* (Pope John Paul II's 1990 encyclical on the Missions), no. 55.
2. N. 8 of 'Faith and Inculturation' in *The Irish Theological Quarterly*, 55 (1989), 145.
3. On the issue of dialogue between the religions see also, International Theological Commission, 'Le christianism et les religions' in *Documentation Catholique* Vol XCIV (No 2157) (6 April 1997), 312-332.
4. *Christianity and the Encounter of World Religions*, 57. The inner dialogue I am suggesting can be related to the notion of 'passing over' to another viewpoint, as outlined by John Dunne in *The Way of All the Earth*, (viii)-(ix).
5. Eric Sharpe, 'Mission between Dialogue and Proclamation' in William R. Burrows (ed.), *Redemption and Dialogue*, 171.

NOTES TO CHAPTER 2 (pp 26-39)

1. Cf. Eric Voegelin, *Israel and Revelation*, 194; see also ibid., 418-427.
2. E.g. The Koran's rejection of the Trinity—Sura IV, 165 in Arthur J. Arberry, *The Koran Interpreted*, 97.
3. Cf. Ninian Smart, *The Religious Experience of Mankind*, 540.
4. See, for instance, the insistence on human responsibility (under God) by Khurshid Ahmed in 'A Muslim Response', in Joseph Gremillion and William Ryan (eds.), *World Faiths and the New World Order*, 182-3.
5. Willard G. Oxtoby (ed), *Religious Diversity: Essays by Wilfred Cantwell Smith*, 31.
6. Cf. R. C. Zaehner, *Hinduism*, 3.
7. *The Bhagavad-Gita* 5:12 (Zaehner edition), 63.
8. *The Bhagavad-Gita* 6:30; cf. Zaehner's introduction, 27-8.

9. See R. C. Zaehner, Hinduism, 63; cf. Ninian Smart, *The Religious Experience of Mankind*, 114 (on Buddhism) and 151-2 (on *The Bagavad-Gita*).

10. Cf. John T. Catoir, *World Religions*, 90.

11. Cf. Smart, *The Religious Experience of Mankind*, 112.

12. Cf. Ibid., 198.

13. Cf. Ibid., 216.

14. E.g. Arnold Mindell, *Sitting in the Fire*.

15. E.g. Joseph Jaworski, *Synchronicity*.

NOTES TO CHAPTER 3 (pp 40-55)

1. Cf. John V. Taylor, *The Primal Vision*, 92-3.

2. Wole Soyinka, 'The Fourth Stage': Through the Mysteries of Ogun to the Origin of Yoruba Trageda', in *Art, Dialogue and Outrage*, 27-39.

3. Donal Dorr, *Divine Energy*, 32.

4. Bolaji Idowu, *Olodumare: God in Yoruba Belief*, 32-62; John V. Taylor makes the point that the influence of Christian missions 'helped to crystalize the concept of a supreme Creator even among those who did not become Christians.' – see, *The Primal Vision*, 81. Taylor also makes a strong case for holding that, in the African view, God is present not in the making of the world but as immanent and involved – see, *The Primal Vision*, 65.

5. Cf. Emefie Ikenga Metuh, *God and Man in African Religion*, 75-6, who deals with the same issue in Igbo religion and notes that it is not marked by such dualism.

6. Soyinka says: 'Ogun stands for a transcendent, humane, but rigidly restorative justice. (Unlike Sango, who is primarily retributive.)'— *Art, Dialogue and Outrage*, 28.

7. Dáithi Ó hÓgain, *The Sacred Isle*, 64.

8. Ibid., 148.

9. Ibid., 66-7.

10. Ibid., 112 and 203.

11 Ibid., 133-4 and 145-6.

12. Ibid., 140.

13. For this account of the nature of Greek goddesses and gods I have relied on Vincent Vycinas, *Earth and Gods*, 174-223. (Vycinas himself has drawn heavily on the works of the German scholar Walter F. Otto.) Vycinas's insightful study of the nature of these Greek divinities enables him to throw much light on the purpose and value of Heidegger's attempt to unveil the sacred dimension of the world in which we live, rather than relying on an other-worldly religion. For a more factual popular account of the Greek divinities see, Sofia Souli, *Greek Mythology*.

14. Bernard Knox, Introductory Booklet to Homer, *The Iliad*.

15. Ibid., 63.

16. Taylor notes that a person's 'brooding anger or envy very quickly can take on an existence and vitality of its own' – *The Primal Vision*, 40.

17. On shamanism see Wendell C. Beane and William G. Doty (eds.), *Myths, Rites, Symbols: A Mircea Eliade Reader,* Vol. 2, pp. 262-282.

18. For a sensitive treatment of the topic of witchcraft see Michael C. Kirwen, *The Missionary and the Diviner,* 30-2, 50-4, 127. Kirwen suggests that in many respects the witch in African religion plays the role which Christians have traditionally assigned to the devil (p. 54). See also Taylor, *The Primal Vision,* 66, where Taylor makes the interesting suggestion that witchcraft springs from 'a rapacious individual grasping of the power-force latent in other beings'.

19. In making this distinction between two levels of transcendence I am attempting to go beyond the somewhat over-simplified view of Taylor who, in *The Primal Vision,* 80, says: 'The Christian, with his theology grounded in the doctrine of the transcendence, must pass through an agonizing abnegation if he is to understand imaginatively how essentially this-worldly is the closed circle of being which is the African world, and how little it needs a transcendent God.'

20. A brilliant and highly successfully attempt to respond to the hunger for Celtic spirituality is John O'Donohue, *Anam Chara: A Book of Celtic Wisdom.*

NOTES TO CHAPTER 4 (pp 56-73)

1. Cf. Michael Paul Gallagher, *Clashing Symbols,* 113: 'There is not so much a generation gap as a credibility gap of languages, where the typical mediations of Church can be experienced as a foreign tongue.'

2. Dáithí Ó hÓgain, *The Sacred Isle,* 216.

3. Cf. Michael Paul Gallagher, *Clashing Symbols,* 114, who speaks of post-modern people who have an 'anchorless spirituality'.

4. Cf. Donal Dorr, *Option for the Poor,* 275.

5. Cf. David J. Bosch, *Transforming Mission,* 191; and Donal Dorr, *Divine Energy,* 136-9.

NOTES TO CHAPTER 5 (pp 76-90)

1. Cf. Aylward Shorter, *Evangelization and Culture,* 4-8; David Bosch, *Transforming Mission,* 409-420.

2. We might add that some of the more recent theology (such as that of 'the anonymous Christian') had raised doubts or questions about the need for mission and about the whole concept of 'mission'.

3. Of course this view is shared by most Protestants, apart from some extreme evangelicals; and in recent years there has been an even greater convergence between the Protestant and Catholic approaches.

4. See Donal Dorr, *Divine Energy,* 63-6.

5. For an interesting example of a somewhat similar summary of the gospel – but designed for a tribal nomadic people – see, Vincent J. Donovan, *Christianity Rediscovered,* 73-4.

6. See Karl Rahner, *Theological Investigations,* Vol V, 113-134 and Vol. VI,

390-8; cf. Anita Röper, *The Anonymous Christian*. See also Paul F. Knitter, *No Other Name*, 128-135.

7. Eugene Hillman, *The Wider Ecumenism;* Eugene Hillman, *The Church As Mission*, 88-99; Eugene Hillman, *Toward an African Christianity*.

8. *The Wider Ecumenism*, 108: 'The sacramental significance of the Church may be fully achieved among a particular people, even though the Church may not be juridically and numerically co-extensive with every single member of this people.'

9. John Fuellenbach, *The Kingdom of God: The Message of Jesus Today*, 270. See also Michael Amaladoss, *Making All Things New: Mission in Dialogue*, 29: '… what I am suggesting is a shift of focus by which building a new world or the Reign of God is not seen merely as one constitutive element among others of the Church's mission of evangelization, but rather the main focus … '; cf. ibid., 40-1.

10. This whole issue is teased out very extensively in Paul F. Knitter, *No Other Name*, 120-204. See also Michael Amaladoss, *Making All Things New*, 234-8; also the clear summary by Michael McCabe in a booklet entitled 'Christianity and Other Religions' (1999) circulated privately by the Irish Missionary Union.

11. *Redemptoris Missio* (1990), 41-60.

NOTES TO CHAPTER 6 (pp 91-108)

1. Cf. Michael Paul Gallagher, *Clashing Symbols*, 110. Gallagher gives an interesting account of the differences in emphasis between the view of Pope John Paul II and the views in the World Council of Churches in relation to the possibility or rightness of a 'Christian culture'; the Pope uses the term while the WCC sees it as 'loaded with cultural imperialism'; see. ibid. 54, 58-61.

2. 'In the Encounter of Christianity and Religions, Syncretism is Not the Goal', *L'Osservatore Romano* (English edition) 26 April 1995, 5-8. Reference to p. 6. This is the text of an address given by Cardinal Ratzinger two years previously (March 1993) to a meeting of Asian bishops in Hong Kong. (In subsequent notes I shall refer to this article as 'In the Encounter'.)

3. Vincent J. Donovan, *Christianity Rediscovered*. The best-known edition was published in 1982 but the book was originally published in 1978 and was based on articles written by Donovan some time earlier.

4. Ibid., (v)

5. Ibid., (vii)

6. Ibid., 24.

7. Ibid., 162. His intention was to give the new churches nothing more than St Paul give to the churches he founded.

8. Ibid., 38: Donovan's programme involved visiting each community one day in the week over a period of about a year.

9. Ibid., 77.

10. 'Report on the Church in Africa, VI (1) Christianity and African

Culture', in Raymond Hickey (ed.), *Modern Missionary Documents and Africa*, 207-245, quotation taken from p. 234.

11. See, for instance, Aloysius Pieris,'Inculturation in Non-Semitic Asia' in, Norman E. Thomas (ed.), *Classic Texts in Mission and World Christianity*, 276. (The article from which this excerpt is taken was published in 1986.) See also David J. Bosch, *Transforming Mission*, 478. For a fairly thorough exploration of some of these issues see Michael Amaladoss, *Making All Things New*, 163-178, 192-8, 242-268. See also Aloysius Pieris, *An Asian Theology of Liberation*, 74-86.

12. See, Joseph Cardinal Ratzinger, *Wesen und Auftrag der Theologie: Versuche zu ihrer Ortsbestimmung im Disput der Gegenwart*, 79 where he objects to a *'Hinduisierung'* of Christianity. Cf. Joseph Cardinal Ratzinger, 'Current situation of faith and theology' address published in *L'Osservatore Romano* (English ed.) 6 November 1996, pp. 4-6. The article is a strong attack on relativism, in the context of dialogue between the religions.

13. 'In the Encounter', 5-6; cf. Joseph Cardinal Ratzinger, *Salt of the Earth: Christianity and the Catholic Church at the End of the Millennium*, San Francisco: 1997 (original German 1996), 35: Faith, when lived, 'forms a life-style and also produces a culture'.

14. 'In the Encounter', 6.

15. Joseph Cardinal Ratzinger, *Church, Ecumenism and Politics : New Essays in Ecclesiology*, 230. (The essay from which this quotation is taken was originally published in German in 1979).

16. 'In the Encounter', 7. When he refers to the church as a 'cultural subject' he adds at once that this subject has 'its own historically developed and multi-tiered interculturality'. I take it that this is to distinguish the church from the more univocal culture of each ethnic group; the church can embrace people of many different cultures.

17. See, for instance, *Salt of the Earth*, 133, where he makes disparaging remarks about 'inculturation' as exemplified in *teologia india* in Latin America, which he sees as an attempt 'to get free of the foreign overlay imposed by Europe'; cf. 'In the Encounter', 7.

18. See, *Ratzinger Report: An Exclusive Interview on the State of the Catholic Church* (Ratzinger interviewed by Messori), 193. (It should be noted, however, that the words quoted are Messori's interpretation of the Cardinal's thought, rather than Cardinal Ratzingers's own words. In response to this remark of Messori, the Cardinal says that there can be no going back to the cultural situation before the results of European thought spread to the whole world.)

19. 'In the Encounter', 7.

20. 'The Cultural Implications of World Mission' – typescript of paper read to the British and Irish Association of Mission Studies Conference in 1991, p. 4 (used with the permission of the author).

21. Aylward Shorter, *Toward a Theology of Inculturation*, 64-7.

22. Ibid., 63. The Indian theologian Amaladoss also stresses the distinc-

tion between the stage of acculturation and that of inculturation – see Michael Amaladoss, *Making All Things New*, 127.

23. Aylward Shorter, *Toward a Theology of Inculturation*, 66.

24. Ibid., 63.

25. Ibid., 64. Shorter seems to attribute this imposition of a uniform subculture to two intertwined mistakes which Catholic Church authorities are inclined to make. The first mistake is to identify the 'cultural patrimony' with Sacred Tradition (ibid., 65). The second is to assume that the patrimony is a universal culture (cf. 'The Cultural Implications of World Mission' typescript, pp. 13-4: Shorter warns against 'a dangerous tendency in official circles to imply that this multicultural patrimony is in itself a universal form of culture.')

26. *Toward a Theology of Inculturation*, 64

27. Ibid., 67.

28. Ibid.

29. In listing these six items I am drawing on an unpublished paper by Michael McCabe, 'Inculturation: Part I: Clarifying the Term and its Theological Foundation', 6-7.

30. See, for instance, R. E. Frykenberg, 'India' in Adrian Hastings (ed.), *A World History of Christianity*, 148-56.

31. See, for instance, Kevin Ward, 'Africa' in Adrian Hastings (ed.), *A World History of Christianity*, 197-200.

32. Examples of the rich spirituality which developed in the Eastern Orthodox Church are the tradition of *hesychia* (solitary contemplative prayer) and the use of 'the Jesus prayer' and rhythmic breathing. On this see, Mary B. Cunningham, 'The Orthodox Church in Byzantium', in Adrian Hastings (ed.), *A World History of Christianity*, 103-4. Another example is the profound spiritual renewal, within the Russian Orthodox tradition, associated with the writers Tolstoy and Dostoyevsky and the philosopher-theologians Sergei Bulgakov and Nikolai Berdyayev – see, Philip Walters, 'Eastern Europe Since the Fifteenth Century', in, Adrian Hastings (ed.), *A World History of Christianity*, London, 308-310. For an account of the missionary outreach of the Eastern Church to the Slavs see, Mary B. Cunningham, 'The Orthodox Church in Byzantium', in Adrian Hastings (ed.), *A World History of Christianity*, 82-5.

33. See Shorter, *Toward a Theology of Inculturation*, 169-170.

34. 'In the Encounter', 7

35. *Evangelization and Culture*, 156.

36. Ibid.

NOTES TO CHAPTER 7 (pp 109-127)

1. Donal Dorr, *The Social Justice Agenda: Justice, Ecology, Power and the Church*, 7-18.

2. Walter Wink, *Naming The Powers: The Language of Power in the New Testament*; Walter Wink, *Unmasking the Powers: The Invisible Forces that Determine Human Existence*; Walter Wink, *Engaging the Powers: Discernment and Resistance in a World of Domination*.

3. See Enda McDonagh, *The Demands of Simple Justice: A Study of the Church, Politics and Violence with special reference to Zimbabwe*, 132, 139.
4. Kairos theologians: *The Kairos Document: Challenge to the Church: A Theological Comment on the Political Crisis in South Africa* (revised second edition).

NOTES TO CHAPTER 8 (pp 128-143)

1. Segundo Galilea, *The Beatitudes: To Evangelize as Jesus Did*, 81.
2. Cf. ibid., 82.
3. Cf. ibid., 80-1.
4. Cf. Robert J. Schreiter, *Reconciliation: Mission and Ministry in a Changing Social Order*, 49.
5. Cf. ibid., 60-1, 77-8.
6. The Nobel laureate Wole Soyinka, in his book *The Burden of Memory, the Muse of Forgiveness*, 23-92, mounts a very serious challenge to the approach of the South African Truth and Reconciliation Commission on the grounds that it effectively condoned criminal behaviour, and did not demand genuine remorse and repentance. Soyinka notes that according to the African way of thinking, reconciliation presupposes that there be some element of restitution or reparation for past injustice and injury. In response I can only say, first, that the South African model did call for remorse; secondly, that the public acknowledgement of guilt went some way towards making reparation; and, thirdly, that the state undertook to compensate injured parties. As I pointed out on page 130 above, the first stage of reconciliation between victim and oppressor is a recognition of the injustice that was perpetrated. In the South African situation the issue seems to be mainly whether, on the whole, the right balance was achieved between the ideal and what was possible in practice. I do not feel entitled to claim that the South Africans got the balance wrong.
7. For instructions on the use of this 'Win-Lose' exercise see, Donal Dorr, *Integral Spirituality*, 220-3.

NOTES TO CHAPTER 9 (144-166)

1. In my account of poverty I have drawn on Hennie Lötter, 'Philosophical Reflections on Poverty and Riches' in *The Challenge of Eradicating Poverty in the World: An African Response*, 9-62.
2. Anthony Giddens, *The Third Way: the Renewal of Social Democracy*.
3. I have spelled out these aspects in more detail in my book, *The Social Justice Agenda*, 109-112.
4. Cf. Donal Dorr, *Option for the Poor: A Hundred years of Vatican Social Teaching*, 364-6.
5. E.g. Juan Luis Segundo, *Theology and the Church: A Response to Cardinal Ratzinger and a Warning to the Whole Church*.
6. Arnold Mindell, *Sitting in the Fire: large group transformation using conflict and diversity*, 165.
7. Ibid., 192.

NOTES TO CHAPTER 10 (pp 167-183)

1. Cf. I have treated this topic in some detail in my book *Divine Energy*, 76-8, 151-2.

2. The methodology they worked out is summed up in, Anne Hope and Sally Timmel, *Training for Transformation: A Handbook for Community Workers*, 3 Volumes.

3. See Pádraig Ó Máille, *Living Dangerously: A Memoir of Political Change in Malawi.*

NOTES TO CHAPTER 11 (pp 186-192)

1. 'Mission as Gathering In: a Biblical and African Perspective' – paper delivered to a gathering of missionaries in Maynooth, Ireland, in 1994 and circulated privately as a booklet by The Irish Missionary Union.

2. David J. Bosch, *Transforming Mission*, 191.

3. See Karl Rahner's article 'Jesus Christ' in *Sacramentum Mundi*, III, 203; cf. Donal Dorr, *Divine Energy*, 143.

NOTES TO CHAPTER 12 (pp 193-201)

1. The links between these two aspects of missionary work are well articulated by Michael Amaladoss in *Making All Things New*, 25-41.

2. Donal Dorr, *Spirituality and Justice*, 202.

3. Cf. Michael Amaladoss, *Making All Things New*, 2, 24.

NOTES TO CHAPTER 13 (202-219)

1. For instance the Maryknoll Missionary Society of Fathers and Brothers defined their mission as being outside the continental boundaries of the USA. Similarly the Missionaries for Africa ('White Fathers') defined their task as mission to the Africans. The Columban missionaries' original constitutions committed them to work for 'the Chinese'. The original constitutions of my own missionary Society used a more generic term, which was still geographical; it described the members as missionaries *ad exteros* ('to the outsiders').

2. Indeed the SMA (African Missionaries) had adopted this approach from the beginning; already in 1856 their founder laid down that they could 'accept missions outside of Africa, provided it be to peoples of colour'.

3. Some missionary institutes have begun to accept the challenge offered in the encyclical. One particularly striking example is the following passage in the working paper circulated by the General Council of the Divine Word Missionaries in preparation for their 1994 General Chapter:

> The SVD mission is called:
>
> – to spearhead the attempt to cross over frontiers. We refer not so much to geographical frontiers but to frontiers of faith, frontiers which relate to the dignity of the human person and frontiers expressing the values of the Kingdom ...
>
> (*Our Mission at the Service of Communion*, p. 15).

4. See Seán McDonagh, *To Care For the Earth;* also *The Greening of the Church* and *Passion for the Earth: The Christian Vocation to Promote Justice, Peace and the Integrity of Creation,* and *Greening the Christian Millennium.*
5. Missionary groups played a very prominent part in setting up and supporting the 'Debt and Development Coalition' which was established some years ago in Ireland as a focus for information and lobbying on the debt issue.
6. Aylward Shorter, *Evangelization and Culture,* 78-9; cf. ibid., 156.
7. Ibid., 69.
8. Ibid., 67.
9. This approach seems to be the theology underpinning the lay missionary programme set up some years ago by the Missionary Society of St Columban. They not only send European missionaries to Asia but also send Koreans to the Philippines and lay missionaries from Fiji and the Philippines to Ireland. If one follows what I have called Pope John Paul's 'situational' way of defining mission *ad gentes,* it would seem at first sight that the church workers coming from Fiji to work in Ireland should not be called missionaries *ad gentes* in the strict sense. But perhaps people coming to Ireland from vibrant young churches see in Ireland a dying church which is objectively in need of mission *ad gentes.*

NOTES TO CHAPTER 14 (pp 222-238)

1. Cf. Pádraig Ó Máille (Patrick O'Malley), 'Mission and Missionaries in African Writing: Creative Writing from Post-Colonial Africa and the Black Diaspora', (unpublished paper) pp. 4-32. I am indebted to my colleague Pádraig Ó Máille for this comprehensive account of how missionaries were perceived and presented in a very wide range of post-colonial literature.
2. See Anne Hope and Sally Timmel, *Training for Transformation: A Handbook for Community Workers,* 3 Volumes; see also Donal Dorr, *Integral Spirituality.*

NOTES TO CHAPTER 15 (pp 239-250)

1. Donal Dorr, *Spirituality and Justice,* 61-72, 212-5; *Integral Spirituality,* 149-185; *The Social Justice Agenda,* 126-143; *Option for the Poor,* 110, 117-131, 179-184, 198-200, 212-3, 370-1.

NOTES TO CHAPTER 16 (pp 251-268)

1. See Donal Dorr, *Integral Spirituality,* especially pp. 118-27.
2. SVD General Chapter 1988, *Mission Spirituality Formation,* 16.

NOTES TO CHAPTER 17 (pp 269-285)

1. Various instances of such 'missionary' initiatives can be found in John O'Brien, *Seeds of a New Church.*
2. On this question see, Richard Cartwright Austin, *Reclaiming America: Restoring Nature to Culture.*

Bibliography

Ahmed, Khurshid: 'A Muslim Response', in Gremillion and Ryan (eds.): *World Faiths and the New World Order*, 182-3.

Amaladoss, Michael: *Making All Things New: Mission in Dialogue*, Anand (Gujarat Sahitya Prakash: 1990)

Arberry, Arthur J.: *The Koran Interpreted*, London (OUP: 1964)

Austin, Richard Cartwright: *Reclaiming America: Restoring Nature to Culture*, Abingdon, Virginia (Creekside Press: 1990)

Beane, Wendell C. and Doty, William G. (eds.): *Myths, Rites, Symbols: A Mircea Eliade Reader*, New York (Harper Colophon: 1975)

Bosch, David J.: *Transforming Mission: Paradigm Shifts in Theology of Mission*, Maryknoll (Orbis: 1991)

Burrows, William R. (ed.): *Redemption and Dialogue: Reading 'Redemptoris Missio' and 'Dialogue and Proclamation'*, Maryknoll (Orbis: 1994)

Campbell, Joseph: *The Masks of God: Primitive Mythology*, Harmondsworth (Penguin: 1959, 1987)

Campbell, Joseph: *The Masks of God: Oriental Mythology*, Harmondsworth (Penguin: 1962)

Carabine, Deirdre and O'Reilly, Martin (eds.): *The Challenge of Eradicating Poverty in the World: An African Response*, Nkozi/Kampala (Uganda Martyrs University Press: 1998)

Catoir, John T.: *World Religions: Beliefs Behind Today's Headlines*, New York (Alba House: 1992)

Cunningham, Mary B.: 'The Orthodox Church in Byzantium', in Hastings (ed.), *A World History of Christianity*.

Divine Word Missionaries (SVD) General Chapter: *Mission Spirituality Formation*, Rome: 1988

Divine Word Missionaries General Council: *Our Mission at the Service of Communion*, Rome: 1994

Donovan, Vincent J.: *Christianity Rediscovered: An Epistle from the Masai*, London (SCM) and Maryknoll (Orbis), 1982

Dorr, Donal: *Spirituality and Justice*, Dublin (Gill and Macmillan) and Maryknoll (Orbis) 1984

Dorr, Donal: *Divine Energy: God Beyond Us, Within Us, Among Us*, Dublin (Gill and Macmillan) and Liguouri Missouri (Triumph), 1996

Dorr, Donal: *Integral Spirituality: Resources for Community, Justice, Peace, and the Earth,* Dublin (Gill and Macmillan) and Maryknoll (Orbis), 1990

Dorr, Donal: *Option for the Poor: A Hundred Years of Vatican Social Teaching* (revised ed.), Dublin (Gill and Macmillan) and Maryknoll (Orbis), 1992

Dorr, Donal: *The Social Justice Agenda: Justice, Ecology, Power and the Church,* Dublin (Gill and Macmillan) and Maryknoll (Orbis), 1991

Dunne, John: *The Way of All the Earth: An Encounter with Eastern Religions,* New York (Macmillan) and London (Sheldon), 1972

Frykenberg, R. E.: 'India' in Hastings (ed.): *A World History of Christianity,* 148-56.

Fuellenbach, John: *The Kingdom of God: The Message of Jesus Today,* Maryknoll (Orbis: 1995)

Galilea, Segundo: *The Beatitudes: To Evangelize as Jesus Did,* Dublin (Gill and Macmillan: 1984)

Gallagher, Michael Paul: *Clashing Symbols: an Introduction to Faith-and-Culture,* London (Darton Longman and Todd: 1997)

Giddens, Anthony: *The Third Way: the Renewal of Social Democracy,* Cambridge (Polity Press: 1998)

Gremillion, Joseph and Ryan, William (eds.): *World Faiths and the New World Order: A Muslim-Jewish-Christian Search Begins,* Washington DC (Interreligious Peace Colloquium: 1978)

Hastings, Adrian (ed.): *A World History of Christianity,* London (Cassell: 1999)

Hickey, Raymond (ed.): *Modern Missionary Documents and Africa,* Dublin (Dominican Publications: 1982)

Hillman, Eugene: *The Church as Mission,* London (Sheed and Ward: 1966)

Hillman, Eugene: *The Wider Ecumenism,* New York (Herder and Herder: 1968)

Hillman, Eugene: *Toward an African Christianity: Inculturation Applied,* New York (Paulist: 1993)

Hope, Anne and Timmel, Sally: *Training for Transformation: A Handbook for Community Workers,* 3 Volumes, Gweru, Zimbabwe (Mambo Press: 2nd revised edition 1995)

Idowu, Bolaji: *Olodumare: God in Yoruba Belief,* London (Longmans: 1962)

International Theological Commission, 'Le christianism et les religions' in *Documentation Catholique* Vol XCIV (No 2157) (6 April 1997), 312-332

International Theological Commission, 'Faith and Inculturation' in *The Irish Theological Quarterly,* 55 (1989)

Jaworski, Joseph: *Synchronicity: The Inner Path of Leadership,* San Francisco (Berrett-Koehler: 1996)

John Paul II: Encyclical, *Laborem Exercens,* 1975

John Paul II: Encyclical, *Redemptoris Missio*, 1990

John Paul II: Apostolic Letter, *Tertio Millennio Adveniente*, 1994

Kairos theologians: *The Kairos Document: Challenge to the Church: A Theological Comment on the Political Crisis in South Africa* (revised second edition), Braamfontein, South Africa (The Institute of Contextual Theology), Grand Rapids (Eerdmans) and London (CIIR), 1986

Kirwen, Michael C.: *The Missionary and the Diviner: Contending Theologies of Christian and African Religions*, Maryknoll (Orbis: 1987)

Knitter, Paul F.: *No Other Name: A Critical Survey of Christian Attitudes Toward the World Religions*, Maryknoll (Orbis: 1985)

Knox, Bernard: Introductory Booklet to *Homer, The Iliad*, Harmondsworth (Penguin Audiobooks, 1990)

Küng, Hans: *A Global Ethic for Global Politics and Economics*, London (OUP: 1998)

Küng, Hans: Global *Responsibility: In Search of a New World Ethic*, (Continuum: 1993)

Küng, Hans and Kuschel, Karl-Josef: A Global Ethic: *The Declaration of the Parliament of the World Religions* (Continuum: 1993)

Lötter, Hennier: 'Philosophical Reflections on Poverty and Riches' in Carabine and O'Reilly (eds.): *The Challenge of Eradicating Poverty in the World: An African Response*, 9-62.

McCabe, Michael: 'Inculturation: Part I: Clarifying the Term and its Theological Foundation' (unpublished paper)

McCabe, Michael: 'Christianity and Other Religions' (booklet circulated privately by the Irish Missionary Union, 1999)

McDonagh, Enda: *The Demands of Simple Justice: A Study of the Church, Politics and Violence with special reference to Zimbabwe*, Dublin (Gill and Macmillan: 1980)

McDonagh, Seán: *To Care For the Earth: a Call to a New theology*, London (Chapman: 1986)

McDonagh, Seán: *The Greening of the Church*, Maryknoll (Orbis: 1990)

McDonagh, Seán: *Passion for the Earth: The Christian Vocation to Promote Justice, Peace and the Integrity of Creation*, Maryknoll (Orbis: 1995)

McDonagh, Seán: *Greening the Christian Millennium*, Dublin (Dominican Publications: 1999)

Metuh, Emefie Ikenga: *God and Man in African Religion*, London (Chapman: 1981)

Mindell, Arnold: *Sitting in the Fire: large group transformation using conflict and diversity*, Portland, Oregon (Lao Tse Press: 1995)

Neuner, Joseph (ed.): *Christian Revelation and World Religions*, London (Burns & Oates: 1967)

O'Brien, John: *Seeds of a New Church*, Dublin (Columba: 1994)

O'Donohue, John: *Anam Chara: A Book of Celtic Wisdom*, London and New York (Bantam: 1997, 1998)

Ó hÓgain, Dáithi: *The Sacred Isle: Belief and Religion in Pre-Christian Ireland*, Cork (Collins Press: 1999)

Okure, Teresa: 'Mission as Gathering In: a Biblical and African Perspective' – paper delivered to a gathering of missionaries in Maynooth, Ireland, in 1994 and circulated privately in booklet format by The Irish Missionary Union

Ó Máille, Pádraig: *Living Dangerously: A Memoir of Political Change in Malawi*, Glasgow (Dudu Nsomba Publications: 1999)

Ó Máille, Pádraig (Patrick O'Malley): 'Mission and Missionaries in African Writing: Creative Writing from Post-Colonial Africa and the Black Diaspora' (unpublished paper: 1998)

Oxtoby, Willard G. (ed): *Religious Diversity: Essays by Wilfred Cantwell Smith*, New York (Harper and Row: 1976)

Paul VI: Apostolic Exhortation, *Evangelii Nuntiandi*, 1975

Pieris, Aloysius: *An Asian Theology of Liberation*, Maryknoll (Orbis) and Edinburgh (T. & T. Clarke), 1988

Pieris, Aloysius: 'Inculturation in Non-Semitic Asia' in, Thomas (ed.): *Classic Texts in Mission and World Christianity*, Maryknoll (Orbis: 1995)

Rahner, Karl: *Theological Investigations*, Vol V, Baltimore (Helicon) and London (Darton, Longman and Todd), 1966

Rahner, Karl: *Theological Investigations*, Vol VI, Baltimore (Helicon) and London (Darton, Longman and Todd), 1969

Rahner, Karl: article 'Jesus Christ: History of Dogma and Theology' in *Sacramentum Mundi*, III, New York (Herder and Herder) and London (Burns & Oates) 1969, pp. 192-209.

Ratzinger, Joseph Cardinal: 'Current situation of faith and theology' address published in *L'Osservatore Romano* (English ed.) 6 November 1996, 4-6.

Ratzinger, Joseph Cardinal: 'In the Encounter of Christianity and Religions, Syncretism is Not the Goal', *L'Osservatore Romano* (English edition) 26 April 1995, 5-8

Ratzinger, Joseph Cardinal: *Church, Ecumenism and Politics: New Essays in Ecclesiology*, New York (Crossroads: 1988)

Ratzinger, Joseph Cardinal (with Vittorio Messori): *Ratzinger Report: An Exclusive Interview on the State of the Catholic Church*, San Francisco (Ignatius Press) and Leominster (Fowler Wright) 1992

Ratzinger, Joseph Cardinal: *Salt of the Earth: Christianity and the Catholic Church at the End of the Millennium*, San Francisco (Ignatius Press: 1997) (original German 1996)

Ratzinger, Joseph Cardinal: *Wesen und Auftrag der Theologie: Versuche zu ihrer Ortsbestimmung im Disput der Gegenwart*, Freiburg (Johannes: 1993)

Röper, Anita: *The Anonymous Christian*, New York (Sheed and Ward: 1966)

Schreiter, Robert J.: *Reconciliation: Mission and Ministry in a Changing Social Order*, Maryknoll (Orbis: 1992)

Segundo, Juan Luis: *Theology and the Church: A Response to Cardinal Ratzinger and a Warning to the Whole Church*, Minneapolis (Winston Press) and London (Chapman) 1985

Sharpe, Eric: 'Mission between Dialogue and Proclamation' in William R. Burrows (ed.), *Redemption and Dialogue: Reading 'Redemptoris Missio' and 'Dialogue and Proclamation'*, Maryknoll (Orbis: 1994)

Shorter, Aylward: 'The Cultural Implications of World Mission' – type-script of paper read to the British and Irish Association of Mission Studies Conference in 1991

Shorter, Aylward: *Evangelization and Culture*, London (Chapman: 1994)

Shorter, Aylward: *Toward a Theology of Inculturation*, London (Chapman: 1988)

Smart, Ninian: *The Religious Experience of Mankind*, New York (Charles Scribner's Sons: 1969) and London (Collins Fontana: 1971)

Souli, Sofia: *Greek Mythology*, Ilioupoli (Editions Michaelis Toubis: 1995)

Soyinka, Wole: *Art, Dialogue and Outrage: Essays on Literature and Culture* (revised edition), London (Methuen: 1993)

Soyinka, Wole: *The Burden of Memory, the Muse of Forgiveness*, New York (Oxford University Press: 1999)

Taylor, John V.: *The Primal Vision: Christian Presence amid African Religion*, London (SCM Press: 1963)

Thomas, Norman E. (ed.): *Classic Texts in Mission and World Christianity*, Maryknoll (Orbis: 1995)

Tillich, Paul: *Christianity and the Encounter of World Religions*, New York and London (Columbia: 1963)

Voegelin, Eric: *Israel and Revelation* (Vol 1 of *Order and History*), Baton Rouge (Louisiana State University Press: 1956)

Vycinas, Vincent: *Earth and Gods: an introduction to the philosophy of Martin Heidegger*, Nijhoff (The Hague: 1961)

Walters, Philip: 'Eastern Europe Since the Fifteenth Century', in, Hastings (ed.): *A World History of Christianity*

Ward, Kevin: 'Africa' in Hastings (ed.): *A World History of Christianity*, 197-200

Wink, Walter: *Engaging the Powers: Discernment and Resistance in a World of Domination*, Minneapolis (Fortress Press: 1992)

Wink, Walter: *Naming The Powers: The Language of Power in the New Testament*, Philadelphia, (Fortress Press: 1984)

Wink, Walter: *Unmasking the Powers: The Invisible Forces that Determine Human Existence*, Philadelphia (Fortress Press: 1986)

Zaehner, R. C.: *Hinduism*, London (OUP: 1962, 1966)

Zaehner, R. C.: *The Bhagavad-Gita: With a Commentary, Based on the Original Sources*, London (OUP: 1969)

Index

Theological Commission
  (Vatican) 19.
Thomas, Norman E. 63, 103, 290.
Tibet 217.
Tillich, Paul 21.
Timmel, Sally 171, 234, 271, 293, 294.
Tolstoy 291.
Training for Transformation
  (agency / programme) 234.
transculturality 205.
Travelling People 279, 281.
Trócaire (agency) 239, 244.
Truth and Reconciliation
  Commission 138, 143, 292.
Tutu, Archbishop Desmond 139.
Uganda 170, 208.
USA (United States) 111, 150, 205,
  216, 240, 280, 293.
values (*see also* ethical/moral
  values).
  Christian 82, 86, 88, 92, 94, 95,
  108, 158, 187, 194, 195, 197, 198,
  200, 201, 222-238 *passim*, 245,
  251, 284.
  constellation of 23.
  feminine 188, 283.
  global 12, 192, 207-8, 260-2, 266,
  268, 282.
  gospel 13, 82, 92, 95.
  reign of God 11, 195, 197-200,
  224, 243, 245, 247, 248, 283, 294.
  religious 10, 21, 22-5, 29, 31, 32,
  37, 40, 42, 56-9, 60, 63, 72, 83, 91,
  92, 107, 196.
Vanier, Jean 58, 66, 159, 168, 208.
Vatican II 77, 81, 84, 85, 175, 167, 196.
Vatican, the 19, 20, 21, 61, 104,
  159-160, 239.
Viatores Christi (agency) 270.
Vietnam 186.
VMM (Volunteer Missionary
  Movement) 169, 208.
Voegelin, Eric 27, 286.
Vycinas, Vincent 287.
Waco 170.
Walters, Philip 291.

Ward, Kevin 291.
West Africa 52, 255.
White Fathers 105, 293.
White Sisters 105.
Wink, Walter 110, 111, 112, 113, 292.
witchcraft 51-3, 55, 288.
women's movement 61, 62, 111,
  209, 277.
World Bank 241, 243.
world order 261, 282.
worldwork 163-5.
writings, sacred (of non-Christian
  religions) 26, 28-9, 33, 98.
yielding power 180-3, 265.
yoga 33.
Yoruba religion 42-46, 48, 49, 287.
young church/es 9, 85, 105, 199,
  204, 242, 249, **251-268**, 271, 294.
Zaehner, R. C. 287.
Zaire 106.
Zimbabwe 124, 292.
Zionism 27.